OPEN CONVERSATIONS

OPEN CONVERSATIONS

Public Learning in Libraries and Museums

David Carr

 LIBRARIES UNLIMITED

AN IMPRINT OF ABC-CLIO, LLC
Santa Barbara, California • Denver, Colorado • Oxford, England

Copyright 2011 by David Carr

All rights reserved. No part of this publication may be reproduced, stored in a retrieval system, or transmitted, in any form or by any means, electronic, mechanical, photocopying, recording, or otherwise, except for the inclusion of brief quotations in a review, or reproducibles, which may be copied for classroom and educational programs only, without prior permission in writing from the publisher.

Library of Congress Cataloging-in-Publication Data

Carr, David, 1945 Apr. 4–
   Open conversations : public learning in libraries and museums / David Carr.
     p. cm.
   Includes bibliographical references and index.
   ISBN 978–1–59158–771–2 (pbk. : acid-free paper) — ISBN 978–1–59158–770–5 (ebook)
1. Libraries and community—United States. 2. Museums and community—United States.
3. Libraries and education—United States. 4. Museums—Educational aspects—United States. 5. Libraries—Social aspects—United States. 6. Museums—Social aspects—United States. 7. United States—Intellectual life. 8. United States—Cultural policy. 9. Politics and culture—United States. I. Title.
Z716.4.C37   2011
021.2—dc23   2011025423

ISBN: 978–1–59158–771–2
EISBN: 978–1–59158–770–5

15 14 13 12 11   1 2 3 4 5

This book is also available on the World Wide Web as an eBook.
Visit www.abc-clio.com for details.

Libraries Unlimited
An Imprint of ABC-CLIO, LLC

ABC-CLIO, LLC
130 Cremona Drive, P.O. Box 1911
Santa Barbara, California 93116-1911

This book is printed on acid-free paper ∞

Manufactured in the United States of America

CONTENTS

PREFACE

These essays have challenged my confidence as I wrote and rewrote them and reconsidered their purposes. As a writer I often find it difficult to live up to the ideas that move me. It may take months to be articulate, yet I am likely to remain unsure. Two observations remind me of this daunting fragility and my obvious limits.

It surprises me first, though it shouldn't, to find that the intention of this collection extends ideas in my previous work, especially the concept that our cultural institutions are both places and not-places. It surprises me to find that I write from an unfinished space inside my life, exposed in the process of writing itself. In the title essay of my 2006 book *A Place Not a Place*, I wrote,

> We will discover our answers only when things are happening, and when we have made places for new things to happen: places where words can be heard that help us to live up to ideas; places where we can contribute our gifts to civic culture: our time, our resources, our ideas; places where we can volunteer and assist; places where we can observe and experience the energy of each other.
>
> When a community has created the right kinds of institutions, its citizens can discover in themselves what de Tocqueville called "the habits of the heart"—the ways that prove and shape our common character. (Carr, 2006)

The museum or the library *as a place* is a beginning, a grounding and a situation that inspires thought. As *a place not a place*, it leads us into a world we cannot find elsewhere, because it is created by the mind in response to experience and knowledge. We carry and sustain it in mind. It is a transaction between a present life and the continuities of the past, a negotiation between living cultures and their futures. While it is a conversation, it is also a silent collusion, a form of promise made. However brilliant and immediate the evidence in a cultural institution, I think that our best responses take us away from the artifact, book, or exhibition. What emerges for us transcends where we are and what we see. We go somewhere behind our eyes, where the real work of art, or science, or fiction, or music, happens within us. Each institution resonates with the worlds it summons for us, and we respond to the resonance by entering an imaginary but equally resonant place.

I think it is also a truth of practice: our places evoke the shadows of writers, artists, inventors, historians, philosophers, scientists, clerics and ancestors, all living still in the resonant traces left to us of their works and days. Among the perfunctory, routine acts and assumptions of libraries and museums, it remains possible to evoke the astonishing and moving voyages taken by others. We often need to draw back the dense veils of scholarship and didacticism for these things to happen, for us to imagine the unassuming thing itself as something new, to see its power, and allow it to break through.

It is further daunting for me to write about this kind of resonance and feeling without immediate doubt and doublethink that tell me to be more grounded, less vaporous, and to write about the steady immediacies of virtuous practice, not momentary awakenings of insight. The doublethink leaves when I recollect myself. We who have worked and thought in museums and libraries, and who have observed our users, will understand the momentary awakenings, the sudden epiphanies of practice: this is the unexpected moment I have taught my students to recognize and live for in their work.

The second and more immediate challenge I feel follows from the unrelenting political news that never seems to include a generous thought. I write these words just before an election of such disappointing character and vituperative discourse that I feel whatever I write will be far too small to change the great empty meanness of our civic culture. I ask if I am needed. Do I have useful words for the culture surrounding me? And yet: this is what I have written, and this is what I believe. Admittedly, I am also unaccustomed to feeling that what I write might have relevance to our national life. My life work has been limited, unfocused, and only intermittently visible: to educate and encourage perhaps a thousand librarians as their teacher, a small number in a large and vibrant generation. In the museum world, I have accomplished even less. I remain outside there. Writing of the kind I am doing now has come to me late. And yet the privilege of teaching and advising about libraries and museums continues to be a fire for my thinking. I am grateful to have slowly become an educator over four decades, to have studied and written about the ideas hidden in great museums, and to have imagined the undervalued, unexplored capacities of libraries and other cultural institutions. I know they can make differences by redefining themselves, and so I remind myself to trust myself and say my beliefs. The idea that libraries and museums have a central place in the articulations of democracy is certain to me.

Although it is a small theme in this book—captured in Susan Jacoby's title phrase, "the age of American unreason"—I am concerned about a wide public disdain for intellect, for reasoned discussion and compromise, and a preference for shallow vacancy when far greater depth and content is required by our challenging and complex society. Commerce, education, entertainment, the Web, desperate media, minor celebrities, vulgarity and flash are all part of this daily world. Yet more sinister, and more erosive to our character as a nation and a democracy, are the forces of greed and power that seem to be (in the Orwell phrase) "more equal than others." I am thinking of oligarchs, heavy with both wealth and bias, who have the resources to command the fascinations and political notions of people who feel themselves distant, ignored, and unheard.

What could bring these passionate but discouraged people into libraries and museums, to engage in a balanced discourse, a conversation about values, an examination of ideas and analysis from multiple points of view? Libraries and museums exist so all people who think can think with information and knowledge they have discovered and collected for themselves. What part of cultural institutions might evoke their enduring trust and inspire their best, most open questions? I will hope for a long enough life to address this possibility. At the end of this political season, and the start of another one, I feel that we live amid limitless arrogance of this kind, and so there is more to be done.

I hope that many people share my feelings about the meanness and the cynicism driving a bleak, barely political, landscape. As a teacher, my worry is about what people will learn from these events. As a man of age who now worries over ideas like legacy and continuity, my great concern is about how and where fresh generations will come to understand discourse, caring, deliberation, reflection, and the constructive acts democracy makes possible. How might new professional generations understand the possible reaches of their institutions? I have sought not to write a political book, but the issues of public knowledge and understanding have arisen on their own. We are in need of smart and careful, thoughtful and empathic people. Democracy depends on intelligent citizens, on readers and thinkers. But I am now no one's teacher, only the author of small books such as this one and am left to wonder about the future of learning and thinking in the world.

Consequently, to the daunting themes I address in this book—the great power of cultural institutions in our communities and erosions of civility in the nation's life—I can certainly add a few more that my book and I are unable to match: the struggle toward inspired public education, our

imperiled literacies, our love of mindless technology, shallow social networks, and school testing. There are more, but I will stop with the hope that
other books are being written now to assess the effects of these phenomena
on the curiosities and imaginations of children and the horizons of their families. And I will also hope that there are educators who dream of great,
human alternatives to what is dominant in the present, remembering that
the future of our lives always dwells in a place Maxine Greene has called
"the not-yet." And so we will wait. Perhaps the inadequacies of this book
will inspire another writer to advance the promise of open conversations in
our generative institutions, including public schools. They too are agencies
of democracy. But there is no simple remedy to deepen shallowness, no electronic remedy to populate emptiness, and no virtual response to dissolve isolation and silence.

Since I have listed my second (and third) thoughts as I prepare this manuscript for submission to a patient publisher, I will also mention an inspiration for hope in the bands of principled and earnest people and
organizations I have found who have taken up the cause of rescuing public
conversation and intelligent public discovery. I find more each day. I have
cited several in the middle chapters, but since every search reveals yet
another promising source, I am confident that there are more collective
minds, resilient and positive, who invite a good conversation for the sake
of clarity, understanding, and the grace of becoming something together.
I trust that we all require that grace and might move together toward it.

Open Conversations is a book for Carol Carr, my brightest and most
open partner in conversation over a lifetime. She helps me to be generous
and kind, and to survive my fears; she alone gave me the abundant possibilities of a human life I would have otherwise lost. No book is large enough to
say what I need to say to her.

David Carr
Carrboro, NC

ACKNOWLEDGMENTS

I am grateful for the opportunity to have written several formative essays and chapters, and to have delivered invited addresses, that allowed me to think and write about themes now more extensively developed in the essays published here.

Zahava Doering and the editors of *Curator: The Museum Journal* published two essays on similar themes: "Confluence" in vol. 51, no. 3; and "An Aspect of the Infinite: New Zealand Talks," in vol. 53, no. 1 (2010).

Thanks also to the Committee on Audience Research and Evaluation of the American Association of Museums for the privilege of delivering a keynote address, "Think with Me," at their annual conference in Chicago in 2007; to the Boston Athenæum, for generously inviting me to speak as part of their bicentennial in 2007; to the New York City Museum Educators Roundtable, for the privilege of delivering an endnote address at their 2008 conference, "Museums and the Unfinished Fabric of Living"; to the Conference on Social Theory, Policy and the Arts, for their approval of a paper, "Cultural Institutions and the Unfinished Issues of American Life," presented at their 2008 conference in Baltimore; to the University of North Carolina at Greensboro, for the generous invitation to deliver an address, "Museums, Libraries, and the Rescue of American Voices: Context and the Common Story in Cultural Institutions," in 2009 at the Weatherspoon Art Museum; to the Visitor Studies Association for the privilege of delivering a keynote address at their national conference in Phoenix, "Valuable Thinking, Variable Knowing," in 2010; to the University of South Carolina School of Library and Information Science, for the opportunity to deliver a series of four lectures titled "Conversations on the Foundations of Library Service," during the Fall 2010 term as this book was in its final stages; to the Aubrey R. Watzek Library at Lewis and Clark College, Portland, Oregon, for the privilege of delivering the Tenth Johanna Sherrer Lecture, "Think with Me: The Possibilities of Public Conversations in Cultural Institutions," in September 2010; to the North Carolina Humanities Council for the privilege of delivering a keynote address on March 21, 2011, in Greensboro; and to the Faculty of Information at the University of Toronto, for the privilege of delivering the Bertha Bassam Lecture in April 2011, devoted to the invisible themes in cultural institutions. Each of these events permitted me to meet wise professionals, promising students, and a generous audience.

Parts of Chapter 5 are adapted from "Confluence," *Curator: The Museum Journal* 51, no. 3 (July 2008). Parts were also presented in the keynote address to the annual conference of the Visitor Studies Association, July 29, 2010, in Phoenix, Arizona. The full text of that talk, "Valuable Thinking, Variable Knowing," appears in *Visitor Studies* 14, no. 1 (April 2011). The title of Chapter 8, "Look at the Unknown," comes from the mathematical problem-solving heuristic in G. Polya, *How to Solve It: A New Aspect of Mathematical Method* (Princeton, N.J.: Princeton University Press, 1960). An earlier version of Chapter 10 first appeared in a different form under the title "Mind as Verb," in H. H. Genoways, ed., *Museum Philosophy: For the Twenty-first Century* 11–18 (Walnut Creek, CA: AltaMira Press, 2006). I am grateful to AltaMira Press for permission to adapt this essay, and for permission to quote from page 131 of my book, *A Place Not a Place* (Walnut Creek, CA: AltaMira Press, 2006).

Some content in Chapter 2 is my interpretation of the inaugural poem read by Elizabeth Alexander on January 20, 2009, as published in the *New York Times*. Some content in Chapter 12 is my interpretation of material published by James Fallows on his blog at the website of *The Atlantic Monthly*, where he is an admired national correspondent. The reader is encouraged to seek out the original texts in these places.

Barbara Ittner of Libraries Unlimited, an imprint of ABC-CLIO, has shown great patience in waiting for this manuscript and its revisions. I thank her for that, and for her encouragement to add Chapter 12.

INTRODUCTION: THINK WITH ME

A great civilization is a drama lived in the minds of a people. It is a shared vision, shared norms, expectations, and values. . . . Societies that keep their values alive do so not by escaping the process of decay but by powerful processes of regeneration. . . . [T]he great ideas still beckon—freedom, equality, justice, the release of human possibilities.

John W. Gardner (1999)

Ancient Greek democracy was inseparably linked with the institution of the agora, the square, a place where political decisions were reached through dialogue as citizens enjoying equal rights talked to one another directly, face to face. . . . The modern era has reached a point of culmination, and if we are not to perish of our modernness we have to rehabilitate the human dimension of citizenship as well as of politics. This is what I consider to be the principal challenge of our time, a challenge for the third millennium.

Václav Havel (1993)

My hope is to remind people of what it means to be alive among others, to achieve freedom in dialogue with others for the sake of personal fulfillment and the emergence of a democracy dedicated to life and decency.

Maxine Greene (1988)

Consider the tsunami, deadly and devastating as it is in actuality, as a metaphor for something that has happened to us everywhere. In little more than a decade, electronic information tools have ineradicably reshaped our awareness, books, civil society, commerce, communication, community, content, culture, dating, education, encyclopedias, entertainment, friendship, government, information, institutions, learning, leisure, literacy, memory, music, news, play, politics, publishing, reading, research, schooling, social participation, visual images, writing, and more.

In little more than a decade, the capacity of a mindful civic life has come to include global AIDS, al Qaeda, ambiguity, ambivalence, avarice and corruption, climate change, crumbling national infrastructures, domestic terrorism, drug trades, earthquakes and tsunamis, economic collapse, electric cars, educational breakdowns, emigration, faith-driven politics, famines, fears, foreclosures, genocides, hurricanes, international jihad, internecine war, joblessness, lasting drought, massive national debt, nuclear meltdowns, plutocracy and technocracy, political revolutions, politicized news, redefined families and genders, 9/11, and more.

In these contemplations it may be useful to remember that we cannot download, curate, or collect any of the following things: altruism, artistry, attention, authenticity, cognition, collaboration, consideration, courage, critical thinking, curiosity, democracy, empathy, esteem, expectations, freedom of thought, generosity, hope, imagination, inquiry, integrity, kindness, patience, respect, responsibility, or wisdom. These things come to us from elsewhere. Where? *When the continuities of our lives are swept away, as we have seen happen around the world, what is our future? How do we feel, how do we think, when our world is in motion? When in the path of a tsunami, what is our relationship to knowledge? What shall we give to each other? Why do we cling to each other? In a tsunami, if we are capable of rescuing others and ourselves, what is the most useful thing to do? What parts of our lives can we understand in new ways? What shall we do for each other now? Which of our losses, which of our strengths, shall we discuss first?*

I advocate the importance of cultural institutions helping people to increase their capacity to grasp, negotiate, adapt, and respond to change in their lives. We are always challenged to do this, at every age, in every era. Unless we live forward with change we become its victims, locked in silence, detached and invisible. We will always be ambivalent and unwilling. There will always be fear. And when the tsunami recedes, our lives are farther away from us, disassembled in the fragments and wreckage of where we used to live and how we used to think. The structures that contained our lives have collapsed. The conversations that informed our lives are impossible. The transmission of continuities that have shaped us stops. We have nothing left of what defined us. How do we change and learn when we lose these things? How do we rediscover and restore ourselves without these things? How do we think about these things after the tsunami?

I contend that there is no one to help our citizens to think about our tsunami, or our choices, or our strengths and losses, other than cultural institutions. There is no one, no other institutions, and no other agencies of democracy that will help us to become something together as people, even in small places of respect and generosity, other than us. It is in fact only in the small places of respect and generosity that this can happen. We have the capacity to survive, the intellect to guide our continuity, and the will to become different.

Several ideas construct the foundations of this book: the potential for cultural institutions to assist their users to think about public issues; the complexities of knowledge and objects and their interwoven contexts; the unknowns that shape us; the intangible traces of experience, and its evidences in language and memory; and the need, if we are ever to know the importance of our institutions, to move our understanding toward the interiors of lives. The human interior is a daunting place, but it is where we have to begin our discoveries of what institutions make possible in private and public ways. I am most interested in what is difficult to explain even as it happens to us: how our intuitions and our aspirations leap toward whatever knowledge we next require, and how we respond, how we think.

Think with me about the user in the art or history museum today, or in a branch of the public library, especially in a large city, where collections are extensive. Think with me of that intentional experience, of going to this place or that for something to know. It is not a perfunctory moment. The choice to know something fresh represents a deep and essential aspiration: a striving for some missing part of the past, or an exploration of some indefinite wanting. The person who seeks details or revelations, an expanded view of the past or an unpredicted insight, needs a bridge to new awareness, to trusted intuition or purposeful reflection, something that cannot be experienced elsewhere and cannot be found without actively wanting knowledge or change.

Even the casual user or traveler will go to the institutions of a city or town as a way to stand in the center of its mind, at the center of its possibilities. Each great library or museum in an inspired city is a concentration of common wealth, a public recognition that the city and its people have dreams, a place where people go to experience the secular ecstasy of standing outside themselves, becoming part of another emerging world. We feel drawn there, to break through, to trade our common experiences in a place that invites transformation, exhilaration, and exchange.

Of libraries and museums—even in small towns, where horizons are closer to common memories and local thinking—we might say they are the centers of that knowledge held by the city for its people. They are also the centers of public aspiration, where private dreams emerge to take shape, and possible actions become real through reflection. The people of a place—even its emigrants and people in transition—can discover themselves and become stronger and different in such places.

This is part of what I believe: intentional experiences of this kind—simply going to the library or the museum and thinking with ideas found there—are forms of promise and design. At their best, our experiences imply the promise of thinking anew, privately and fearlessly; and then, designing an experience of one's own. Every cultural institution is in its own way about courage and fear; it invites us to use the first to reduce the second. It is for breaking through to new experiences: breaking out of routines and somnambulism, and out of stagnation and ignorance. We are, I believe, at our strongest when we trust ourselves to think anew amid confusion and ambiguity; when we trust and renew our questions; and when we open our lives to the unknown, to experiences we have not yet lived. At such times, we are made of courage and fear—and dreaming as well.

We are thinking now of purposeful users: people who ask and reflect. We think of people engaged by complexities, questions, and unknowns that remain unfinished, always open. These are the users who *complete* a cultural institution by their presence; later they continue the influence of the institution by the examples and continuities of their lives. Think with me about what the presence of this user in the cultural institution implies: an intention to experience something new; an anticipation of engagement and, perhaps, immersion in something deep and unpredictable; a repertoire of previous experiences and memories evoked or newly wakened; and adult knowledge, arrived at as an experience of adulthood without schooling. Embedded in the user, these implications compose the energies of use. Intention, anticipation, openness, memory, and knowledge are the principal variables of cultural experiences.

Abundant cognitive energies are essential to rich experiences and intellectual change; there is no need to create fresh motives, for they are embedded in us. Our work is to evoke and nurture. If we can understand and respect these personal engines, we may make a difference in cultural places. Lives bring complexity; we might want to know something about the user's formative educative style and continuing interests, some of the passions and unfinished issues of one life. We might want to hear these expressed because they are the indicators of a progressive life, a life moving forward. And in this way, the user—with energies awake, dimensions in change, and possibilities unknown—enters the place for thinking.

The user enters this place, library or museum, and finds it to be a kind of floating world where experiences are brief, evanescent, and public; most likely gentle, certainly edifying, often quite dreamlike; intense but momentary; puzzling, variable, transient, and in most ways solitary. Experiences matter in the moment, yet may matter more when they are over. What does it mean, to contextualize the intellect of this user in this floating situation of serial experiences, each potentially different from its predecessor? How does each of us rework a fabric out of all we know and discover, all we have been, and all we want to be when we are in the presence of something new?

A life rises to itself through anticipation and awareness, trying out and taking in multiple experiences. The rising life needs trusted resources, mentors, living exemplars, and a repertoire of instrumental behaviors and strategies. A person needs to be comfortable with ambiguity and risk, flexible, adaptive, and willing to respond to both advances and setbacks with reflection and self-renewal. A life that gradually emerges from routine requires energy, persistence, motive, and the courage to see and listen, to think and act. The evolving life rises toward the possible.

Think with me about how we fold our lives over and over intentionally—almost like origami, to make something recognizable out of something plain—and the delicate, invisible work of problem solving in a cultural institution, where the problem is the construction of an aware self. The user negotiates and improvises in an uncharted world, keeping questions open. This working mind at work in a collection is ultimately what cultural institutions are challenged to study, to ask about, to illuminate. We study the interiors of our institutions, but we also need to study the interior lives of men and women in their times, human beings making lives among all the formidable yet tacit dimensions of the complex social and intellectual space that the institution provides.

That word "uncharted," above, is perhaps a generous way of saying we are adrift. There is a reason for our popular culture to feature television programs about people lost on an island with scary others, in an accidental situation that cannot be explained; or playing out false roles as survivors in a fabricated and deeply meaningless contest. Not just vapid entertainments, they may also constitute self-help training, reminders that whatever world we have cherished in the past no longer exists in the present. We are ourselves increasingly insular, living through a series of accidental events. A program televising simulated social fear and desperation, it turns out, is a tutorial for life amidst wreckage, vapid competitions, and the fading promise of rescue from somewhere else. Often I too believe that we all need rescue from such shame, but that we must do it ourselves, and with luck we will have the agency of people we trust.

Think with me. To enter a strong cultural institution is to experience a place so deeply in motion that it necessarily puts *us* in motion. Our thoughts are both here and not here, moving among objects and tools and yet also within an idea or an image of our own. This is one way to understand cognition in the situation provided: it is an uncharted, moving territory, a situation for thinking, an experience of elevation and surprise. Responding to great works and concepts, discovering new paths, we are less tangible to ourselves. We think; we combine and adjust our thoughts; we try out what we tentatively see and have the words to capture. We negotiate and improvise our passage, pausing for insights to take form.

And yet, beneath these elevated sensations and hidden dimensions is our need, the true engine of the human path. What is it we need? What is it we want? What do we need or want to become? What is this wanting we have? We might know it in a slightly parallel form when we read. Our wanting and desire for complexity and experience to appear to us and engage us are proven each time we open a book. One of my students, after a discussion of reading groups, wrote to me, "All people who read the story become part of the story forever, just like the story becomes part of them forever." She continued, "In the same way, when lots of people read a story and especially when they talk and write and think about that story together they become something together." Her words pervade this book.

Think with me. What if the museum, the library, the zoo, the history collection, the children's art studio, the science and the natural science collections, what if they are all about becoming something together—becoming thoughtful together, and striving to imagine together? What if our collections could be seen as structured situations, even maps, for finding our way together into the unknown and back, ways for sorting the contextual intangibles we all recognize in our lives, so we might imagine and understand the possible difference a single idea might make? What if we could hold an idea before us, exploring its meaning among other people and other minds? The idea before us also has its origins, and a place among other ideas, other interpreters, other forms of knowledge, other memories central to other lives. Context is an inevitable confluence of different voices in the continuing fabrication of experience. These voices say no context is identical to another.

Each context has its own energy and its own surrounding themes. When we try to understand or isolate one context from another, we are at a loss. One contextual nuance has meaning only among others. Each context evokes potential ambiguity or disintegration. We experience our lives through these tensions: I am a man, a husband, a parent, a librarian, a professor, a writer, a reader, a photographer, and other things all at once, responding to my life as a construction of perpetually undernourished contexts. Librarians know better than others that such contextual abundance means an abundance of new information and knowledge, each adding new energy and new ambiguity to the flow of problem solving. In a difficult cognitive journey, there is nothing to do but to think your way forward, to negotiate a balance among the contextual intangibles that present themselves, and to work toward coherent thoughts. When we think at our best, contexts enrich each other and how we see the great complexity of things. Museum or library use, it seems to me, is not about learning, but about experiencing and thinking—organizing, connecting, always under the uneasy tensions of multiple contexts. At times we may be like witnesses to a conflict or a rescue, or survivors who live on to think, remember, and testify from the truths we craft for ourselves.

Think with me, the place must say. Museums and libraries, any or all, are not about learning anything; they are about thinking anything, experiencing anything. They work well in response to questions, but they are not examinations and they are not schools. They derive their integrity from knowledge, but they are not judgmental of people who know nothing. They inspire scholarship, reading, inquiry, communication, community, engagement, writing, drawing, and conversation, but they are not curricular. They assist every form of literacy, but they are not schools. We may be in the museum or the library because we went to school, and we may think of ourselves as having been schooled; we may be educators and scholars ourselves, but cultural institutions are not schools.

I have come to believe that our most important professional questions ought to be about the thoughts of the user, about the interior, wordless experiences, the pauses, the interpretations, the conversations with the situation, the times spent engrossed in confusion—working a way out of it by thinking. I will always aim my attention toward the things we cannot see: the invisible actions, the invisible traces, that place that is not a place except somewhere in the mind, the thing that has not happened yet, the people we have not yet become, the immanent aspect of the infinite.

And so, in both the library and the museum, I am most engaged by the idea that our experience is a process occurring under our eyes but not visible to us, its effects not immediately apparent, a dreamlike and intangible thing that constructs and alters us. However, there are sometimes visible, sometimes audible artifacts of thought in our institutions, and they are typically associations and questions, indicators of wanting to know more, to know what it is possible to know, and to know where and how knowledge might be found. People observe and speak; consult directories, maps, and catalogues; pay attention; and take their time. Our experiences in these places will always be unfinished. In a museum or library, the question "What more do you need to know about what you have seen?" will help us to understand a great deal. When we ask this question, we ask, "What kind of thinking has taken place for you here? What new unknowns did you discover? What kind of thinking do you need to do tomorrow? What possibilities has this experience opened for you?"

Frank Smith, whose work I admire greatly, categorizes important critical thinking acts. Classifying, comparing, and conceptualizing are among them, as are differentiating, evaluating, grasping, questioning, recognizing, searching, verifying, and weighing—these are just a dozen critical-thinking operations from his list of forty (Smith 1990: 95). The list comprises what we actually do when we are thinking well. Smith says we apply these operations to such issues as accuracy, ambiguity, arguments, assumptions, authenticity, and authority—and those are merely the first six words that lead his list of sixty-four critical dimensions (96).

The brain is not an information-processing device, any more than it is a passive, reactive device. The brain does not seek or respond to information in the world—the brain imposes meaningfulness on the world.

It is an active, experience-seeking, reality-creating organ. The enormous quantity of knowledge that we accumulate as we go through life is not the purpose of life but a byproduct of experience. We learn the worlds we create. The brain is constantly generating possibilities of realities that may or may not exist objectively, and our experience of these realities constitutes our life and our identity. (Smith 1990: 47)

Smith says, "The brain does not respond or react to the world; it creates the world. . . . Imagination is not something to which we must deliberately turn our mind; it is the fundamental condition of the brain" (Smith 1990: 46). And this: "The brain is more like an artist than a machine. It constantly creates realities, actual and imaginary; it examines alternatives, spins stories, and thrives on experience" (12). This is why we ought to study thinking, remembering that John Dewey said the word "mind" is principally a verb, perhaps most importantly and most invisibly a verb. Dewey says mind is not something we have, but something we do; we attend, we care and feel. To mind leads us to see, and engages us in "active looking after things that need to be tended; we mind our step, our course of action, emotionally as well as thoughtfully" (Dewey 1934 [1987]: 268). Minding is questioning. For Dewey, the infinitive "to mind" is defined by intellect and applied attention. It signifies memory and purpose.

We need to worry about mind in all its uses, noun or verb. Think with me about the present moment in our national life and its meanings for cultural institutions. Educational evaluation has been tied to tests, not to curiosity or invention, nor to the subtler forms of literacy and interpretation. Imaginative, flexible educational policy must overcome a polarized and uncivil public arena and accountability demands. Compromise and patience are rare or invisible. The abbreviated cognitive processes that characterize the World Wide Web cause me to wonder what kinds of young scholars, thinkers, learners, and readers are we now creating? What kinds of adult learners will they become? How will they learn to think critically in the ambiguous parts of life? Have our children been compromised and narrowed by our schools? Have we, and their parents, been diverted from the construction of living minds?

Whatever your response to these questions, perhaps you will agree with me that a generation prepared for the test in a culture of shallow competition is not likely to be a generation that trusts complex personal experience as the basis for learning. Nor will an insular generation easily understand the perspectives of others, nor will it fully grasp the importance of cultural institutions to civic society, and to democracy. Nor will it easily respond to my questions "How do we think and trust in times of fear? How do we come to understand American variances in culture, knowledge, and context? How do we speak and think together with others?" Educational arrogance, no matter how broadly practiced, cannot replace the cultivation of trust and intellect in a time of ambiguity.

Think with me about what a museum or library forum might suggest about human differences, historic events, or alternate ways to think and strive for knowledge worthy of trust. Think about how our institutions might assist us to understand the lives and families of others near us. Assume with me that creative and responsive lives, lives of wanting more than they are capable of providing, are everywhere. I think that they are likely to be motivated by a desire to complete the unfinished parts of their worlds, and to fulfill the imagined possibilities of their experiences. Our work is founded upon respect for such common wanting.

It appears to me that our task each day is to reconfirm what is fragile, and to understand how we are strong. We can rescue a civic life of insight and expression, and make a more thoughtful community possible, first by imagining it as a situation of possible ideas and conversations. If uncertainty is valuable to thinking and therefore important to our institutions, how shall we define it and how shall we use it? What do we *not* know in our world that we might explore and experience together? How shall we demonstrate through what we provide that thinking well can be a form of apprenticeship, and that there are many masters of thought and understanding to be heard before we will feel certain of whatever truths we must craft on our own?

A democracy requires intellect in its citizens. We ask questions and listen, and perhaps we ask again. We avoid judging, we encourage the narrative to continue. Tell me more, we can say. We can see how one life varies from another in family, in resources, in choices, in education, and in happiness, and how it differs in health, in civic participation, and in employment and avocation. We all differ in these and other parts of our lives, but they do not make a difference that prevents us from understanding each other.

A democracy requires that we spin and weave our own strands, yet we are also in part woven into the strands of others. Our hopes, anticipations and hardships may be private, but we can cull a lifetime of stories from our conversations. Whole families and communities are in these stories. And yet, it seems to me that, even with so much to say, we are largely without places to speak and present ourselves, without ways to express what we see and know, in ways that reach toward the experiences and knowledge of other people in the same culture. Consequently it also seems to me that without rescuing voices and experiences, we will not live up to the possibility of sharing a common world, or filling it with something that will last beyond our selves. We will be faint mysteries and vague shadows to each other, and to those who follow us

In my experience, museums and libraries are the cultural instruments most able to approach the complexities and ambiguities of our lives. They are places of artifacts, records, and documents, but they are also

not-places, meaning that when we occupy them we are in process and
motion; they cause us to think of some place or thing beyond ourselves. They
allow us to construe meanings elsewhere. Cultural institutions deepen,
inform, and encourage—even elevate—their users toward reflection. As we
experience them, we are likely to become more complete, more open, and
our awareness and language are likely to expand. Museums and libraries
are resonant places: they imply affinity, continuity, and safety, and they
promise a place of sustenance and advocacy. They suggest the possibility
that there is more to think and imagine.

I propose to reinvent American cultural institutions as places for the
expression of American voices, and to explore the ways we have of discovering possibilities, changing our perceptions of complexity, and reinventing
our attention. My idea is to use these American cultural instruments, already
dedicated to the invisible actions and meanings of lives, to recover the lost
voices of living Americans. We should be asked to live up to these possibilities, to give attention to the promises inherent in our lives. Clearly, my ideas
are not new. In American public libraries during the early decades of the
twentieth century, people became something together, against the odds,
against the challenges of immigration, bias, and an economy on its way to
a crash. And I know there has never been anything simple or simplistic about
the United States; its complexity is overwhelming and extraordinary because
it has always been grounded in process, expansion, reinvention, and the persistence of democracy as the method of its own becoming as a nation. It has
lurched fitfully toward fairness in my lifetime and will continue to challenge
itself with good ideas and bad.

Our nation is continuously unfinished; accordingly, our cultural institutions are about the democratic process of coming into knowledge, informing
our minds, and moving our feelings. We must come to be comfortable with
the open end of civic hope, with the striving that never ends. In contexts
large and small, the nation cannot hide its errors or losses, but it also cannot
hide its fears, nor can it obscure its resources and energies. We will always
want to see the nation evolve openly, through informed acts carried out with
purpose, undertaken fearlessly, by thoughtful people. What it cannot bear, it
seems to me, is fear of others whom we do not yet understand, or a failure to
be curious about the possible dimensions of lives we cannot yet see. To be
called incurious—implying preknowledge of answers before the statement
of a problem, or simply not caring to consider the crafting of truth—is the
most damning epithet for the mind I can imagine.

Our institutions can help to bring communities to their questions, to the
knowledge that helps to inform their responses, and to the ideas and values
that will shape our policies and plans. We especially require new thinking
to discover the experiences that will last within us, for rebuilding our institutions, and for growing new fields of ideas, sown by our own lives—out
of which we might harvest and nourish what our great communities,

institutions, and people want to become. Children should be present to see adults do this, so they will never believe that thinking critically and the public applications of thought begin elsewhere with other people. Children might also come to know that libraries and museums exist for exactly this kind of transformation by deepening what we think about, and how we think about, differences.

For all we hear about Main Street, there is only one kind of place where we might go to discover our own voices. That place has an unrealized role in reconstructing American trust through face-to-face forums and community conversations. If the nation is capable of becoming engaged in this immense work of rediscovering itself and what we have become, we must be thinking with each other.

We still have our resources and our tools; we will continue to have an economy of banks and auto makers; and we have an economy of information, moving too fast to see—at least until we do our jobs and slow it down. We still have greed and the extremes of capitalism; we still have generosity and compassion. We still have people moving into our nation to become a part of it and to become part of us, and perhaps, unknowingly, to rescue the future by transforming us. We may have these things, but I think we do not have very much, or enough, of each other. This weakens us.

Think with me. We need to replace ruthlessness and selfish individualism with becoming something together. As we can see in pockets of our past, it will not be the first time we have done this. It will begin with stories told in places where we live, to others who sit near us. Over time, we all will be unafraid to speak in the safe places we have made for discoveries, reflections, and voices. If we teach ourselves to speak, listen, and think together, our places, our libraries, will open us to ourselves—to something courageous within ourselves—and move us toward the possibilities of self-rescue that every civilization needs.

As I began the last chapters of this book, an opportunity to speak in Portland, Oregon, brought me to that beautiful city, where, in the Portland Art Museum, we saw a transformation mask, worn in sacred dancing of the Kwakwaka'wakw people, made in the late nineteenth century of red cedar and fur. The transformation mask is two masks, one within another. The outer mask is a dark, heavy-browed face of the animal world. The inner mask is a human face, mortal, wide-eyed, seeming to be taking in breath as he is revealed by awe, the human within the animal spirit. I was moved to contemplate this image of transition from form to form, animal to person, person to animal, as I envisioned the dance. I would want this book, about transformation of a worldly kind, to capture even a slight aspect of that deep power.

We can never assume that the future requires no inspiration, or that our thinking is of little consequence, that our gifts of memory and fabrication, being merely personal, do not have infinite dimensions or consequences for citizenship. We are not without our masks, and we are adept at hiding our faces. And yet we too can be revealed in awe. Of museums and libraries, I hope it will be said in the future: *Even though people were uncertain, they were unafraid to question together for the common good, using institutions where knowledge was treasured. They identified the unknown and worked to illuminate it. They helped to reconfigure fears and doubts into previously invisible strengths and possibilities.*

The essays in this book are about cultural institutions as places for the renewal of lives by other lives, the construction of ideas by other ideas, and the generation of thoughts by other thoughts. Therefore they are about friction and transformation. They attend to the places, both grand and humble, where we have made ourselves safe from autocracy, authoritarianism, and theft of the revealing, inquiring spirit. This is a work of advocacy for a renewed era of public thoughts and explorations, ways of knowing and becoming stronger together, beyond schools and teachers, in the continuities of life as it is lived. I believe that there is useful, enticing, and provocative thinking to be done in this living experience, and so in this book I ask you to think with me.

CHAPTER 1

Our Places

Our places, being the kinds of places they are, will be defined not by what they contain, but by what they begin, evaluated by what they inspire, and not by what they complete. They invite and incite the longing and wanting, the close and hidden need, the desire carried by learners who hope to become something more. They are engaged and charged by things unseen, ideas unspoken, inventions that have not happened yet. That is, stories not yet created to rescue and console us.

They are at their best when at capacity, full up to closing time. They are at their second best when empty of everyone: the collection waiting. In an empty world, or when we are ourselves empty, they are still full. In a hollow world, when we are feeling hollow, they are still resonant and relevant. When we are bereft in an impoverished world, they are our treasuries. In a shallow world, they are permanent, defiant, and deep. They are rich and common, private and crowded, lofty yet often worn, steady and changing, conservative and transformative, exhaustive and still incomplete, filtered and yet revolutionary, contained and infinite, overflowing and underfunded, loved and exploited, admired and certainly foremost on the list of the taken-for-granted. And yet the fresh day always arrives and never ends early: these are places where the living promises of lives and the living aspirations of communities are nurtured.

What is their foundation? The concept of democracy. Who are their allies? Questioners and seekers. Unfinished persons. Every generation. Who are their enemies? The arrogant, the certain, the myopic, the fearful, the limited, the cheap and miserly. What do they require? Multiple forms of courage, to create the edges and circumstances that serve and inspire human beings. What is their task? Restoring the nation. Why do we need these places? Because we are human beings, always in the process of becoming new. And so we want to move forward to embrace our own lives, safely and fearlessly; we want to shape our own becoming among people in a place we can trust, with help we can trust.

They are, in all their forms, essential instruments of democracy. Knowledge is what we use when we need to rescue ourselves and each other, and so we need these places to hold and provide it. At their best, they are fair and open, like no other public institutions anywhere. In everyday civil exchanges and conversations in such fair and open places, we acknowledge that we are all equal occupants. What we come to see and know about ourselves and what we feel possible for ourselves when we are present make it our place, a source of energy and a match to the dry imagination. What we do in it, what bridges we construct, makes it into an engine of connection to a larger world.

When we stand up for these places, we assert that knowledge, not economy or government alone, makes a community. We see ourselves in a story, even if it is a story of flaws and errors, or a record of change and impermanence. Knowledge of the story moves us forward, an evolutionary force: the more we know and the more complex our knowledge, the more we evolve. What we must love most about our places and our communities is neither their outcomes nor their achievements, but the ways they have of making people want to become somehow more: smarter and more connected to each other, perhaps, and therefore safer. With knowledge and literacy, time and place, the public can read and flourish in confidence and privacy. When institutions and communities do not do this for their people and themselves, it is a failure of democracy.

They teach us to know that our communities are deep mines of memory and rivers of progress. Knowledge constructs a community by moving from person to person and from generation to generation. We transmit our ways of doing things and our ways of seeing things from where we are. At our best, we are capable of moving ourselves toward breadth and understanding. We can remind ourselves of great changes in time, and the gradual, forest-like evolution of our culture. When knowledge allows our community to become broader, more inclusive, and more open, our ways of speaking and understanding also grow more capable of expressing shared integrity and mutual respect. We regenerate our culture after losses. We learn the acts, words, and values of inclusion; and then we might even come to see ourselves differently: more inclusive, less judgmental; more mindful, less thoughtless.

Every life teaches, every life is a lesson, but every life needs a voice and a place. We become stronger when we speak about our lives; we tell our stories to each other, and our thoughts become more connected and more resonant simultaneously. Our greatest strengths may come to us slowly over time, but our discoveries and insights can strike us like lightning to a kite, with a surge and a promise. We find courage, trust, and empathy in ourselves as we find knowledge, and as we think fairly among others. We may feel powerless under the condition of the world as it is, but every experience carries an implication for what it might become, and what we might know next about it. It is always within our power to learn more. Every bit, every byte, every piece or page—each one is an aspect of the infinite, and something for us to examine in the largest frames of life. But when we are listening and speaking among others, something more will happen to us. We will think of how people live and experience their knowledge, how they create and constantly revise its lessons, and how they imagine themselves more fully into the future.

If we are a community, information and complexity will nourish and awaken us. Challenges will define our ethics and character. If we are learners, our conflicts require us to become stronger and more resilient. Differences among us engage both our conscience and our spine. If we are a community, we engage in civic discourse, conversations about how we expect the world to be, and how we can wrestle with it toward the better. We are given this task by our lives, if we can bear it: to live up to the challenges of knowing everything we can know—but then to go for more beyond it, to make something greater of knowing and thinking, and to make something more of ourselves. Our task is to know, and to express, as much as we can, and to listen with care, and to want more than we can possibly hold.

The irony, to me, is that some are tempted to think that these places are no longer needed: that they are luxuries amid a generous web of universal access. The belief is generalized that everyone has the tool at hand (not true) where all possible past and future information has been made freely available and easy to find (even less true). People can buy their own information (not so), can watch their own brand of news (not really), and can get information sent to them with neither work nor judgment required. In this unreality, we no longer need experiences, because the virtual is superior to the real. What more could a person require? And so, in hard economic times foolish people say we can reduce our support for these places because they are redundant. But practice tells the truth: people seek billions of items each year, and show up millions of times each day. Something unending continues to happen in cultural institutions.

UNFINISHED ISSUES

Our places continuously open the closed doors of lost memory and past indifference; they are capable as well of returning us constantly to the unfinished issues we carry with us as individuals and as a society. Every day we are driven by what we do not yet know, the questions we ask privately, the moments we carry from faith, family, and memory that do not go away. I also count as unfinished our failure—or our inability or our fear—to engage in essential conversations about the public but often unspoken themes of human lives, such as race, gender, family, war, home, and hope. We all share a need for respect and generosity in our assumptions about each other. Among our unfinished issues, I would include our great cultural losses: I think of the world that is shy of poetry, the missing lessons of history and memory, the lost knowledge of human differences and human experiences, and the disappearance of conversations that last into the night. There are public unfinished issues as well: the role of faith, the limits of individualism, identities and responsibilities, freedom to speak, and the foundations of democracy, among others. Our institutions are capable of helping us to address this list. They compose a form of mind for our culture that is always fluid, expanding to contain emerging thought and possibility, gathering fresh evidence to renew our conversations.

They remind us that knowledge is a living process that moves us forward, resistant to vapid simplifications and insipid superficialities. Media do not help us to do this; often their task is to mask authenticity, to entertain us, to sell us things, and to weaken our attention in order to make the pitch easy. For the most part, they do not lead us to personal depth or a cultural narrative to grasp. We need a story we recognize that comes from a living place and the talk of smart, probing people. To think with each other, we often need the questions and controversies of other intelligent observers. These can appear only when living people, their voices, their memories, and their reading and reflecting lives as well, are present together, the real in place of the virtual, the near in place of the distant, the community in place of the talking head on screen.

Our living voices also can address the endangered conscience, always at risk. The weaving together of many-stranded experiences into a community narrative strengthens our connection and responsibility to others. Every opportunity people have to gather information and establish a fair point of view will nourish their consideration, ethics, and conscience. These experiences are conducive to self-reliance and intellectual self-respect. They construct a lasting fabric for a community.

They remind us of ourselves and our experiences. When our technologies have reduced everything that requires reflection and conversation to the virtual, how shall we rediscover the authentic in ourselves? How shall we become our own persons under the influences and constraints of narrow entertainment, simplistic politics, and anti-intellectualism? How do we live an authentic life that we can trust to be our own unless we can sever it from phony distractions? We learn nothing from surrogates on reality shows or performers without art. We are more than sources of applause. People need to be able to see themselves as they are woven into the tapestry of their times and cultures, not viewed on jumbo screens, standing outside life as mere consumers, visitors, audiences, and victims of its accidents.

The tapestry of a trusted life is woven in our places, in the living environments of our culture. As information and its contextual meanings increase and our places provide connections and explanations in the presence of complexity, the need to understand entire patterns of life increases. The events and issues that influence our views of community, nation, civilization, and universe need to be grasped where we live, among our own values, cares, and intentions. We require critical thoughts; we need to express them, and we need to listen to them. We require a wide view among complex collections. Knowledge—given, discovered, combined, inferred—contextualizes a community. A rich cultural environment can become a mirror of local human needs, a community artifact.

AN ORGANISM, NOT A MECHANISM

How different, how constricted and vulnerable, our lives as citizens would be without our trust and experience in these places. At a meeting of the American Association of Museums in May 2010, I commented about a presentation by the Los Angeles County Museum of Art and the Queens Museum of Art in New York, each describing their ways of serving communities outside the conventional scope of the art museum through library collaborations. I admired these museums and their libraries when I spoke.

These programs, I said, *are evidence of how a cultural institution can be an organism, not a mechanism, how it can be responsive and adaptive. How the borders between institutions can become permeable and no longer reflect the conventional limits of what a museum can be for its citizens. Each institution is able to "see" and "sense" the lives of users, and open and respond to them in different ways. When acting in this way, the institutions can "touch" and "feel" the textures of lives. They can "listen" to their users, and they can invite and speak in a generous way when they respond.*

It is always important to allow the user to become your teacher. Responsive institutions are capable of taking in and adapting to complex information about families, cultures, languages, and personal experiences. This means that they are mindful and flexible as well as sensate. They come to hold particular knowledge of the community's living cultures and to use that knowledge to change the museum as a cultural place—in part simply by diversifying and respecting the people who use it. Libraries have always been about the people who use them, about those living cultures; it's something museums can learn from them.

Both museums and libraries are underestimated instruments of American democracy. When people engage with cultural institutions, they become, by definition, more connected, more informed, more powerful and aware, less isolated and less silent. These museums give a place to immigrant populations negotiating their identities under new conditions of social membership.

They make their families more connected to the culture they inhabit. They become better communicators. This extends the strengths of individuals, addresses the likely imbalance between fear and courage (as we must understand it in all of our increasingly powerless lives), and heartens the disheartened (as we must understand that only museums and libraries can do). This is an underestimated part of our capacity as institutions.

Collaborations of this kind—between similar institutions with comparable missions and collections—require not only an understanding of how much is shared between the two places, but also an understanding of what is complementary (that is, not shared or duplicated, and not compromising for either institution in the relationship). Each place brings its own authenticity to the relationship, but working together creates a mutual integrity of commitment, service, and promise that neither can have alone. This trust takes time. Collaborations require a long run to work. A sustained willingness to work and think together can't happen without trust.

Finally, collaborations of this kind require several strong, visionary, convinced champions of cooperation—people willing to negotiate and design in order to make the collaboration work. This happens when people have confidence and trust in their institution and what it gives to people's lives. Cautious, insular institutions can't do this; only bold, engaged museums, libraries, and human beings can.

When our places redefine themselves and think in fresh ways, they increase their capacity to develop new designs for service that do not reduce their historic or traditional gifts, but extend them into our transformed society. They become formative. The museum and the library are capable of mutual regard for their users, and of the embracing behaviors, connections, and identities that construct and extend living cultures. When that regard is established—and when it is explicitly served—the links between institutions become clear, helping citizens to understand that the commitments of each institution to knowledge and literacy are simultaneous and robust. These places are not competitors in a democratic society. In collaboration, both institutions have greater capacities to reflect the people of the place back to themselves. Each can demonstrate that a deep experience of art or literacy is also a deep experience of information and cultural knowledge. And they are likely to be perceived by citizens as naturally collaborative places. It is true about both people and institutions that collaboration need not compromise the independence of either partner, but will strengthen both.

Wherever I have seen collaborative programs between museums and libraries that advance literacy and citizenship, programs and spaces that respect visual facility and alternative ways of learning, and professionals who strive to know and explore the emerging identities in their communities, I have also observed that these collaborations are intuitively correct (similar intellectual values prevail in both places), educationally sound (cultural products and cultural diversity stimulate a desire for more information), and structurally smart (two institutions support each other, enhancing common strengths).

In my observations of the Queens Museum of Art and the Queens Library, in a community more densely populated with immigrant families than any other in the nation, I have understood the constructive effect of collaborative services. As a museum and library forge an active and engaged library partnership, both institutions can gather the experiences and energies of a community and recombine them as part of an underlying cultural presence. These experiences and energies are captured and held not only in the work of artists, including those enabled to find new American voices through collaborative museum and library programs, but also in the presence of its residents who become competent in the ways of public citizenship. As institutions with respect for the aspirations of their citizens and their living communities, the Queens Museum and the Queens Library are engaged in the construction and capture of cultural knowledge and value. This is especially important in a society where boundaries are open to expansion, and where extraordinary change is happening between generations.

Because our institutions, our places, have the power to aggregate, display, and reflect these energies, and because they are natural advocates for literacy, citizenship, and the common good, they together have an instrumental effect on lives nearby. Like no other institutions, they can assist different communities to generate new ideas for themselves, and to have new ideas about each other, while capturing human continuities and aspirations in common languages and artifacts. This is a new form of generativity in our places as we know them. It is becoming something together. It is regeneration and renewal, the adult life work. And it is confluence: becoming ourselves through gathering and practicing what we value together. Our places exist for this confluence.

CHAPTER 2

Beginnings

It may seem strange, but we might begin to understand the open possibilities of public learning in cultural institutions by observing a person asleep and dreaming. We have no need for the details of the dream or its images in order to tell that something is happening that we cannot see in the brain and the body of the dreamer, dreaming as we watch. The sleeper may experience fear or passion invisible to us, or vivid, extraordinary and mysterious struggles we cannot see. The closed eyes and dormant body are in motion, but even the agitated sleeper is unlikely to wake as the dreaming mind works. The dream leaves its traces, as a harrow leaves a groove. Each of us is touched by dreams when we wake, but what has happened to our minds remains elusive and provocative, especially when a dreamed image recurs throughout a waking day. What part of my life is this? The faint trace stays, then we sleep and dream some more, because our minds are always in motion. It is this motion that will help us to understand.

Or, we might begin to understand the possibilities of public learning by imagining a person at a moment of great excitement and elevation, listening with countless other listeners, to a poem on a cold January day in Washington, D.C. We are watching one particular listener with care, from a small distance. As the ceremonial poem surrounds us, we hear the words together: they are about the daily work we do, the way we ignore or notice each other as we pass, our silences amid the chaos, and the words we might say if we were to speak. The poem is about the traces of infinity in this everyday chaos: memory, lineage, recollection, sorrows, and joys, all of them with us as we listen with this person, whose head is gently bowed, eyes shut. The poem, on this day, is about the language we use to become something, to be something with others. It is also about the moment of safety we need in order to savor what is happening, as we are about to enter the next unknown, the next invisible thing. The closed eyes of the listener are not the closed eyes of solitude, prayer or sleep, but an awareness of something we cannot see. Watching, we may believe it is a moment of looking inward. The head moves downward, mouth opens and eyes shut tighter, head nods once, a breath is taken deeply through the open mouth, almost a sigh. Ready now, on this remarkable day, to move forward. Eyes are open now, the head nods again as though in a brief agreement, and they squint against sunlight, straining to see the distant person, tall at the center of this moment, so far away we can only trust.

We dream and we aspire. We find our dreamings and aspirations through words. And even if we cannot see what will happen next, we carry an invisible courage into the everyday. We do these things because we are alive and human, each in our own dream and aspiration. It is the dreaming and aspiring that will help us to understand.

This essay and all of the essays in this book are about ourselves, dreaming and aspiring, entering—as we do each day—whatever is not yet clear to us. But this collection is not a work of psychology or memory, thought, mind, dreaming, or the meaning of poetry, and yet my true intent is to see how all of these things—and yet other more invisible strands of experience—might help to advance and illuminate the forward motion of one progressive life. "Progressive life" as I use it means "life moving forward," as I believe all lives must. Lives that do not refresh and renew themselves or flow toward a new aspiration are at risk of stagnation and immobility; they are vulnerable to despair. This is also true of cultures. As I write about the possible roles of cultural institutions in progressive lives, I also envision new ways of conversation that might enhance the understanding of national experience for us all.

Though we may not be scientists, each of our lives gives us a rich and seemingly impenetrable complexity of empirical experiences. Think of it as the immense, cumulative data of what we observe and feel, even in mundane and uneventful circumstances like going to a movie or a local reading group. The living life is our laboratory for experiments in moving forward—our unfolding, our trying out—in order to become ourselves. To see the possibilities of public learning may begin by imagining one life dreaming in an open, nearly transparent way, one life in imaginative progress. To see these things will remind us that none of us is ever finished nor is our course fixed or fully known; in our lives, something is always about to happen, even as we sleep. And, when we wake informed by our dreams, we want something more to happen for us, we want something different to begin.

WHEN THE MIND UNFOLDS

When the mind unfolds like a roadmap in a museum or library, our unknowns and our experiences momentarily combine to create us in the world as questioners. Our questions may help us to complete our thinking, or extend its possibilities. Unfolded by our words or memories, opened by our question, we will always remain unfinished, but we have become different. Even changes of the smallest kind can inspire and remake us and outfit us for a new voyage. We are at our best when we are restless and uneasy, testing, questioning and doubting, moving forward into an evolving comprehension in an evolving world. Or, at least, aspiring or dreaming to do that, and looking for help.

This book has been assembled—or it has been itself unfolded—in a tentative way, in admiring regard for "the evolving self" described by Mihaly Csikszentmihalyi (1993) as a way of striving for greater complexity, fulfilling its potential complexity and capacity.

> To help guide the progress of evolution it is not sufficient for a person to enjoy merely any kind of life, but a life that increases order instead of disorder. To contribute to greater harmony, a person's consciousness has to become complex. Complexity of consciousness is not a function of only intelligence or knowledge, and is not just a cognitive trait—it includes a person's feelings and actions as well. It involves becoming aware of and in control of one's unique potentials, and being able to create harmony between goals and desires, sensations and experiences, both for oneself and for others. People who achieve this are not only going to have a more fulfilling life, but they are almost certainly more likely to contribute to a better future. Personal happiness and a positive contribution to evolution go hand in hand. (Csikszentmihalyi, 1993, pp. 207–208)

I also write with regard for what adult educators have described as "possible selves," understood as "an individual's conceptions of future selves, including the selves that are ideal and hoped for, as well as those possible selves that one fears or dreads. The concept of possible selves encompasses both the culturally determined and the self-constructed aspects of the self" (Rossiter, 2007, pp. 5–6). The possible self is a tentative path for a life, depending on the capacity of the person for understanding outcomes and values, for projecting these from now into the future, and for "instrumental behavior" as a series of constructive strategies toward an energetic new state. "In effect, possible selves build a bridge between the current state and the desired future self" (Leonardi, 2007, p. 20).

Possible selves, it is important to say, are also about an interpretation of the present self, in the process of becoming different. "An individual's repertoire of possible selves is not just any assortment of roles or identities that one can imagine, but includes only those possible selves that are psychologically accessible and personally meaningful" (Rossiter, 2007, p. 6). The possible selves of one life may be diverse, revealing, and surprising. They confirm self-renewal and mature vitality, a way of reweaving the fabric we might once have thought to be complete and firmly, tightly woven. Instead, we find the fabric to be unfinished and always open.

ASPECTS OF THE INFINITE

These essays assume that aspects of the infinite lie hidden in everyday lives and understandings, discovered in memory and perception, often appearing in the unfinished issues that shape us invisibly. I write to suggest, if not to grasp, the value of cultural institutions as instruments of service to the open, possible lives in every adult. For decades, I have kept in mind the vital concept described by Gordon Allport as the "proprium," an image of human becoming. Allport (1955) describes as an example how fundamental and essential our native language is to us, and how much of our perception and expression depends on having it. And yet, he writes, its use is "ordinarily felt to be quite peripheral to the core of our existence" (p. 40). Take it away, however, and we would rapidly understand how our language creates a central projection of our selves and our ways of thinking about our lives.

> So it is with the myriad of social and physiological habits we have developed that are never, unless interfered with, regarded as essential to our existence as a separate being.
>
> Personality includes these habits and skills, frames of reference, matters of fact and cultural values that seldom or never seem warm and important. But personality includes what is warm and important also—all the regions of our life that we regard as peculiarly ours, and which for the time being I suggest we call the *proprium*. The proprium includes all aspects of personality that make for inward unity. (Allport, 1955, p. 40)

The proprium comprises our senses of physical self, identity, the ego, the progressive extensions of the self toward what we value, our rational agency, and the self-images, private and public, that represent us in the world. Enfolded in these elements are aspects of the self-image that compose our aspirations, our idealized selves, the human being we wish to become. In one form, the self may bundle an array of delusions; but at its most valuable and functional, that self can use the propriate image as a cognitive map for identifying and planning motion toward a reasoned goal, based in reality and entirely attainable. There is, Allport says, an imaginative use of the proprium, with power to give one life the integrity and form that comes only from strongly conducted pursuit.

"Propriate movement" or "propriate striving" is motivation, the human being's way toward realizing aspirations, persistence against obstacles, an urge toward transformation in accord with a design. "Striving," says Allport, "always has a future reference. Along with *striving*, we may mention *interest, tendency, disposition, expectation, planning, problem solving* and *intention*.... People, it seems, are busy leading their lives into the future, whereas psychology, for the most part, is busy tracing them into the past" (Allport, 1955, p. 51). Then to this construction of the striving future self at the center of the proprium, Allport adds that "the self as *knower* emerges as a final and inescapable postulate" (Allport, 1955, p. 52). It is this knower—synthesizer of the self, weaver of the fabric, author of the narrative—who strives to design the life a human being leads. In this sense, a designed life is not stainless or impervious, but rather a life that is not dominated by disorder, accident, or dysfunction. I see it as our wanting not simply to know but also to become different, to understand and experience something fresh, to reflect on it and perhaps to transmit part of one's self toward others. This wanting is, to me, the parts of the self we are most likely to consider "warm and important" as we live. Learning, however we think of it, has no truth without them.

I first read about the proprium in *Self-Renewal*, one of John W. Gardner's fine and sensible books (Gardner, 1964). I continue to write in gratitude for Gardner, a genius of social life. There is no more dedicated and persuasive advocate for self-renewal. The concepts that guide *Self-Renewal* continue to guide me after four decades. In passages following his discussion of the proprium, Gardner writes about the compelling search for fresh knowledge (i.e., "modern science") that is robust but comparatively shallow when juxtaposed to a deeper frame for the human being.

> Man has never been satisfied to let it go at that. He has throughout history shown a compelling need to arrive at conceptions of the universe *in terms of which he could regard his own life as meaningful.* He wants to know where *he* fits into the scheme of things. He wants to understand how the great facts of the objective world relate to him and what they imply for his behavior. He wants to know what significance may be found in his own existence, the succeeding generations of his kind and the vivid events of his inner life. He seeks some kind of meaningful framework in which to understand (or at least to reconcile himself to) the indignities of chance and circumstance and the fact of death. ... He wants, in the worlds of Kierkegaard, 'a truth that is true for me.' He seeks conceptions of the universe that give dignity, purpose and sense to his own existence. (Gardner, 1964, p. 102)

Gardner confirmed for me that the deeper frame of our lives—often masked by the reductive terms "learning" or "education" or "skills"—is rarely construed in public as the complexity it is. When those terms are used in their political (rather than personal) senses, there is a quality of separation among them from the ongoing continuities of life. When we hear or read "education" or "learning" in the news, it is likely not to be about transformation but about a commodity we must go somewhere to get, where we are measured and clad in acceptable administrative ways, and defined nearly always by the horizons of others, and not by our own undiscovered dreams.

WANTING

Actually, of course, we have many ways to think about the wanting that inspires us to learn; dreaming is just one. We also know that our wanting to learn is diverse and persistent, and the words we use to name it are extensive and evocative. We ache to know. We covet or crave knowledge. Inspired by Frank Smith's lists of words related to thinking, this is my list of words for wanting or striving to know: we strive, envision, itch or lust, we search and struggle. We aim, anticipate, ask, aspire, attempt, build, design, desire, determine, dream, endeavor, essay, expect, fantasize, go after, go for, hope, hunger, imagine, intend, long for, need, picture, plan, prepare, project, propose, purport, pursue, require, see, and seek knowledge. We ask. We are tempted by knowledge, we wish and thirst to know. It is to die for, to try for, to undertake, to visualize, and to yearn for. We are seduced by knowledge, we are intrigued, we are lured, and we become addicted. But "learning" is a cheapened word, not a word to be used with ease. It begs for specificity, and it alone cannot take us far.

Does "learning" mean that I have undergone a transformation and have now grown or become different from the man I was? Does it mean that I have discovered or realized some elusive truth, following an adventurous pursuit? Is it a conquering? An overcoming? A triumph? Does my learning mean that I have solved a problem, broken through a barrier, and unraveled tangled evidence? Have I mastered a process of understanding complexity? What did I experience? Did my learning extend or expand my vision or perspective, allowing me to perceive insights or see some at-last-revealed secret thing? Having learned, did I construct something, assemble it from separate objects, make connections, make sense, put the pieces together, and make them fit, finally constructing something whole? What was it: transformation, discovery, breakthrough, mastery, vision, insight, construction, or a synthesis of all these? When we next hear some expert talk about "learning," perhaps we could ask, "What kind of learning do you mean? Can you tell us what 'learning' means?" And when we use the word as experts ourselves, perhaps we too can say what, of all its forms, we mean? And, finally, when we explain it, we might acknowledge that neither quantities nor test scores are relevant. Instead, we might speak of invention, design, curiosity, connection, determination, and resilience, or of fearlessness in the midst of change.

We will hear "learning" commonly whenever the discussion or the news moves to the state of the schools, where it becomes a nearly meaningless word. In that discourse, "learning" represents a measurable commodity, and almost surely an artifact manufactured in the small world of schooling. However, in my lexicon, to be a *learner* remains a special honorific, as it is to be a scholar or a student; I will always want to be among such people, working to make progress against bewilderment. In cultural institutions, people think and grow, reflect and expand their capacity for the new. They also work to overcome the effects of their underimagined and overmeasured schooling. Of course, even in these pages the word "learn" will appear, despite its deficiency in capturing the variation and complexity we hide beneath it.

"Learning" is the word we tend to use in place of "thinking" or "thought." We also use it instead of "experience," meaning how people move toward greater complexity and more able craft, or how they combine a strong complement of tools in order to act on an unknown. There is a truer vocabulary that matters far more than "learning" does: thinking, moving, crafting, acting, trying out, building, saying, and experiencing. I also value the idea of being able to articulate a lesson learned, of grasping an experience that helped to make a difference or a decision, or helped to name a fresh idea. Look back: how did you learn this?

The dissociation is evident in common parlance about education: there is a concept called "readiness to learn," we complete our "formal education," and we must master "twenty-first-century skills" before we are ready to take an active role in the current century. These ideas imply a set of well-meaning curricula, an ideal efficiency, and the implication of completion and finishing something off. Each diploma confers evidence of success, a victory. But they are not always connected to the vivid, compelling events of an inner life. They are not even (to me) the primary way we change. Rather than "learning" and the other words, cultural institutions are about construction, transformation, configuration, and observation. They are about experiences that matter and stay with us, leading to the possible; they are about thinking anything.

I express these beliefs and cite my early readings in gratitude; I always want to turn readers toward them. Although I have no mentors, I would have welcomed the chance to study in the shadows of many: Allport, Gardner, Dewey, Emerson, Maxine Greene, Jack Mezirow, Erik H. Erikson, Frank Smith, and Donald Schön. However, each has given me a gift in the anthropological sense: an exchange that deeply connects minds and enacts obligations of respect and reciprocity. I am too presumptuous, neither a philosopher nor a psychologist, merely a librarian. And yet, wanting so much, I have always been a reader in search of consonant voices. I know that my colleagues in museums and libraries have also given me equally binding gifts; I give them whatever I can offer in return, my gratitude first. It would take a lifetime to grasp them all.

Old as they may be, ideas like reciprocity and becoming never disappear; rather, they become more central to our lives as we are challenged to live responsively and thoughtfully. Old as these ideas may be, they appear in this book, written in 2010 as the nation reaches the end of its first decade in a new millennium. It has been an ambiguous, difficult period characterized by wide variations in trust and truth, and a painful struggle to think clearly when we cannot see clearly and (echoing John W. Gardner) there are no easy victories.

WE GROW

Yet the single formative fact of our lives has not varied: by necessity we grow through striving for something, and we become more complex as we do. We also grow through resisting something. At times, we may resist and hide ourselves from change, but a life in progress will grow far beyond the comforts of any easy, thoughtless way. We work to restore ourselves and feel a capacity for resilience. At our best, we resist shallow simplicity and we resist ignorance, even when it is prolific. We grow toward new choices, designs, beliefs, and complexities in our lives. We grow toward a more precise language to define and remind ourselves. We grow with an intuition that survives despite modifications forced by technology, schooling, and media. We allow our beliefs to evolve. Thinking with each other in the open places we have made, our tentative understandings of experience and possibility allow us to know and shape a living world. Our thinking in this way can supplant stagnation with authenticity and power.

My work over forty years has been to observe and to teach, to express my own ignorance and uncertainty aloud, and to remind myself and others that my voice is mine alone, neither thoughtful nor artful enough to offer much beyond my own questions in the unique surrounding territory of my unknowns. Therefore I know that no one can create thought or understanding for another person, or teach with a claim to the truth. As a librarian and teacher, I know that it is possible only to assist progressive lives, and to provide structures and tools as we can. Moreover, it is possible to assist or influence only those who admit us to their trust. No one will every learn anything because we say they must. It is unethical, impossible to do more.

As I say, my unknowns are mine alone. When I write about possibility and promise, or about ways of thinking and learning in civic lives, I also know that such things may not exist widely or plainly for everyone to see. I worry about this invisibility, and doubt my ideas as no one else can. Still, as an advocate for lives that flourish, and as a teacher of professional practices to assist the mind's unfolding, I suggest this following handful of principles—call them beginnings—early in this book. They have been guiding possibilities for me, precepts of public experiences in cultural institutions.

Cultural institutions collect what once was created, discovered, or gathered to solve a problem, to answer a question, or to provoke one.

Our institutions are not only about what they contain and the questions we ask in them; they also refer to a world elsewhere.

The most important content of a cultural institution is neither shelved nor shown: it is the original setting or problem, from another time or society, or a microscopic world in a laboratory, or a macroscopic world in an observatory; in an artist's studio, a writer's desk, or wherever this particular world begins.

The unknown in the thing before us is the need, question, or desire that required it, the provocation it makes, the change it inspires in us, the open question it still asks. Where is the aspect of the infinite in this thing?

Wanting to understand, we overestimate the value of order, logic, and category in museums and libraries. We confound order with explanation. It is received, replicated, expanded, and reified; ideas of order preserve illusory control over intangible experiences. Until we move beyond the order, to a place that remains wild and original, we inhabit a bloodless world, thinking it is real.

Following blueprints, we build libraries and museums to provide systems and structures as ways to find patterns or connections. Our aspirations may be worthy and useful, but cultural institutions may work best when accidents and surprises occur, when boundaries are crossed, or when our expectations are overturned like apple carts and we must rely on something we have not expected.

An overturned apple cart is a gift. Even in great collections—as in all great fiction—amid great experiences and anticipation, something is meant to be overturned.

In our work, we constantly invent practice; nothing is given to us. We create practice by acting and speaking. We create institutions by causing things to happen in them. We adapt to the present, and to people in the present.

Advocating the goodness of our institution's mission or collection, and the great value of our knowledge is not persuasive, and not even constructive. It becomes constructive only when an institution acts to create the presence of knowledge in its community.

An institution's evidence of value appears in its power to cause change outside itself. Its tacit mission is to address the lives and aspirations of people outside the place. To be useful, the place draws outsiders in, helps them to use the place, slowly incites their questions, and then begins a public conversation, knowing that there is no easy trust.

We look from our own place. We live on evolving horizons, shaped by both designs and accidents. Our strongest experiences cannot be entirely saved, repeated, evaluated, tested, or described or remembered in detail. They disappear like dreams unless we are challenged to curate them.

However, our questions and thoughts do not disappear; they continue to lead us, even when we think we have moved on. Every thought about knowledge moves knowledge. When we reveal, describe, and talk over our experiences, knowledge folds upon knowledge. Patterns evolve when people think and decide, and as they use language with each other. And yet we can say only what we have the words to say, and, lacking words, something will always escape us. Our challenge is often simply to use words; words make observations possible and prevent their disappearance, their evanescence.

SHAPED BY STORIES

I often think that, without museums and libraries, some experiences would be impossible, and therefore some knowledge would be impossible. Cultural institutions prepare us for situations where the conceptual, the fluid, the permeable, the variable, the comparative, the extensive, the ineffable, and the incomprehensible are all present in spaces, collections, connections, structures, patterns, comparisons, and differences. What are the dimensions of these things? Even in a measured universe, it is not possible to say. But we do have stories to keep. Museum stories and library stories are the same connected stories: people lived; events happened; contexts became more complex; time passed; people changed; stories were recollected and told; memories, records, and artifacts survived. From where we stand, we look for what is present and what is missing in the story, in order to tell it, restore it, and discover its contexts in our contexts.

Every person's world is shaped by stories, by unknown maps and timetables, invisible cultures and languages, formative voices, all unseen and unheard by others, sometimes invisible to the person as well. They may or may not reveal themselves, and by these uncertain guides, we begin. We name the world as we encounter it, and the names appear, perhaps tentatively, in our conversations. Except for mortality, there is no limit to our capacity for an inner experience of the outer world. Nor is there a limit on our capacity to miss the inner experience entirely, having been distracted by the outer world. We learn most from the changing contexts of lives and experiences, including our own, but we have to look, or we cannot think beyond the moment. It is always a struggle for us; but we dare not look away from the experiences that lie in an encounter with complexity, and so we are drawn in.

We confirm, we change, we connect, and, when we can, we speak about our thoughts. Our capacities to attend, to ignore, to reflect, and to inquire share an infinite dimension. We walk into that which we cannot yet see—the endless, invisible dimensions of our strongest experiences—if we are aware and moving forward in our lives. These are the beginnings of things—ideas that seem to me to describe our observant lives in process. Because their origins are obscure, the ideas that move us are necessarily incomplete, but they promise more. My intentions are to suggest the need for open conversations in public; to describe practical possibilities for cultural institutions, especially public libraries and progressive museums; and to encourage ways to think beyond the great collections that only begin to define our possibilities and capacities. If we are capable and passionate—and if we devote our advocacy to a new vision of our institutions—the richest moment will endure.

CHAPTER 3

Flourishing

The few remaining places open for our missing public conversations are public cultural institutions: libraries, museums, science centers, historic sites, and public spaces where knowledge, human differences, public policies, and common ideas can be explored without a rush toward resolution. Our need for fearless experiences and conversations—civil, public, informed, open, reflective, welcoming, unfinished—increases with the complexities of our experience. Above all other reasons, this need for comfort with complex tasks and lives, and an understanding of contexts, has sustained cultural institutions. They are places for negotiations between ourselves and the knowledge that composes a society; they are places for finding what it is we are striving to become, what is possible for the nation, and the missing parts of our lives. In their best instances, cultural institutions are participatory and open; they invite active, progressive engagement; they are inquiry centered, holding knowledge to assuage great unknowns. They are ideal places for breaking through silence with dialogue. They encourage thought and reflection and therefore enhance human capacities. They help us to flourish as people.

The concept of civic flourishing is not a purely economic concept. It refers to more than the ways of consumers and markets. In the largest sense, the flourishing of differences is the most visible characteristic of a strong and thriving community, evidence of energy, resilience, and ethos. A similar indicator is a robust complement of open places where new ideas can be addressed over time, but this will require comity, goodwill, and imagination. A flourishing community is likely to comprise economic health for a wide array of workers; philanthropy and volunteering in community causes; shared attention to public safety and health; diverse, democratic citizen engagement in shaping civic choices; evident ways to express opinions to leaders; acts of respect and concern for people across differences of age, origin, and wealth; acceptance and exploration of those differences; situations for responsive and successful learning apart from schools; and government practices that exemplify continuity and integrity. Perhaps these are ideal indicators, but when a community is at its best, I think that evidence of broad engagement will be apparent in some way. None will be realized perfectly, and no single example will be achieved without the presence of others. A community is a complexity; it often grows from the bottom up, and flourishes from its edges in.

Civic flourishing requires an invitation that reaches the edges, and comprises robust public conversations about the values and intentions of a community's purpose. This talking work occurs in the councils and agencies serving community aspirations: policy-making bodies, police and fire departments, hospitals and clinics, political parties, public schools, and leadership groups. It also occurs informally when people congregate to volunteer, seek opportunities for public service, or read and discuss ideas in an atmosphere of independence. Wherever citizens think and communicate together for the good of the civic space—separate from politics or self-promotion—a contribution to the flourishing community is made.

Libraries and museums each have a stake and a purpose in advocacy for civic flourishing; in particular, libraries have a specific and direct role in the cultural deliberations that affect all community thriving. A public library occupies a critical place in a community, providing essential resources for civic progress: a flexible collection of current and useful information, access to technologies, professional attention to the issues and topics likely to make a difference, and a neutral space for public conversations and social learning about the future. In an environment of possibility and uncertainty, public libraries assist good (exploratory, useful, purposeful, and clarifying) public thinking. Democracies strengthen themselves when libraries are encouraged to fulfill the purpose and promise of a community.

For museums, the value of social and civic engagement may be slightly less obvious, but the stake and purpose of the museum have an even larger context than the library. Every museum—collections of history, natural history and art, or a time and place, and living collections of flora and fauna, geology, and astronomy—is a situation for the explorations of definitive themes, the construction of knowledge, and the complexity of objects and the humanity they represent. Understanding details of the past. Grasping the perspectives of genius. Weighing the evidence of living environments, evolution, and human behavior. Redefining the anthropological record. Transferring lessons from other times and cultures. There is no end to these contexts and the differences of opinion and response that surround them. Nor is there an end to the relevance of museum collections to the questions of the current age. Today's front page calls up histories of faith and conflict, geographic dominance, tribal cultures and social practices, global economy, global weather, global communication, and global commerce. It is difficult to imagine a theme of gravity and value that does not have resonance in a museum collection, however hidden its evidences may be.

Cultural institutions should be seen as agents for both their societies and their communities; that is, for human safety and connection to the record, and for the human pulse that causes us to cling together. Our changing experiences of society and knowledge in the first decades of the new century offer cultural institutions an opportunity to participate in the necessary rethinking and possible redefinition of the nation. Opportunities of this kind are always the result of difficult cultural tensions and complexities that create challenges to citizens, great needs that only knowledge and its generation will meet. We know them well: economy, education, diversity, tolerance, gender, and peace. Only libraries and museums are prepared to address these tensions as neutral agencies—not for solutions, but for citizens to know and explore their thoughts and voices in a fair environment. My premise is that the function of cultural institutions is to help us to live more fully within our lives, and then to move our lives forward, toward something we have not yet seen or language we have not yet spoken; toward the breaking through, the transformation of the imagined into the possible.

A STORY TO TELL

I imagine that there is no one living in the world for whom this is not in some way an aspiration: to thrive in brain and body first, as part of a family and a culture, and then to imagine and dream. To experiment, to think, invent, admire, to deepen understanding, to know, to challenge, to uncover, to say. But also to see our own place as a part of a larger culture where we are nourished by continuities and the promise of being remembered as having been present and alive. After all else, our wanting is to have a story to tell that is our own. There, in that untold story, is where the passion and the obsession of what we do and what we are reside. We cannot revise our story until we have told it to ourselves, and understood it for ourselves. That understanding is the source of integrity. Nothing can displace or supplant this wanting for personal truth, not entertainment, fantasy, or technology. In cultural institutions, our work is to start something in that story that does not want to stop and will not disappear.

Our situation at the start of this century can be expressed in configurations of pervasive, essential tensions and imbalances. We live among multiple, divergent, conflicting, often harshly different experiences. We have felt physical attacks, losing human lives and confidence, and yet, in our wounded civilization, violence is popular entertainment and vengeance is a political value. Narrow political ideas and religious expressions are at times indistinguishable; politics, race, and faith separate and reduce us. Cynicism

inures us, and critical thinking challenges us. Consequently, the possibilities of informed and provident thinking escape us. Education is reduced to its least constructive function—the test that classifies (and too frequently fails) its taker. We gaze at the desert of public life with an absence of depth and trust, aware of the incapacity of inquiry, literature, art, and history to express useful lessons. Only acumen, courage, and intelligent human relationships offer respite from our fears. Our anticipations are often reduced to instincts alone, having neither map nor compass for this unexpected landscape.

Think with me about a handful of tensions and burdens in American experience as I write in late 2010, still a time of war and an election season of tension and distress. Think with me about the possible responses of progressive cultural institutions, and about the ways that museums and libraries might contain information and create public discourse in response.

First: we are in an extraordinary, restive, unruly, and corrupted financial environment forcing many citizens to leave behind their assumptions of security, safety, and the future. Among a vast number of American lives, expectations and beliefs in the future have been reconsidered, perhaps abandoned. Income inequality and economic vulnerability are rife, driven by marginal ethics and the extremities of capitalism. Identities are under forced reconstruction, and the touchstones of an individual life—the lives of families, and the futures of children, work, health care, and housing—need to be rethought. Few leaders appear to grasp the impact of these losses on trust and optimism. For many citizens, a politicized economy discards the values and achievements of personal integrity and responsibility. How should citizens plan to live when their lives can be so radically reconfigured by the acts of others?

Second: our population is changed and continues to change. While the aging of healthy generations makes the nation less young, immigration, birth rates, multiple faiths, new languages, and living cultures combine to make the nation more complex, less uniform and homogeneous, more blended, and less white. The nation is less isolated from the living cultures and faiths of the world; consequently there are fewer degrees of separation from deeply different experiences of family and work, growing up, entering adulthood, and striving to become a person of honest accomplishment. No simple understanding of "the American people" will ever work again. With every new arrival, in my view, the quotient of aspiration and hope in the United States is renewed. Others disagree, as they may; but we hear fearful misinformation about, and viral blame and fear of, *the other*, unattached from causality or evidence. There is for me, the grandson of immigrants, a kind of shame in this, in a nation with historic themes, where we have never resisted diversity.

Third: we observe losses of citizen confidence in education, government, religion, health care, political parties, banks, and corporations. And so we

must satisfy and reconfigure our need for trust elsewhere, somewhere, as we also experience a renewed awareness of the economic distances between citizens. While we cannot easily sustain or plan lives, careers, ambitions, or home ownership, or live by even modest design, without economically stable lives, neither can we live without trust or confidence in our national resilience. We need to reinvent some of our institutions, just as we need to reinvent ourselves. Until we do, with neither a supportive economy nor a sustaining ethos, we are increasingly vulnerable to accidents of all kinds, foreclosures, health crises, emotional depression, and other personal assaults on our well-being and self-control, even as many of us are required to reconfigure our lives and dreams. These discontinuities are not abstract: they are personal, and they happen to us. They challenge American resilience and a democratic belief in future possibilities.

Fourth: out of the losses of April 19, 1995, and September 11, 2001, we have drawn only limited lessons, confused our founding values with our fears, and too easily sustained a residual climate of suspicion and insinuation. We live with terrorism; we live with worldwide violence. A patriotic war of dubious justification was prosecuted in the name of the American people; during that war, the unprecedented imprisonment and hidden torture of enemy combatants became routine. A political climate of anti-compromise, bullying rhetoric, and simplistic polarity has meant the disappearance of reasoned debate and the erosion of privacy. Complex realities of American history and life are distorted, denied, or simplified, and broadcast to millions who have neither opportunity nor need to question. It is difficult to question fear. Opinion shapes evidence. There is neither vigorous nor articulate response from weakened, struggling mainstream journalism. As one consequence we have no rational or useful public dialogues, no aggressive public corrections of error, no open conversations among leaders with different political beliefs, no models for compromise or common ground, and no significant debates at election time. In a climate of obduracy and intransigence, it is difficult to explore alternative thinking or to clarify clouded realities. We become susceptible to distortion, misinformation, and demagoguery. The inconvenience of mutual, loyal, authentic engagement for the common good has been forgone, replaced by cynical and well-funded political design.

Fifth: we might add that literacy is in change, knowledge and books are changing forms, and perhaps reading itself is in eclipse. (The resulting controversy ironically thrives on the internet: *What will happen to books? Click here.*) Our dominant tools are small but demanding electronic devices, conveying small but demanding electronic messages, foreboding the death of attention span. Triviality addicts. In any given week, leading television programs are devoted to inconsequential artificial reality, talent, dancing, cooking, fashion, modeling, and weight loss competitions. Though we suspect immigrants, we make heroes of vampires. Simultaneously, the political favoring of mechanistic school testing makes it reasonable to won-der, *What happens to the future of abiding curiosity, personal reading, unre-stricted imagination, and conversations that provoke ideas?* The American mind is starving, we might think, and these conditions constitute crises in nourishment. I believe that our fearful ambivalences, narrow and opinion-ridden information sources, and vapid entertainments have cognitive impli-cations for our understanding of human abilities and differences, and our sense of the nation's changing face and intellect.

Sixth, and equal to all these, in my view, is the invisibility of adult learning in all of our discussions of education and literacy. Having confounded schooling, education, and learning with constant testing, we have done little to strengthen or motivate adult-learning experiences toward the skills of critical thinking, investigation, and synthesis. The five tensions and burdens I have listed here are challenges felt deeply in adult lives, where the practices of informed thought and reasoning cannot be overvalued. It is in adult rela-tionships, economies, social connections, understandings of history, and responses to crisis that our public knowledge is founded. And it is only when our children hear us speaking to each other as we address ambiguities, ask-ing questions and seeking answers, that they have mature models of dis-course and independent learning. We educate children so they are not powerless; we ought to educate adults for the same reason. In a competitive culture we easily can feel far behind others, unable to reconcile the disconti-nuities between our expectations and realities, especially if we have lost our jobs or our visions of possible lives for ourselves. When we are unaware of complexity and history, we are at risk of simplicity and arrogance, some-thing we can never afford. In these tensions there are commonalities: a lack of trust, unsatisfied aspirations, the fear of fear. Such unprecedented adult crises tell us that our world requires new ways to think and act toward their resolution.

OUR WHALE

In 2008, the great novelist E. L. Doctorow spoke at a convocation of the American Academy of Arts & Sciences and the American Philosophical Society, remarkably titled *The Public Good: Knowledge as the Foundation for a Democratic Society.* His first words were a question, "What does it say about the United States today that this fellowship of the arts, sciences and philosophy is called to affirm knowledge as a public good? What have we come to when the self-evident has to be argued as if … it is a proposition still to be proven?" (Doctorow, 2008, p. 76). The title of this brilliant address was emblematically American, "The White Whale," invoking the immensity of our unknowns and our daunting awareness of them.

Melville in *Moby Dick* speaks of 'reality outracing apprehension': apprehension in the sense not of fear or disquiet but of understanding; reality as too much for us to take in—as, for example, the white whale is too much for the Pequod and its captain. It may be that our new century is an awesomely, complex white whale, scientifically in our quantumized wave/particles and the manipulable stem cells of our biology, ecologically in our planetary crises of nature, technologically in our humanoid molecular computers, sexually in the rising number of our genders, intellectually in the paradoxes of our texts, and so on. (p. 80)

Doctorow asks, "What is more natural than to rely on the saving powers of simplism?" Perhaps, he speculates, "We are actually engaged in a genetic engineering venture that will make a slower, dumber, more sluggish whale, one that can be harpooned and flensed, tried and boiled to light our candles—a kind of water wonderworld whale made of racism, nativism, cultural illiteracy, fundamentalist fantasy, and the righteous priorities of wealth" (2008, pp. 80–81).

As John W. Gardner points out, the prospects given to us by our fears rather than our hopes are not new, but are an inimical part of us. We are hesitant to enter a national conversation about our values and aspirations because it is so often the realm of zealots and politicians and so rarely anything like a calm talk among citizens, even citizens who disagree with each other. However this is what we need to do. If, as Gardner says, we are participants in a national drama, we must understand our sources and our scripts: citizenship, processes, laws, settings for explanation and adjudication, ways to regenerate ourselves, and ways to revise our errors. And we need to understand that what happens in drama is transformation, self-realization, an understanding of flaws, the articulation of lessons for other generations. Long before our current tensions, Gardner emphasized a reasonable stance. "That we have failed and fumbled in some of our attempts to achieve our ideals is obvious," Gardner wrote. "[But] we have an uncelebrated capacity to counter disintegration with new integrations" (Gardner, 1999, p. xv).

In *Ill Fares the Land*, published just before his death, Tony Judt (2010) wrote in a similar but less optimistic way.

The case for reviving the state does not rest uniquely upon its contributions to modern society as a collective project; there is a more urgent consideration. We have entered an age of fear. Insecurity is once again an active ingredient of political life in Western democracies. Insecurity born of terrorism, of course; but also, and more insidiously, fear of the uncontrollable speed of change, fear of the loss of employment, fear of losing ground to others in an increasingly unequal distribution of resources, fear of losing control of the circumstances and routines of our daily life. And, perhaps above all, fear that it is not just *we* who can no longer shape our lives but that those in authority have also lost control to forces beyond their reach. (p. 217)

When we do not listen and speak in civic culture, we do not think or grow in civic culture. When we do not strive to understand complexity and instead embrace the simplistic, we betray the complex future we have made possible by our gifts. No simple explanation or plan will last for long. We are challenged by our own need for self-renewal and recovery of confidence. When people look *away*, not *toward*, when people look *alone*, not *with*, and when people look *at*, not *for*—and still cannot say what problem it is we need most to solve—there is work for the cultural institutions of the nation. Judt recounts how the disillusionments and failures of government in addressing environmental change, health care, and the financial crisis "have accentuated a sentiment of helplessness among even well-disposed voters. We need to act upon our intuitions of impending catastrophe" (Judt, 2010, p. 166). He immediately begins his next chapter, "Recasting Public Conversation," with the words, "Most critics of our present condition start with institutions" (p. 167). And we too might well begin with the few institutions already high in trust and use—our cultural places—where knowledge, information resources, and informed guidance are present.

Judt's words are resonant. In 1991, Robert N. Bellah and his associates recognized that "we live through institutions," using this simple declaration as the first chapter title in *The Good Society*.

We need to understand how much of our lives is lived in and through institutions, and how better institutions are essential if we are to lead better lives. . . . Our present situation requires an unprecedented increase in the ability to attend to new possibilities, moral as well as technical, and to put the new technical possibilities in a moral context. The challenges often seem overwhelming, but there are possibilities for an immense enhancement of our lives, individual and collective, an enhancement based on a significant moral advance. One of the greatest challenges, especially for individualistic Americans, is to understand what institutions are—how we form them and how they in turn form us—and to imagine that we can actually alter them for the better. . . . It is hard for us to think of institutions as affording the necessary context within which we become individuals; of institutions as not just restraining but enabling us; of institutions not as an arena of hostility within which our character is tested but an indispensable source from which character is formed. (Bellah et al., 1991, pp. 5–6)

We know that such institutions as schools and hospitals, government bureaucracies, and law enforcement, beneficent as they are, exist to "fix" us, to improve or repair us, to regulate us, to make us better, to straighten us out. We know that we are vulnerable to them and dependent upon them, and when we are in them, we want to be out of them. In nearly all cases, institutions as we know them tend to make us cautious and submissive. Moments when they help people to speak together, to communicate about their experiences, or to become something together are rare. And yet it is clear that community health, community safety, community economy, community governance, and community education have doors that open into each other, inextricably interdependent. And each of these spaces is suffused with information and dependent on essential community information resources.

IN OUR PLACES

Bellah and his associates were writing 20 years ago, before the emergence of the technical fabric now engulfing world cultures, altering every sense of continuity and connection. To put this technology into a "moral context" is to understand the consequences of technology on our ways of being and connecting among each other. Our senses of each other, our integrity, our expectations, and our patience among each other are no longer created by the experiences of the past, where respect, affection, and generosity are grounded. The technological fabric has been—and will be—pervasive and increasingly brilliant, but its moral and cognitive consequences, and our awareness of its ways of influencing us, will be negligible without the continuous reweaving of another shaping fabric of our lives, made of the threads that tie us to time and place, and to each other, and to the democratic impulse.

In our places, we need to foster an imagination of that constructive impulse. We need exemplars and forums. We need to redefine words, as Judt also says, by using them, "recasting" them in public conversations. "If we do not talk differently, we shall not think differently," Judt writes (2010, p. 171). Begin by defining the ideas of flourishing, well-being, and the common good; they seem to be lost concepts as I write them. Consider social courage, innovation, creativity and collaboration, and invention and leadership in public critical thinking. My guiding questions for those who care for our cultural institutions begin with taking responsibility. What have museum and libraries newly undertaken to construct a sense of the possible in our culture? What is it that these institutions and their collections *say* to us? If we live through institutions, how do we live through *cultural* institutions? How have they proven to be instrumentally relevant and engaging to the most lives? What has encouraged the user to say, "This matters to me.

This is applicable and moving; it changes my thinking. I want to know and think more about this, and ideas like these." How often have our institutions said, "Come think together with us and we will remind each other of our capacities. We will consider together the known, the unknown, and the possible-to-know. Our collections are illuminating. Our work is to expand the attention they make possible. Our work is to discover and diffuse their generative ideas, together. What is the difference to be made here for you?" These things have not happened yet.

Among the facets and possibilities of thought and understanding, what is the value and strength of the individually crafted truth? In a nation of a thousand languages, what language do we require for the conversations we need? How do we reject the facile and embrace the complex without fear? How do cultural institutions sustain their place in public trust? How do we craft a new and lasting question—perhaps an unanswerable question—with the user at its center? Is it possible to find more difficult questions, with more essential unknowns? Neither institutions nor citizens change easily, certainly not until the burden of stasis and mistrust outweighs the burden of change. Information and access without human transmission, without a reasoned form of context and dialogue (and the tensions implied), are not knowledge. Nothing is changed, including our own thoughts, without an understanding of tension and dissent. But there is now, as I say, abundant tension and dissent in American life. How might we think of it? What should be done to assuage it, and moderate it toward conversation? And, then, what will we learn?

I am convinced that the essential skills of this or any century have been understood for years: marshalling collective energy, holding dedicated conversations toward contemporary civil understandings of civic differences, critically thinking together, and articulating formative aspirations. They are not new skills but lost skills. I am also convinced that cultural institutions are the central instruments of American democracy—libraries alone more than museums alone, but in collaboration incomparably vital to the restoration of these lost skills to the nation. Each life has its own complexities, energies, depths, and balances. Everyone is in transition, constructing and reconstructing one continuing life. But we all develop, discover the possible, and are transformed by our pursuits in everyday human contexts, among other people. And yet, "Most people don't feel as though they are part of any conversation of significance" (Judt, 2010, p. 172).

Under what conditions and in what contexts is change most successfully constructed? One life observes another life, and other experiences. For each person, the formative continuities are woven within one life, but they remain responsive to the strands of other nearby lives, and likely to be invisible even to the living person. Each strand—our health, family, education, and work, for example—is a separate tightrope, subject to tension, distress, and conflict, and each has the power to reshape our aspirations. Pluck the tightrope and we will wobble; we may fall. Extraordinary activity in one strand can cloud the details and importance of attending to other strands. Successes, failures, refinements, accidents, or explosions on one strand will affect the flexibility and continuity of all others, causing the need for new knowledge, or new thinking, or new models and ideas. It is at these times of need, I believe, when people require ideas or solace, they are drawn to a long view of experience, and they are drawn to knowledge, to want wisdom, insight, and consolation.

Crises, accidents, needs, questions, and the unfinished issues of adult life—the chaos of being human—make us ready and open for new information, new perspectives, and the possibilities of fresh knowledge. Configured by these variable factors and relationships, we practice as much conscious self-development as we can sustain, but we often cannot do it alone, without conversations, without history or art or knowledge, or without able mentors and more informed others. I believe that the work of the cultural institution is in the unfinished, fluid parts of human practice and experiment; our work always waits in the continuous ambiguities of knowledge and experience.

How can public libraries and museums sustain and participate in the aspirations of citizens? How can cultural institutions help to fulfill the purpose and promise of a community? Our responses to these questions ought to be relatively simple. By their existence in a community, libraries and museums hold evidences of knowledge, work, and thought in collections of documents and objects. As public collections, a community's cultural places provide logical situations to ask questions, to think beyond the local and toward the universal. When we inquire with such breadth, we must also ask questions that turn us inward. *What questions and ideas motivate us? How are we a community of learners? What do we want to happen for ourselves and for others?* These questions also imply the value of our institutions to our larger intentions for survival and growth and awareness of other cultures. We enter our communities for hope and intention; we want to lead lives of social purpose and engagement; we want the common structure and public safety a community provides. We turn to a common place as a form of rescue from isolation, and a form of protection from danger. We live through institutions because we hope and work to flourish.

WHAT FEARSOME THING

What fearsome thing can a library or a museum prevent? What is made real when citizens create a center for information and inquiry? How does a modest institution embody a heroic landmark of democracy? What do citizens construct by coming together to build and sustain such places by their presence? If there is a critical heroism in the everyday, it is a self-rescue from silence and passivity, and a turn toward intellect. When a public library opens its doors to a community, an important thing has happened, vital for something that Aristotle expressed, the "human flourishing" (Noddings, 2003, p. 10) of our lives. When the library opens, the community also opens to itself and says it believes in its future, in its aspirations for its children, its families, its businesses, its civic values, and its imagination. Even more than our schools, the library and the museum are about the future we strive to construct every day, because they are adaptive and responsive to a changing world hour by hour, to nearly limitless depths. Each time a person enters the collection with a question, its purpose is proven.

When they open and sustain a library or a museum, the people who live in that community have contributed to their common wealth and changed their common futures. Although we seem to have relegated important words to the past—the *commonweal*, the *common good*, and the idea of *commonwealth*—their concepts remain alive among us in our activities and alliances. Libraries are about the common aspirations of a community, where *common* means *mutual*, *public*, and *reciprocal*, words of distinction and democratic resonance. A community builds and sustains a library to educate itself across generations, to do its jobs better, and to exalt knowledge over emptiness and learning over failure. A community with a library, like a community with a museum, a fire department, or a newspaper, is not entirely shaped by accidents. Such communities can find ways to explain themselves in times of uncertainty and restore themselves in times of crisis. They can address the unknown as those without memory or an archive cannot. They have fulfilled the fundamental assumptions of democracy: people who live together can think together, and can come together to become something together. They can decide together, and make differences for each other together.

A free public library is a rare place in the world, a place constructed so that democracy can happen. Like the firehouse, the food bank, the hospital, and the police, the library in the community provides a place of safety and survival—from catastrophes, storms, hunger, job loss, cancer, and snakebite. When accidents do not drive our responses and possibilities, we can begin to design a life, a possible self. The library puts its citizens in touch with tools as the living craftspeople they are; it offers them the vast designs of knowledge as architects require; and it provides informing resources and strong materials that allow their user to envision a bridge, and then to construct it. And then, tentatively, the builder crosses the bridge in order to build something more on the other side.

The library means that the stories of lives being built in a place—lives lived every day on its streets and in its schools and businesses and homes—can have a progressive meaning and a useful purpose. In the simplest of acts, opening its doors, the library invites its people to become something different, one by one; in its greatest acts, opening its people to the larger world and to conversations about the possibilities of human flourishing, the modest institution invites its community members to overcome, in Tony

Judt's words, "the democratic deficit." Judt writes, "One striking consequence of the disintegration of the public sector has been an increased difficulty in comprehending what we have in common with others" (Judt, 2010, p. 120).

THESE ARE MY THEMES

These are my themes: community, memory, trust, knowledge, help, and fearless change, all among the essential qualities of our republic. We would not live in a place without these things because we find them to be essential to our lives and hopes. Cultural institutions have survived in the United States because they have served the American democratic experiment and sustained the relationship between American citizenship and knowledge. Their presence is evidence that fear and ignorance are enemies of a viable society. Nor would we live in a climate of suspicion, or cynicism, or arrogance, or the smothering falsehoods that neither nourish trust nor help us to craft the truth.

At our best, when we find and reject these things in our world—fear, cynicism, and falsehood—we turn toward the authentic for confidence and certainty. We want something we can regard as true and restorative. We look for nearby lives and experiences, for evidences of humanity we might emulate. When we look at our past with open eyes, we find its compromises, even its cruelties; but then we turn toward each other for models of how to live now, how to be different, calm, and unafraid of both the past and the future. Though we will all differ when we speak, our very speaking is our national treasure. And when we need to talk with knowledge and conviction, we will depend upon a fair place that gives us authority and strength.

This is not to deny the evidence of the recurrent theme of anti-intellectualism, closed, narrow thinking, and viral, erroneous thought described by Richard Hofstadter (1963) and Susan Jacoby (2008). They are well documented every day on television and in public life. What Hofstadter described as a "national disrespect for mind" has a long history, amplified in the middle of the twentieth century by a wide embrace of McCarthyism, greed, materialism, and the complacence of Babbittry. A generation later, in an extraordinary new age, Jacoby refers to a much larger dimension with an American twist: "People throughout the world must cope with social, economic, and technological changes that call traditional verities into question, and the empire of mind-numbing infotainment knows no national boundaries. Yet the United States has proved much more susceptible than other economically advanced nations to the toxic combination of forces that are the enemies of intellect, learning, and reason, from retrograde fundamentalist faith to dumbed-down media" (2008, p. 30).

There are some principles and ideas that cannot be disavowed in museums and libraries. Knowledge and freedom of thought are intimately interdependent. An environment that constrains knowledge constrains trust. When budgets weaken libraries and anti-elitism regards museums as luxuries, a community has been made less capable and less just. When their collections are diminished, the capacities of communities to absorb knowledge have been changed. Current evidence about science, society, and culture is central in a democracy; a probative memory is essential to creating a working model of the past. However, because knowledge implies distance and perspective, because it may require the revision of accepted truths and their removal from local contexts, and perhaps because knowledge evokes for many the residual effects of schooling, its presence implies unwelcome diligence and intensity, and the possibility of failure. Rocket science is, in fact, challenging. So are the forms of knowledge we require: environmental science, community dynamics, local economics, public education, social welfare, and the mutability of common life. Consequently, a need for knowledge and a fear of knowledge tend to occur together.

When a community opens a library or creates a forum in a cultural space, it invites all the risks of democracy—disagreement, reinterpretation, and questioning—a brave and essential thing. Democracy requires us to become comfortable with our own deliberation and slowness, to mistrust easy answers and glib assumptions. When we do not have information and trust in our lives, we should want them, and we should do our best to create them. We should strive to find human qualities of careful thought, generosity, and kindness, combinations of intelligence and fearlessness, to lead us in finding our way toward truths we each must craft. We should not be satisfied with isolated truths; we want a vision of what is possible for us all, for our families, and for our common aspirations.

Think with me. Progress toward a community's civic possibility is difficult for us to see, because we are so small in a world so large. At times we need to find a sense of order and structure, because a constructive life requires us to weave together many goals and many hopes, sometimes slowly. When our issues and problems are diverse, we may need to weave many fine strands at once. For the strength and beauty of this fabric, we need to discuss and share our knowledge in our communities. A commonwealth of weavers, turning to each other, will help everyone to know more. When we turn to each other, stories and lessons will appear, with the qualities of woven strength.

SO FAR

I think that each of us needs to keep mindful of where we began and how our evolution is going, so far. I find myself thinking of my parents and the world they knew; I think of where they came from, and how the world has changed since they were born more than a century ago. I think of our growth as individual human beings over the life span. We need to know their lessons and the signs they interpreted, the events in their lives that made them feel strong, or ashamed, or powerless, or misunderstood. Thinking of my parents, I recognize that each of us needs to know the ways we have to shape the future as more than a series of accidents and heartbreaks. I regret that their lessons are now lost to me.

And those many events that we still cannot understand? Those mysteries represent to us the dearest knowledge we require in order to live with integrity. They hold the lessons we need to realize, or else we will not fully see or feel our experiences or, as needed, forgive ourselves for our errors. Our guiding questions and unknowns are expressions of value, investments we make in what we still search for and the persons we still hope to become. We would not live without these unknowns or the processes of thinking that surround them. We would not live without mystery, we would not live without questions, and we would not live without a record of our world to keep us both safe and humble.

Cultural institutions and their themes emerged in my life slowly. As a young man in my twenties I was drawn to work in the library because, after five years, I could neither trust nor ethically participate in schools as a teacher. Thirty years before the No Child Left Behind Act, I saw that schools were overwhelming, narrow, competitive, and constraining, and not very good places to learn. In my experience, they strove to make successes out of smart people; but by design they also made failures out of other smart people as well. By "failures," I mean people who come to think they are less valuable and less capable than they actually are. Such people, branded early, are at risk of becoming self-fulfilling prophecies, with compromised imaginations of the possible. This is simply unwise, because the fates of communities depend on the uncompromised capacities of the citizen. I have experienced this kind of self-devastation, being a failure at school, and have never fully recovered from it.

Forty years ago, when I was working and thinking among the constraints and damages of public education, my reading allowed me to envision a different circumstance for useful, educative experiences. As a librarian, I envisioned an infinite conversation in progress every day. Knowledge became a process and not a thing to me: I loved how it resisted capture, management, and reduction. Knowledge wants to be connected to other knowledge, I learned; it needs to be part of living, as a leading experience moving toward difference and change. I subscribed first to John Dewey's idea that mind is principally a verb and second to his idea that every experience is a moving force. We are generative, minding this culture both for our lives and for the future, however distant. Regardless of our vocations, we must think about the future as though each of us bears the guiding responsibilities of a teacher. As a teacher, as a librarian, and as a museum observer, I am driven by Frank Smith's idea that the brain is more like an artist than a machine (Smith, 1990).

My work in libraries informed my life and helped it to be transformed toward an advocacy I never knew in schools. I found my perspectives could easily transfer to museums and science, history, and cultural centers. Gradually I was able to express what I saw each of these places to be: not a place to *keep* things but to *hold* them in trust for us; not a place but a process that refreshes a common life and the common good. Our places do not merely keep collections safe; they also keep *us* safe. I came to see that knowledge makes a person's life exactly as it makes the life of a community: the cautious exploration and application of knowledge assist both the person and the community to emerge from crisis and respond to its challenges, to find continuity and possibility, and to discover common strength almost as a form of surprise. It is the surprise of that constructive knowledge that transforms and strengthens us.

Consider a crisis of health or economics, the loss of a job or the need to be educated in order to qualify for a new one. Imagine the challenges of someone we love fading from us, disabled, sick, or in danger. Think of a child, learning disabled or depressed or anorexic, or all three, or balanced on one or another precarious edge, and not yet strong enough to remain safe without our caring. In the larger frame of the republic and the society, imagine our schools, our economy, our public health, our Constitution, all critically important to us, and all in need of our thinking. How shall we rescue each other?

Part of our work now as a culture is to regenerate ourselves as we have often done before, recovering our balance after wars or losses. We reinterpret our possibilities, we renegotiate our values, and we find that the meaning of our success has changed. There will always be dramatic, adult, continuously unfinished issues we need to pursue with each other in the open places we experience. Speaking and listening, asking and answering questions, and seeking and presenting information in public are part of the pursuit. Jerome Bruner (1986) writes that if we believe "that a culture itself comprises an ambiguous text...constantly in need of interpretation by those who participate in it," we must be concerned with the role of language as a critical part of our practice and participation. Language is not simply a tool; it is a definitive condition of our interpretation and engagement.

> So if one asks the question, where is the meaning of social concepts—in the world, in the meaner's head, or in interpersonal negotiation—one is compelled to answer it is the last of these. Meaning is what we can agree upon or at least accept as a working basis for seeking agreement about the concept at hand. ... [T]he reality is not the thing, not in the head, but in the act of arguing and negotiating about the meaning of such concepts. (Bruner, 1986, p. 122)

And so, if we are to flourish, we are required to talk, and also to see and experience together. These acts are the essential moving forces in our lives, and the living ways we have of sustaining the value of knowledge and the possibilities of collaboration. Bruner writes,

> [A] culture is constantly in process of being recreated as it is inter-preted and renegotiated by its members. In this view, a culture is a much a *forum* for negotiating and renegotiating meaning and for expli-cating action as it is a set of rules or specifications for action. Indeed, every culture maintains specialized institutions or occasions for inten-sifying this 'forum-like' feature.... [They are] ways of exploring pos-sible worlds out of the context of immediate need.... It is the forum aspect of a culture that gives its participants a role in constantly making and remaking the culture—an active role as participants rather than as performing spectators who play out their canonical roles according to rule when the appropriate cues occur. (Bruner, 1986, p. 123)

We are challenged to converge, and challenged to discover ways for our lives to change, to vary from orthodoxy and convention, so that we are able to become more than the spectators in our national life we have too often taught ourselves to be.

CHAPTER 4

Unfinished Lives

As a librarian and a teacher of librarians, I am especially interested in three things: information and knowledge in a progressive society, everyday decisions as opportunities for the construction of a lasting and integrated personal identity, and the continuity of institutions that rescue, record, and freely provide the traces of human experience. Each of these things—worldly knowledge, personal integrity, and cultural survival—is something that we create, requiring human sensitivities and decisions. We gather a repertoire of concepts and ideas from the enduring, challenging experiences we witness. We collect, remember, reinterpret, and rearticulate them among others. The record evolves through ambiguities and interpretations, and through confronting the complexity we cannot escape. Memory, complexity, and what remains unknown within us—these things make us mindful people.

A strong intelligence may be made out of loose parts and fragments, but it is grounded on integrity and identity, evolved over time. Lives and ideas evolve simultaneously, feeding each other slowly, sometimes reluctantly, by what we understand through the evidence of experience. This gradual emergence of an engaged adult life is a way of presenting an authentic face in the world. None of us has it easy in this evolution; becoming ourselves takes time, but it also has moments of cliff diving. When we are challenged by crises, we are required at times to act without deliberation or planning. When we are at an edge, we act or we fall. On level ground, when we are not engaged by what we see and do, we risk stagnation and drift. Our growth is not an academic or political exercise of finding a costume and a suitable character, nor is it a life defined by technology or the hum of a social network. It is about constructing a grounded self, neither a luxury nor a performance. Eventually we must present ourselves to the mirror in a true form, our authentic form.

We are, as John W. Gardner said, problem seekers; in order to fulfill our aspirations, we require engagement in a local world where lives are lived, in the company of open questions and unfinished issues. Our work is to ask good questions and communicate with others as they ask their own questions, similar to ours, and yet different as well.

Our imminent future lies in the exercise of public imagination to address the unfinished aspects of both our private and common lives. This means finding a voice, and finding a place and a way to speak among others. It means creating a fair, depoliticized (or at least depolarized) conversation that will assist people to think clearly about what their culture and society ought to be. It means selecting resources that strengthen us, finding alliances that make us bold, and discovering a language that inspires confidence and self-reliance. This is uneasy work, at the unfinished edges of ourselves.

Uneasy, because individuals and societies, even those driven heavily by faith or theory, must always construct themselves authentically through challenges and the tensions of striving, rather than by the depth of their beliefs or the thrust of their idealism. If people want growth with integrity they will follow their desire with a design, and then continue the difficult work of living it out, talking, reflecting and adjusting as they go. It will require compromise as all excellent progress does. The more complex our tensions, the more valuable our arrival at understanding them will be. Wanting to understand democracy, we are challenged to practice it well, work thoughtfully within its constraints, and trust each other. When people describe and discuss together the tensions of democracy as a method of community practice, they become more aware of commonalities, and more likely to grasp the patterns and possibilities of change. Seeing patterns and possibilities, they can begin to design together the constructive change an entire community may require.

Our negotiations with the future happen when issues arise to face us. Change can create public dramas out of civic aspirations and ideals—but also out of personal dramas and fears. They can be moving and consequential dramas, bearing lessons and epiphanies. But ungrounded or artificial dramas can also introduce more fear, and intrude on our conversations and prospects for grasping complexity. In every community there may be many of these dramas, starting in concern or trepidation, then moving quickly into conflict. It is unlikely that the drama will move easily toward a resolution through polarized arguments. But resolution is not the only point; conversation is also the point. The *course* of our involvement is as significant as any outcome or compromise we might craft. The pursuit of a new possibility itself shapes us and shapes our communities. The drama requires our moderation and caution. It requires goodwill, openness and patience. We know that a community's conversations must be gradual and conditional when we work toward becoming something together, because they are deliberate processes of growth. There is no need to harden our lives needlessly in order to survive among neighbors, or to withdraw from others, assuming that our insularity must not be broken down.

AT OUR BEST

As individual actors in these dramas, when we perform at our best, we become more attuned to what we think and feel. Even in pain or disappointment and uncertainty, we grow. The drama—though we may stand apart, observing—shapes our need to imagine possible ways to live. This is our fate in a democracy: to imagine for ourselves, improvising our lives on a public stage. We are driven by our unknowns and unfinished issues; they have consequences in our imaginations and conversations. They affect the ways we make commitments to policies and the promises of change. Engagement with the future can lead us toward our best strengths. Even when we are disappointed, we are not lost. Emerson says that there is a "scientific value" to moments of challenge and change. He says, "These are occasions a good learner would not miss" (Emerson, 1983, p. 1087). Crises may open our lives to change, but without generative contexts, our lessons are difficult to experience and confirm.

Even when there is much public desire for growth and progress, as there ought to be in a culture that constantly aspires to renew and protect itself, citizens may be unaccustomed to speaking about their evolving lives and the implications of change. At times of crisis—the loss of work or safety, the immediate threats of environmental catastrophe, or the collapse of an economy—we may not know how to speak up, and we may be too distressed to speak forcefully and rationally. We may create our own eloquent private voices, but mostly we are silent about our aspirations and fears. We often live in silent communities, with no place to speak or think together. Even so, we may take steps toward ideas, but they live inside ourselves, and we have no keys to unlock them. Existing ways and places to speak and present ourselves to others not only are rare and unfamiliar but also may be vulnerable to shallowness, compromise, or politicization. We have not been well prepared as a democratic people for democratic talk; our rich and efficient society, rarely pausing and frequently thoughtless, tends to cheat us of this opportunity. The bumper sticker that repeats the words of the Gray Panther activist Maggie Kuhn, "Stand before the people you fear and speak your mind—even if your voice shakes," does not tell us just where to stand, or how to articulate our mind, even in that unsteady voice. Nor do we know who will respond.

We lead particular, local lives; our lived experiences are not often meaningful apart from the families or places where they occur, and yet the importance of a local life is easily lessened and made insignificant. National test-crazed education moves knowledge away from the complexity of a local economy of knowledge. The expanding internet is anonymous and distant, even when it is pervasive. Social networks replace the textures of direct interactions with brevity and superficiality. Diverse voices are gone from the radio, as are diverse musics. Angry people and tasteless entertainments populate broadcasting, where inane commercials overwhelm vapid content. The press has no robust dialogue with its readers, and the local news seems on the verge of being simply irrelevant. Older forms of local communication—hometown radio, the town meeting, and Main Street encounters— are largely gone from the landscape.

And we become less patient, less likely to speak to each other. Except for religious gatherings (where people tend to listen and practice as expected) and entertainments outside the civic sphere, there are few events that bring people together for a common focus, and fewer still that exist for steady and open civic discourse. No matter how much entertainment we purchase and devour, we cannot fill ourselves. There is too much that is commercial but purports to be essential, too much that wants to entertain in order to sell but is irrelevant to useful thoughts. Everyday cognition and the social processes that serve a coherent culture suffer from useless noise, and so does our repertoire of responses and resources. We are surrounded by stimuli, and yet we are unsated.

WE ARE UNFINISHED

When I speak to audiences of professionals, or address gatherings of readers in libraries, or docents in museums—and always when I speak to students in professional schools—I remind them that our thoughts and questions are never finished; given our lengthening lives, they have no end we can see. Our lives, I tell my audiences, are configured by the unfinished issues we have made our own by thinking and asking, reading and questioning. We carry them with us. The issues may have come to us early, from growing up in our homes and families, through training in faith and ethics, in response to dysfunctions in our intimate or closely observed relationships, or as a result of early experiences in schools. They may come to us through nearness to illness and death, or through war or disaster. We retrieve enigmatic evidences from memories and dreams; we hold aspirations and hidden ambitions. Or more simply, our unfinished issues are those we long for. We long to travel, to serve, to teach, to perform, and to read. But because we do not do these things as we wish, our aspirations remain open and unfinished, as do our lives. If we feel them intensely and deeply, these closed doors and untried keys, our unfinished issues configure our lives and shape our wanting out of our deficits.

Unfinished issues and unfinished lives are at the center of useful and generative experiences in cultural institutions. Our wanting moves us there, we look for paths in response to our continuing motives, and we become different because we have found something that carries our thoughts and interests forward. The unfinished issues that drive us, the longings, will never be done with us, nor will we be done with them. This is as it should be: the knowledge that configures our thinking is not meant to be complete but to evolve in complexity and interest over time. We may address a question specifically or obliquely; we might find a new book or a fresh exhibition; we might hear a public radio interview that promises something relevant to ideas we have kept active for decades. We may find ourselves looking for scholarship, seeking expertise and conversation. Or we may find that an odd insight occurs to us when we do not expect it, a casual moment that creates a revelation.

When I list my own continuing, unfinished issues, it is an undisciplined, long list, and it includes the themes of the book in your hands: becoming an informed independent thinker, creating a reflective democratic society, and becoming something together in a common place. Here are a handful of other items, all more personal and less professional, that will always be on my list—a list that is itself unfinished, of course. The list has been empirically derived from scanning the teetering stacks on my office and living room floors, the bookshelves in four or five rooms, and my desiderata list of several dozen new titles.

The First World War
Buddhist Practice
Stone Tools and Human Intellect
Holocaust and Memory
Ukiyo-e
Literary Fiction
Genius
Wolves, Coyotes, Dogs

There are many other themes that I cultivate to a lesser extent by form or theme: essays, diaries, and storytelling; handwriting; police procedural fiction; the African-American story; fierce carnivores, wild birds, and ocean life; photography, poetry, and pottery; and collecting, collections, and collectors. But the eight above are the major themes, having attracted my interest and inquiry for about three or four decades. Only the first of my themes arrived in my life through a direct connection: my father enlisted in the Canadian Expeditionary Force in 1917 and served in Europe. All the other themes have been my own projects, derived from my own adult contexts. None of them has its origin in teaching or schooling. I have collected and kept track of many books about these topics, and if I were to enter a good bookstore this afternoon, I would look for more and scan my desiderata list as I search the shelves. I plan museum visits to see relevant collections.

I bookmark websites that address my themes, and I seek out new reference books about these themes.

I am interested in multiple facets of these many topics: histories, theories, stories, examples, biographies, reflections, museum exhibitions, and other living individuals who think about them. Consequently, it is challenging to survey the landscape fully, and in the process of searching I am likely to find more interesting works on ancillary or even completely different topics. As long as I can remember things, I will remember these topics. I will carry them wherever I go. I can imagine a future of questions, each helping to shape my unfinished life, each the promise of possible knowledge, and each the center of its own constellation. I can also imagine a future of documents, readings, and conversations. Interests, ideas, concepts, issues, anticipations, and questions are characteristics of a thinking life. It is difficult to imagine a life without them, or without something to engage us and cause us to imagine.

Most continuing questions are best when broadly stated, while cultural institutions are driven by specificities, details, and examples. The fit may be approximate. As any reference librarian knows, a question generates connections, decisions and strategies. We find that just below its surface are ambiguities, imprecise cultural and psychological themes, and the need for new, more specific language. We may be offered promising choices and (in even small collections) significant depths of knowledge. Or we may not. When we experience these points of choice or discouragement we may come to understand the enticing variables of lifelong learning and adult intellectual growth, clarified by the multiple paths opening to us.

OUR NEED TO HEAR AND SEE

Museums and libraries exist to cultivate and help us to articulate the unfinished parts of ourselves and to follow the paths they open. We begin to find our questions sustained, deepened and broadened, extended into the past, and then brought up to now. As we adapt to a cultural institution and its collections, we also may come to understand how it attends to human knowledge and its generation. Each place is organized by differing systems and patterns. Our progress among these variations often requires a set of limits (era, geography, or event) or a sharpened approach to evidence (letters or documents *only*, Asian ceramics *only*, feminist scholarship *only*, or Native Americans of the Southwest *only*.) A narrower, tightened question gains in focus, though it may diminish in breadth.

What do cultural institutions offer in common? Authenticity. Complexity. Evidence. Ambiguity. Assistance. They evoke our generative selves, and we are given the chance to discover, explain, and connect. They require our collaboration and work. They are structured to lead us into infinite new questions. Using Mihaly Csikszentmihalyi's signature idea, we can see that cultural institutions are able to assist us as we strive to discover the flow of mind and to "fulfill the potential complexity of [our] selves" (Csikszentmihalyi, 1993, p. 212). This is what scholars, observers, and independent learners do, setting a pace for their own design, and constantly making the world they see into something more detailed, more intricate, and more interesting.

In my experience, conversations in cultural institutions draw out particular kinds of thinking essential to the pursuit of what we most need. As we think among collections, we find that they inevitably require us to clarify and interpret concepts, evaluate and compare pieces of evidence, and reflect carefully on the implications of new knowledge. No one can do this for us. Taking my graduate students to museums, I offered some cognitive possibilities for them to consider during their time in the setting. *Establish contexts*, I told them. *Think big, look for implications and consequences. Expand your thoughts. Develop complexities. Construct concepts of difference.* I suggested these instructions as pertinent observations a person might make in these institutions, whether considering a living butterfly in the science museum or a Civil War kit among historic artifacts. None of them, of course, would ever be spoken or provided by the museum itself as a way to suggest the cognitive dimensions of its collections. My intention in offering these intrusions on my students was not to teach history or science, but to suggest underlying tacit dimensions like context, difference, comparison, and complexity. I wanted my students to generate further thoughts at various levels of detail. Grasping "concepts of difference," for example, would cause them to understand the difference it makes to have tools, rather than have none, or how the extinction of wolves might change the living world for generations.

I see my suggestions to students as the basic logics of any museum experience, not very different from the logics of information discovery, or the application of a heuristic or other checklist, as might happen in a library. The final cognitive possibility I provided for my students is both the most important and the easiest to ignore as we work alone. It is also the basis for all of what we might call "learning" in the contexts of experience: *Articulate*, I told them. Find and use language to capture your insights. With language, we establish contexts, describe the dynamic places that surround us, notice the natural and social complexities of living systems, and the difference a good discovery clarifies. Away from the institution, our thinking continues to expand along with our ability to say and describe our experiences. Without our minds engaged, even epiphanic moments pass us without their traces making a difference to our wisdom and awareness.

Motivated by fears, we have lost possibilities of entente, respect, and reconciliation among different faiths, ethnicities, and political cultures. In the decade following our losses in 2001, too few cultural experiences have addressed what Maxine Greene calls "the dialectic of freedom" (Greene, 1988). Throughout her extraordinary presence as an educator and philosopher, Greene has emphasized the deep power of experiences with art objects and performances to open interior spaces and awaken our humanity.

> [The arts] have the capacity ... to enable persons to hear and to see what they would not ordinarily hear and see, to offer visions of consonance and dissonance that are unfamiliar. ... [T]hey have the capacity to defamiliarize experience: to begin with the overly familiar and transfigure it into something different enough to make those who are awakened hear and see. (Greene, 1988, pp. 128–129)

I would argue that, in times of trouble, we want critical, trustworthy information, offered in response to our questions and our fears. Such knowledge can awaken and inform us as the arts do. There are countless instances where citizens can be transformed and engaged by a reduction of polarities across differences and cultures, especially regarding such life-altering divides as poverty, education, nutrition, and public health. The tensions already cited in Chapter 3 are elusive and complex themes for adults to grasp. Genocides (historic and contemporary) and the protection and nurturing of children, it goes without saying, are among these life-altering divides. We have not discussed these things enough, and yet no one can ever know too much about them. Nor has our society fully embraced education for lifelong thinking, social engagement, and other intangible but critical outcomes for citizenship. Every day, the morning newspaper adds further fundamental themes to this account of neglect: there are crises of shelter, health, sexuality, and cultural fragility amid disaster. I list these themes because they are unfinished, and always will be unfinished, in our experience. There are beginnings to be undertaken and promising conversations to be joined. In my view, they are among the continuously open needs that fearless and responsible cultural institutions are constructed to address.

How might our urge to understand—our wanting to think and talk about our culture and its unfinished issues—be served by robust forums in museums and libraries, amid objects, experiments, information, and art; or on public broadcasting; or in fresh conventions of willing and gifted thinkers? How might the educative but nonjudgmental nature of cultural institutions, grounded in both intellectual and egalitarian values, assist community expression and understanding? How could these places of culture contribute as forums for constructive advocacy, toward renewal and responsibility in our national life? If we wish to grasp the critical issues of our lives and argue usefully toward understanding them, I believe that we need to embrace complexity and ambiguity as the real conditions where we live and grow. As Csikszentmihalyi (1993) writes, "[A]bilities do not become effective unless developed through appropriate, socially constructed activities—that is, through patterned, voluntary investments of attention that result in learned skills. Complex skills are built up by complex activities" (p. 170). When we reject complexity for its opposite (not only simplicity but also ignorance and confusion), we embrace what Csikszentmihalyi calls "psychic entropy," mindless disorder that impairs functioning and leads to dysfunction, fear, and rage.

WHAT IS COMPLEX

What is complex? Race, culture, economy, education, health care, gender difference, secrecy, privacy, military policy, and our Constitution. Also, immigration, the internet, energy, jobs, small towns, outsourcing, torture, literacy, numeracy, and the American family. Howard Fineman's 2008 book *The Thirteen American Arguments: Enduring Debates That Define and Inspire Our Country* leads us to national themes in greater depth: the limits of individualism, the role of faith, and local versus national authority. "Who is a person?" "Who is an American?" (Fineman, 2008). Fineman's important subtitle makes his intentions clear: these arguments are indeed "enduring debates that define and inspire our country." Just as they are in cultural institutions, definition and inspiration are pervasive themes in cultural change, but they can be defeated and erased from awareness when we have no institutions unafraid to address them in public.

If citizens in our society are ever to become something together in the twenty-first century, we need to understand the implied quality of "argument" as a process of thinking and reasoning, speaking carefully together without anger. We can and do live with acute ambiguities, as we always have, and yet we do not see the education in them, and it is our loss. We need to argue about them some more, in places we can trust. The front pages of every newspaper in America are shaped by open, historic questions. A headline in 2010 addressed the permanently unsolved slayings of the civil rights era (Defenders Online, 2010), and a few months later a murder from 1965 had been resolved at last (Brown, 2010). The nation is unfinished, just as our own lives are carved unknowingly by the unfinished issues of faith, family, work, school, community, economy, and the ethics given to us by the formative experiences of growing up. Certainly we need to argue in informed ways about the foundations of the present.

If our unknowns drive us, they will of course have consequences on our imaginations and conversations. When we rise to speak and pose questions, we will think about them. And when we find the language to ask or to observe, we will have given the unknown our personal voice. Encounters with gender, race, and politics are made more poignant—and possibly more awkward—by the combination of intimacy and strangeness we feel when they arise, but our voices will soften the distress. Our need for deeper discussions will inevitably reveal more that we need to speak about, more that is both intimate and strange to us, and more that will alter our perceptions of justice, action, and equity. But if this pursuit shapes us, and shapes our communities, so does the failure to pursue the most intelligent and engaged parts of ourselves. For silent, thoughtless people, atrophy is destiny.

Where shall we speak with each other? Our civic lives attract unknowns, complexities, and tensions; we need to address them where they matter most. In my view, these national conversations have to retain local voices; to address the unknown in pertinent ways, we need to be among familiar voices and faces. Some towns have formal ways of meeting, town halls, and places for congregations of citizens to express themselves. We want something central and public, a dispassionate space in our community, with democratic rules and procedures.

How shall we conduct and deepen our discussions? Who will draft a few introductory rules and find the right language to frame and begin a rich, multifaceted argument? What procedures will our discourse follow? How shall we engage the experiences and hopes of multiple generations? How shall we summarize and communicate what we have talked about? How shall we pursue information and documentation pertinent to our conversations? How can we extend our thoughts to the nation's leaders and legislators? People can decide these things together. It is a way to start.

But where? As a teacher, I know that being present and local are important to the discussion: while the internet is convenient, it fails to place people face to face for a couple of hours, and it's open to others beyond the community. It also tends to be inherently shallow and anonymous. It opens us to intrusions and misperceptions we cannot address immediately. We must come together for our conversations, face to face in a public setting. Our questions will require us to linger, to think again, and then return to express new thoughts, tentatively but without fear, together. We will develop patience.

THIS NEED

This need for fearless, patient discussion—civil, public, informed, open, reflective, welcoming, and always unfinished—is why we support unfettered cultural institutions in American communities, generous to their people, and attentive to the aspirations of their citizens. Libraries may be the best examples; they offer evidence and information that is deep, potentially limitless, and fast. Librarians build permanent collections of flowing knowledge to inform our inquiries and conversations, and they generate a sense of integrity and possibility through reference services, public programs and book discussions. Museums also create spaces that radiate the concept of going beyond the everyday, taking on the unfamiliar through the imaginations, reflections, and voices. Libraries, museums, and their communities construct the American landscape, in local ways, in local terms, and in the presence of faces we know and cannot turn from.

We need to have discussions and arguments in every community where the need appears to define and inspire civic lives. But we also need these moments in order to "disclose," in Maxine Greene's words, "the incomplete profiles of the world" (Greene, 1988, p. 129). That is our foremost need as citizens, and it is time to speak to it in cultural institutions. The details of our encounters, of our coming together to talk, will remain to be determined. Perhaps they will begin with "One-Book" projects, single works read together by entire communities, as the Center for the Book in the Library of Congress has documented across the nation. Perhaps they will begin with a librarian, or with a mayor who asks the community to think together.

Whatever their forms, public conversations might be guided by five principles.

1. *The principle of valuable complexity.* Our need is to resist simplicity and seek evidence in detail. To acknowledge complexity among our themes and ideas is to begin the processes of critical thought and intelligent response. Complexity also leads us to understand our limits for accessible, reliable, and current information, and the value of consultation and interaction with informed others. Deliberations and compromises may be uneasy; but when conversations remain open over time, their issues recur in new and different forms. The possibilities of becoming stronger together, through thoughtful arguments, are in themselves complex and essential to a common future.

2. *The principle of public discourse without conclusions.* There are no terminal contexts of inquiry; all of our ideas must remain dynamic and open to the arrival of new evidence, and new configurations of continuing issues. This is reflective practice applied to the user's experiences in cultural institutions, where we act thoughtfully, then think actively about our observations and experiences, renewing them in our lives and keeping their implications open.

3. *The principle of cultural service.* Providing a place for thinking and questioning is a form of cultural service for empowering citizens, encouraging them to stand up and ask questions derived from a larger world. It seems likely that the values and issues we need to understand are intimately woven among each other, and so they tend to extend toward an almost infinite array of observations and conditions. In the renegotiation of the ambiguous text that is our culture, we ought to understand and value the notion that there is no place where the arguments of a culture will stop.

4. *The principle of transparent values.* When issues are opened before us, and when a cultural institution undertakes the responsibility of inviting conversation, the setting must be transparent if it is to gain the trust of a community. Accord on processes and documentation, an agreed-upon vocabulary and rules of discourse, a time to assess, a time to conclude, a set of inviolable rules of courtesy, and an open-book approach to organization are necessary.

5. *The principle of becoming together*. In our schooling—and in museums and libraries, perhaps as a result—we tend to emphasize individual, private thinking as the essential conditions of experience. The individual's outcomes seem to be the point, especially in competitive school environments. An effect of this emphasis may be that we see ourselves encapsulated for life by schooling and how well we competed there. When we overcome our educations and learn to communicate fresh and often difficult thoughts, critically examining our own weak assumptions so they might crumble into the past, we are prepared to become together what we cannot become alone. Of those who gather to converse in the places we create and sustain, it ought to be said that their lives, minds, and discourse remain open and unfinished, always about to be new.

CHAPTER 5

Living Strands

The coast of North Carolina is peerless on a sunny day. Ocracoke Island is on the Outer Banks, across the Pamlico Sound from the mainland, almost three hours by ferry out of Swan Quarter. On Ocracoke in March 2007, my wife and I began the day by walking the beach, taking a look at the spare white lighthouse, then exploring the nearly empty town before I spoke at the public library at seven o'clock that evening. It was early in the season, so not many places were open and only a small number of visitors were on the sand or in the shops. In brisk early March, the small town had just begun to resume its identity as a destination for fishers, bikers, and northern migrants.

We found a bookstore and bought some books. We crossed the street to a clothing shop and browsed. Three minutes later, another couple arrived in the clothing shop and, welcoming them, the shopkeeper asked, "Where are you folks from?" The couple replied, "New Jersey," the Garden State, where I lived and taught for my entire life until 1998. I wandered among T-shirts and hats, and on my way to the door I moved myself near the couple and asked, "So, what part of New Jersey are you from?"

He said, "Small town. Whippany."
I said, "Interesting. I grew up in Whippany."
He said, "What was your address?"
I said, "Ninety-nine Troy Hills Road."
He said, "That's my address."

And so it was his address, my address. We talked about the house, its history, and my recollections of it, not having seen it for about 15 years, since the day I drove my mother past, on her way to the nursing home where she would die.

I had not entered the house in 40 years, but still kept a floor plan and a geography of the property—the lawn mowed, the hedges clipped countless times—in my imagination. That house (as it was in my childhood) no longer exists except as I remember it. I have seen it in photographs, and now it shelters others' memories. They do not erase my own: on any night, I could wander through it alone in the dark and never stumble once.

At my lecture that night in the Ocracoke Public Library, I mentioned this encounter in the clothing shop and the thoughts that followed me—and still follow—from it. Had the storekeeper not asked his question loud enough for me to hear it, I would not have known the couple came from New Jersey. Had I not followed my homeboy predilection to address other lost wanderers from New Jersey, I would not have begun that small, odd conversation. We would not have met. Had the time been altered by a moment—another coffee at the restaurant—this meeting would not have happened. Two unrelated men whose lives have been shaped by occupying the same house four decades apart meet by chance in a place 600 miles away. A question is asked and answered, and they speak to each other. Which of these things is less likely: the shared house, the shared presence, or the shared conversation? How often, because such questions are rarely asked or such conversations never begun, do we walk unknowingly among people whose lives bear extraordinary confluence with our own?

I have never used the common word "coincidence" to describe this meeting, nor have I gazed mechanically at my inexplicable encounter through patterns of the explicable; there is no explanation. We cannot reduce an unlikely experience to a concept or a coincidence, except at risk of missing the reality at its center. That meeting was no illusion; it was a demonstration of something beyond description or explanation. My questions have not abated. How are the evolving strands of our lives braided together? How can we reconcile the orderly patterns and disorderly revelations of our lives? What traces have I left behind? What other, less exact or more predictable congruence might we share with others? What might it mean to find an unexpected commonality with a stranger? Under what circumstances would we express these commonalities? How do we integrate our small lives with larger stories? How do our insular and private worlds bear resemblance to the worlds of others?

AOTEAROA

Less than a year earlier, in 2006, I had been invited to speak at several places in Aotearoa/New Zealand, including Massey University in Palmerston North, a city on the northern island of the nation, surrounded by a district called the Manawatu, a brief drive from the black sands of the

Tasman Sea. I was given a special chance to meet students in a seminar devoted to museum work, so I planned two small activities about objects and thinking. One task involved using everyday writing instruments, placed on a common table and organized according to various systems: ink or graphite, barrel color, size, cost, elegance, brand, specialty, design, and so on. How we arrange such objects, I wanted the students to see, reflects how we value their differences or interpret their functions. My lesson was simple: we can simulate interesting collection dimensions and complexities when we empty our pockets.

The second activity for the class asked students to present an object of their own, brought from home; to tell its story and identify its place within their world; and to talk about why they had chosen to bring it to the class. I asked them: What strands, woven through experience or narrative, bind the inanimate object to you and give it a special status in your living world? We spoke around the circle of the room, holding up our objects: a stuffed cat doll, treasured from early childhood; a great-grandfather's pocket watch and special fob, from the nineteenth century; a polished seashell, a favorite decoration; a treasury of photographs; and a Maori design on a simple necklace. Each object was different, and each story was similar. *We hold our objects dear*, the class said one by one, *because they have touched us, and we have touched them over time, over our lives. They hold solace for us.* These were heartfelt relations, animated by memories and connections, and by energies of other lives and places as well as their own. They seemed to say, *When I hold this object, I recover a sense of myself. When I talk about it, its value moves closer to my center, and so do I.*

Students are generous to each other; each class member appreciated the expressions of the others as I sought to evoke a memorable context. "See these strands of memory, connecting us to objects. How many deep, common themes appear in the objects we have carried here today?" The last student to speak changed the entire conversation in a minute. He had been preceded by a student with a pearly seashell, polished to become an object of decoration, neither especially personal nor evocative. We agreed it was lovely to see, and then we turned to the final student and his object. The young man held a common dark stone in his palm, also neither remarkable nor vivid nor inspiring: just a small dark stone. I took a mildly joking stance; how important could this stone be? "This stone was given to me," he said quietly. "It comes from Antarctica, from Mount Erebus." The entire class grew still. The stone became more important.

Mount Erebus is an active volcano, 11 hours by air from Auckland, the site of the worst disaster in New Zealand's aviation history, the 1979 crash of Flight 901, a sightseeing flight with 257 passengers and crew, mostly New Zealanders, all lost.[1] In that small nation, its impact has been wide, deep, and long. Beginning to grasp this, I asked the university students, "Do you see what has happened here? You have come from all over the nation to this university, out of different communities and ways, yet each of you knows this event and can feel it. How many more unspoken strands of awareness might you share? And how might they lead you to conversations about common lived experiences?" I also realized how significantly excluded I was from this knowledge, as one who had no living connection to the experience. I was not in New Zealand in 1979, but then, I realized, neither were these students. At the Museum of Wellington City and Sea a few days earlier in our journey, we had seen a stirring, largely silent film about the *Wahine* disaster, depicting the April 1968 sinking of a commuter ferry with significant loss of life during an unprecedented storm in Wellington Harbor, just outside the museum's doors. In easy sight of land, the foundering ship was captured in devastating news film, and in firsthand reports of loss, endurance, and suffering.[2] Like the students I would go on to meet a few days later in Palmerston North, the museum users in Wellington that day seemed to view these events as the tragic lumber of national identity.

From these experiences I have taken these things:

> We do not know what others know.
> Much of what we know, we know together.
> Much of what we become, we become together.

In both of these places I became aware of the confluence of unspoken or hidden experiences in social environments, the consequences of presentations that unlock and open a private self, the confirmation of the near past,[3] and the value of initiating communication that breaks silence.

Our lives comprise simultaneous open strands spun further each day, and it is along these strands that we accumulate experiences. These strands are fixed to specific anchors such as our bodies, our families, and our work, but the events they accumulate are ordered and placed by chance in time and space. Until we speak about these accumulations of experience, we will not understand either differences or similarities among us. This is not to say that we grow through the revelation of secrets—although we may—but it is to say that when we disclose patterns of becoming, we allow ourselves to construct more transparent lives, the basis for shared respect and civility. We know together best when we are together, speaking to each other in occasions of engagement. These are neither accidental nor casual engagements but artifacts of human experience, of asking questions or being together in hope of hearing a story refreshed and retold. In cultural institutions, they are moments of design and intention, occasions when experiences are summoned, not merely summarized.

I have wondered if our institutions should be seen as maps for finding our way together into the unknown and back, ways for sorting the contextual intangibles we all recognize in our lives, so we might imagine and understand together the possible patterns in our experiences. What if (I have wondered) these places are ways for us to find our paths toward each other? Is it possible that we are allies in revealing the social construction of our living culture, what Václav Havel (1993) called "the human dimension of our citizenship"?

When we conceptualize a generation or a community as a single unit, as in "The [Blank] Generation," we do it disservice. Similarly, when we regard September 11, 2001, or the experience of Hurricane Katrina as singular experiences, we do an injustice to the immense variables of human experience. We must learn to see a mass of contexts and histories, each with its own traces of the truth, possessed in infinitely variable ways. These ways are the contexts of lives, the bases for our thinking and speaking together. It is perhaps no more than a fond dream, but I think we are more open with each other than we know, even in our insular worlds; among people we grow to trust, we present ourselves in authentic ways. I think it is likely that our shared, congruent, and resonant experiences are more extensive than we know. Naturally, like my inexplicable meeting in Ocracoke, or my seminar in Palmerston North, explicit confluences may be rare among our experiences. But the possible adjacent worlds we might share in these situations are typically unrealized as well. The shared experiences of time, place, and generation that inhabit us may require only a particular question or conversation, or the appearance of stimulating evidence, to evoke a narrative. Were we to breach our guarded privacies we might hold our own lives more readily up to light, to become less opaque parts of larger patterns that might well inform our ideas of our connections and ourselves.

My lessons are artful, perhaps, and insubstantial. My suggestions are speculative and simple. But we do not know what others have seen; we know even less of what others, having lived in their own experiences, have made out of them. The rivers of experience carve different canyons for each life. We are carried along, alone, unless we rescue ourselves.

STRANDS

A few years ago, teaching about information as a formative element in adult lives—and our need for information as a kind of insatiable hunger—I wanted my students to understand the complex variables of an individual life. I drew a long line at the top of the white board at the front of the room, from side to side, about 18 feet long. "This strand is *one life*," I said, as I scored it into nine segments, each one a decade of human living. In an approximation using my keyboard, it looked something like this:

A|——10——20——30——40——50   60——70——80——|位

The first mark along the line, at the left, I said, is Birth, and I marked it with *alpha*. The last mark on the right is Death, at about 90, though it might be sooner or later. I marked it with *omega*.

Then I drew another strand, with marks at intervals to match the first line above. I told my students that this line represented the *biological* strand of our experience, the basic living foundation, influenced by genetics and diet and exercise. The strand I drew on the board was a somewhat mechanical and banal perspective on the person as a progressing independent organism, growing physically more complex over decades, and inevitably declining toward death.

BIO |———|———|———|———|———|———|———|———|———|

Very early in this strand, I told them, a human body experiences neonatality, birth, and physical growth into childhood; and soon after the first decade ends, it experiences puberty and adolescence. By age 20 (the third mark), adolescence is over and an adult specimen has arrived, a physically mature entity with a fully adult body. Later in this strand one cannot predict the fate of the physical body. Decade by decade, I told my students, the body ages and endures, and over time might experience illness, accident, depression, obesity, addiction, chronic conditions, or (of course) robust health and continuous strength until, say, a century mark is in sight, a long life nearing its end.

Below BIO line, I drew another, again marking it off into nine decades. "This," I said, "is a person's *family* life," comprising the relations among generations and intimate and extended families, but not simply a set of relationships.

FAM |———|———|———|———|———|———|———|———|———|

Families, I noted, involve complex tensions, secrets, passions, and binding experiences. And then, of course, there are the genetics, except in cases of adoption, but the genes are part of the upper, biological strand. Notice, I said to my students: the strands connect to and affect each other. The experiences of this familial strand are more complex. They will include childhood memories, evolving responsibilities and trusts, growth into autonomy, and adult participation as a family member. It will also include the partnerships and parenting that adulthood is eventually likely to include, the creation of an independent home, and all the risks of adult relationships: loss of a partner; estrangement, dysfunction, or divorce; dissolution and reformation of the home; caregiving to aging parents; family stress; and family deaths. Like the variables of a biological life, the variables of a family life are unpredictable and diverse. One change affects another within a family. But a change in the physical body—illness, pregnancy, or a chronic condition—also has an impact on the family. The principle is simply made by these two strands: one strand affects another. I wanted my students, most in their third decades of life, to consider the family patterns they had experienced, how the family adapts in order to survive, and how it might grow or fracture under stress.

Eventually, five further strands evolved in my tracing on the board of the variables that configure a human life. My lines and segments began to look like a chart. There are many other variables in any life but my small set was sufficient for my teaching. It was a simple illustration, and it remains simple, as my purpose remains simple. If we consider the strands of our own lives and understand how they evolve simultaneously, accept how they might affect each other, and see how they might create a need for knowledge, then we might better understand human differences among other people. (The full chart, in its revised and complete form, appears at the end of this chapter.)

For example, to consider the strand of a person's diverse *education* increases our awareness of the gain and incorporation of complex skills, from preschool, to formal education, to learning over the span of one life. Education includes self-education, being mentored, learning at work, and learning from experiences such as travel, health or financial crises, adaptations to technology, consistent museum and library use, civic engagement, leadership, memberships, and personal reading. How many other variables might appear in the inventory of things we have learned or the people we have learned from, or the situations that taught us the most? How easily can we answer the question "Where or how did you learn this?"

When I added the strand of *economy* to the growing set of variations in one life, perhaps the greatest source of individual complexity appeared on the board. In the early decades of our lives, we are dependent on others, and our first jobs tend to be supplementary, not primary. They help us to learn economic independence. By the beginning of our third decade, however, the complexity expands to include trying out a career, managing finances and housing, food, transportation, making investments, signing contracts and leases, meeting obligations and responsibilities, and paying taxes. Unless disrupted by job loss, our ability to manage our finances and needs must be uninterrupted and expansive. We know the effects of national and international economic fluctuations and disparities, losses and transitions in careers, and even foreclosures and bankruptcies. We also know that these things can affect health, family, and education. Assuming other strands are stable—not very likely—variations in our economic vulnerability may make the largest differences in our personal lives. We manage until our retirement, when our economic state again changes and brings new challenges.

If an economic strand is the greatest source of complexity in lives, our multiple participations in *society*, the fifth strand, are probably the most obvious and attractive. Our networks and connections, especially in these days of friending and tweeting, are ways to demonstrate that we matter to ourselves and to each other. We keep up with each other, and it makes us feel less alone. But this is also the strand that involves our altruism and civic engagement, our relations to the state and nation, our service to ideals, our participation in politics, and our ways of serving, volunteering, and championing a cause. This strand is where we find our rootedness among others and our sense of belonging in a neighborhood and its community. At another level, it is also about national identity, continuity within a culture, and responsibility to the structures of government and law. The linear idea of a strand perhaps suggests the wrong metaphor for this dimension of our experience; the variables embedded in social life might better be displayed in concentric or overlapping circles, or in a web. But it is over the life course that the social dimension progresses, accrues, and increases. We participate in more circles, or the web filaments proliferate. Our connections to others change, fade, and disappear as new engagements cumulate and expand. But what fades and drops away from us still leaves a trace on us. It also can reappear. Because we are looking at one life over time, it is not at the center of a concentric social web; rather, it is an expansive procession or wave, or a widening parade along this particular strand. This dimension can endure and grow throughout a life, never diminishing if we are lucky.

The permanent dynamics of our *beliefs*—faith, political values, ethics, fairness, and philosophy—also do not disappear, if we have been attentive to their strand, the sixth. While they are the most ethereal of our shaping forces, they are also where we become accustomed to questioning, testing rules, discovering authenticity, and forging a working ethic that permits us to conduct conscientious lives. Our mature beliefs guide us to be true, we might say, but a robust relationship with faith and philosophy is more likely to emerge from conflict rather than calm. I think mature beliefs (even of the devout) can be variable, adaptive, private, and personal. They allow us not only to see ourselves, but also question ourselves. We may turn to our beliefs for guidance, explanation, solace, and reflection; we may also turn to them for unbending ethics. Faith, politics, and ethics evolve, it seems to me, from trust in others, observations and participation in systems, the integrity of leaders, and the tensions that decisions require. They may also evolve from forces we cannot see or describe. Faith, we know, has a political side; it also endures or crumbles in crises. We may use this strand of our lives to address the value of capital punishment, for example; or we may use it to determine a gratuity in a diner. Our ideas of justice, goodness, forgiveness, and generosity evolve as experience evolves, and they never disappear or become irrelevant to us. I have found that maturity also causes haunting recurrences of lapsed behaviors, failures to be generous, and reluctance to speak out. We learn from this strand by what we have and have not done for justice.

In the seventh strand, I added further complexity to my students' lives by briefly outlining *the stages of human development* as described by Erik H. Erikson, reminding them that, as all the complex engagements of one worldly life are going on, our psychological lives have their own tensions to resolve in order to progress toward a strong identity, successful intimacy, generativity, integrity, acceptance, and advanced age. (Erikson and Erikson, 1998).

When I describe these strands, I often feel the need to offer an apology; they are so simple and everybody knows about them, I think. But my young students needed to see these strands on the board, layer after layer, in order to envision one life growing more complex. My older students saw their lives and the lives of their elders as variants on my chart. I asked them all to think of their parents and grandparents, to recall some crisis or transition that made a great difference to their families, and to see how an event on one strand—military service or a sudden death, for example, or a financial reversal—might affect the steadiness of another strand, such as a belief in fairness or an article of faith. Such observations, I felt, are essential for seeing the lives of adult information users as they may be shaped by multiple tensions. When we serve the cognitive lives in our communities, it is vital to see that each one carries an individual, unspoken history of tensions and resolutions.

THE INFORMATION STRAND

To make this clear, I knew that the final element in my boxy chart of one life's strands was essential, but I did not add it for a few months, until an hour or two before a lecture at the University of South Carolina. The final strand I added to this model of a life is devoted to *knowledge*. It is the strand that is most original to the human life, because it develops in response to the challenge and complexities that happen along the other strands. It is intellectual and multidimensional, and it is the strand over which we have the most personal and continuous control. I told my students that the need for knowledge is most intense when change happens to us, when we need to adapt our thoughts to new conditions, or when a crisis of health or family, for example, shocks and dazes us. We desperately seek information when a crisis affects the continuity of a life. We keep mindful of our health, especially. If our educational plans go awry, we need to find a different path, and probably adapt our personal economy and family responsibilities. If a marriage ends, we cannot afford to be passive, but perhaps we also cannot afford to return to school for vocational training. When these things happen, we need to know more, we need to find information that is fitted to our need, and we need to be able to trust it or trust its source. We might also want more than knowledge or guidance; we might need a person whose work is to provide empathic help and professional service. We might need a collection that awakens us to possibilities we have not yet considered.

This is the larger purpose of these bare ideas. The continuities of one life are simultaneous, interconnected, and likely to be invisible even to the living person. All the strands in one person's life begin and end at once. All strands evolve differently for individuals, and yet all strands are connected. Events in the context of one strand have effects on other life strands. Extraordinary activity in one context will have resonance elsewhere. Extraordinary activity in one context will cloud the details and importance of attending to other strands. Crises and disasters are not possible to contain on one strand. All strands are potentially equivalent in their power over our aspirations. The driving systems of each strand need to work reasonably well for progress toward what we want to occur. When we are unable to find social or familial or economic support for our dreams, I told my students, we must often struggle to know how to sustain them.

The strands are neither fixed nor preordained; they are configured in variable ways by the possibilities presented in the course of experience. We develop and are transformed by human contexts; these are unpredictable. We may practice conscious, reflective self-development, and we respond to challenging situations when we are required to grow. When we live up to the crises, accidents, needs, and aspirations of one life, our questions and unfinished issues make us ready for new information. This is when human beings can turn to cultural institutions, and to the contexts and situations provided there, for knowledge and help.

We should understand further that the acts of constructing an adult self occur over time and under extremely variable conditions, making the dimensions and dynamics of change less predictable. We may have no control over these conditions. We anticipate, hope, or fear the future based on much that happens early in our lives. Our parents affect our opportunities and attitudes toward ambiguity and risk, and toward independent thinking. We may or may not have mentors, models, advisors, or guides. The presence of siblings helps us to understand the experience and individuality of other selves. Social and economic class variables, and demographic and geographic conditions, all affect our awareness of paths and possibilities and our ability to pursue them. In emergencies, resources and support will vary. Leisure and reflective time, early literacy, access to current information resources and technologies, and opportunities for travel also vary according to social and economic status. Persons vary in physical and intellectual skills and energy, talents and interests, persistence, motive, flexibility, adaptation, and the ability to think anew. In some cases, disabilities are present, diagnosed or undiagnosed. People vary in their responses to advances and setbacks and in their progression toward adulthood.

There is neither a map nor guide for this. We have experiences we have not anticipated. We observe events that we cannot fully describe. Our thinking narrows, then it broadens. We perceive a nearby idea that helps us to change our minds. We know someone who becomes our model, our teacher, or our mentor. Our questions begin, then they expand, then they contract or change into other questions. We begin again and we look again. As we want to know more, we observe more deeply. We see sequences and patterns in events, acts of great unexplained genius, inventive juxtapositions, ideas that sweep across contexts, and strong but unclear and ambiguous relationships between forces and phenomena. We perceive continuities and variations among objects and ideas, and if we backtrack we find more than we had anticipated.

We have indelibly embedded some events as common witnesses in the way that the students in Palmerston North carried the flight of 901 within them a generation after it occurred. Our semblances to other experiences may be closer than we imagine, and we may not be the strangers we imagine ourselves to be. But we may also have witnessed other events from afar: the rise and fall of a great life, the collapse and disappearance of a futile movement, or the rise and success of a grand one. We may have endured an economic downturn or military service and think of them as watersheds in our experience. My mother talked about the Great Depression, my father about the Great War. Both experiences made them different, perhaps in more formative ways than any other thing they experienced. These experiences become parts of our self-construction. But we have also witnessed and recorded smaller, more intimate events, and these too have made us experienced and thoughtful.

We live amid or on the edges of events each day, and we keep private memories and responses. Among others, we are capable of shifting and adjusting our observations of lived experiences in order to extend the common ground shared; we find empathy and mutuality where we can. We are able to speak to each other with encouragement in acts of progressive reciprocity. Soon we are less strange and more known. Across our extreme differences, there are grounds in memory and experience for the conversations we need in communities and cultural institutions. We are able to think ourselves together into the future. Our conversations can make every fragment we remember and harbor, and every jagged shard that emerges as we reflect, join and live.

STRANDS: CONTINUITIES AND POSSIBILITIES OF ONE LIFE.

Timeline header: A... | 10 | 20 | 30 | 40 | 50 | 60 | 70 | 80 | ...Ω

Strand	Early life	Adolescence / Young Adult	Adulthood	Possibilities / Later life	Ω (Old Age)
BIOLOGY Growth, Sexuality, Health	Birth, Infancy [PHYSICAL GROWTH → FULL PHYSICAL GROWTH] [MATURITY →]	Childhood [PUBERTY → SEXUALITY, EXPLORATION →] Risktaking; Youth Adolescence [ADULTHOOD →]		[HEALTH POSSIBILITIES, VARIABLES AND FACTORS →] Accidents, Addiction, Chronic Illness, Depression, Diet, Exercise, Genetics, Health Care, Health Insurance, Obesity, Physical Activity, Smoking, STDs, e.g.	
FAMILY Generations, Relations, Transitions	Treatment as a child, central to adult attention, among parents and siblings.	Treatment as a growing person, gradually more responsible for self. [AUTONOMY →] Adult participation in the family among all generations.	[PARTNERING →] Childbirth, adoption [PARENTING →] Creating a home	[POSSIBLE FACTORS →] Proximity to family. Strengths of relationships. Possible loss of partner. Disaffection; infidelity; estrangement; divorce; subsequent sexual relationships; re-partnering; step-parenting; dissolution and reformation of the home. Aging and caregiving. Parental decline and dependence; loss of parents, family deaths.	Surrogate families, companions, caregivers
EDUCATION Socialization, Schooling, Learning	Pre-School / Grade School / Middle School	High School / College / Graduate School. OTHER FORMAL TRAINING: PROFESSIONAL STUDIES, CURRICULA, FACULTY, STANDARDS, EVALUATION. OUTSIDE SCHOOLS: MEDIA, LANGUAGE, APPRENTICESHIPS, ORGANIZATIONS, CULTURAL EXPECTATIONS, HOUSEHOLD INFORMAL LESSONS, PERSONAL LEARNING		POSSIBLE WAYS OF LIFELONG LEARNING. Parenthood experience. Health experience. Crisis experience. Economic experience. Work-inspired experience, work-required experience. Successes and defeats. Experience driven by adaptation to technologies. Household experience. Travel experience. Avocational experience. Networked experience. Art and craft participation and observation. Museum and library use. Community experience. Civic and political experience. Self-rescue. Reading, personal engagements and conversations, focused study, curiosity, unfinished issues.	
ECONOMY Consumption, Contribution, Outcomes	[COMPLETE ECONOMIC DEPENDENCE ON OTHERS]	First Employment, Independence [Limited, part-time]	Career try-out; career choices, adjustments; financial independence; savings, housing, transportation; investments; contracts; obligations; taxpaying; debt, repayment	[RETIREMENT →] DEPENDENCIES AND RESPONSIBILITIES Family, Home, Stability, Anticipations [FACTORS →] Economic fluctuations: wealth and security; job insecurity or loss; career loss, financial loss; career transition; foreclosure; bankruptcy	Family, leisure; travel; mentoring; part-time employment. Rediscovery of possible selves.
SOCIETY Networks, Altruism, Civic Life	[INTIMATE WORLD → PARENT FAMILY →] Play Friends, School Friends	[SMALL WORLD → LARGE WORLD → PUBLIC WORLD →] High School World to College World to Military Service to Volunteer Service to Travel	[EMPLOYMENT →] [FRIENDSHIP FAMILY →] [PERSONAL FAMILY →] [PUBLIC MEMBERSHIPS →] Political and civic engagement; volunteerism; rootedness; championing; civic or political causes; undertaking new ventures, responsibilities; practicing non-work leadership and service	Continuity, expansion or contraction of civic connections; transitions in activity, passing responsibility to others	
BELIEFS Faith, Politics, Ethics	[RECEIVED FAITH →] Early Faith and Ethical Training	Questioning, testing rules; hypocrisy; authenticity; personal beliefs	Applied ethics in work and society; political judgments	Mature faith is variable, adaptive, private, and personal. Faith informs a view of self and the external world. Faith can appear and disappear, may be challenged by events, varies in understanding events, losses, successes. It is often a source of solace and explanation. Political opinion may evolve from beliefs, ethics, and faith leaders. Ethical beliefs evolve from observation and participation in systems, under conditions of tension. Ideas of goodness, forgiveness, and generosity evolve as experience evolves. Some of free will affects attitudes toward thinking and learning. These issues never disappear.	Reconciliation, acceptance, transmission, lessons
SELF (Erikson) Identity, Memory, Experience	I. TRUST vs. MISTRUST (Ego, drive, hope) II. AUTONOMY vs. SHAME (Skills, autonomy) III. INITIATIVE vs. GUILT (femaleness, trials, experiments) IV. INDUSTRY vs. INFERIORITY (Competence, ability)	V. IDENTITY vs. ROLE CONFUSION (Complexity, self, peers, variations)	VI. INTIMACY AND SOLIDARITY vs. ISOLATION (Affiliations, relationships) VII. GENERATIVITY vs. SELF-ABSORPTION OR STAGNATION (Work, family, community)	VIII. INTEGRITY vs. DESPAIR (Fulfillment, contribution, meaning, contentment vs. failure, worthlessness, regret, disconnection)	IX. ADVANCED OLD AGE (Managing the challenges of daily life; acceptance)
KNOWLEDGE Information, Wisdom, Insight	The continuities of one life are simultaneous, interconnected, and likely to be invisible even to the living person. They cannot be fully observed except from with the life. All the strands in one person's life begin and end at once. All strands evolve differently for individuals. All strands are connected; disasters are difficult to contain on one strand. All strands are potentially equivalent in power over us. All strands are configured by possibilities and variables. Events in the context of one strand have effects on other life strands. Extraordinary activity in one context will cloud the details and importance of attending to other strands. Extraordinary activity in one context will have resonance elsewhere. We develop and are transformed by human contacts. We practice conscious, reflective self-development, and respond to challenging situations when we are required to grow. When we live up to crisis, accidents, needs, aspirations, our questions and unfinished issues make us ready and open for new information.				

NOTES

1. The crash was evidently caused by the failure to communicate a revised flight plan, thereby diverting the aircraft 45 kilometers off its typical course. Assuming the ground below was flat, the pilot had descended to an altitude of 610 meters to provide closer views of the monochromatic landscape, where the white mountain could not be differentiated from the white ground. Debate on blame is extensive. See www.nzhistory.nct.nz/culture/erebus disaster and http://library.christchurch.org.nz/kids/nzdisasters/erebus.asp.

2. The incident is described at www.wcl.govt.nz/heritage/wahine.html and http://christchurchcitylibraries.com/kids/nzdisasters/wahine.asp.

3. On that same trip, in Dunedin at the southern coast of the nation, the Otago Settlers Museum contained an exhibition of shipwrecks suffered in the cold seas during the great Scottish migrations of the nineteenth century. The journeys, the losses, the privations of survivors, and the sheer number of documented cases seemed appalling and numbing. The tenacity and courage of the age—and the foundation of the nation in these catastrophes—helped me to understand how people come to know something together.

CHAPTER 6

Open Conversations

The best professional advice, I have found, is tentative and conditional. Experience, the authentic teacher, happens only in a situation, a complexity in a place, among people with intentions you might fully understand only if you are there. There is no service, experience, connection, or reflection in the abstract. The best advice is deferential and unassuming; it is often difficult to articulate. Open conversations begin with people who question, willing to engage and converse with others. While it is daunting to start any new forms of engagement with users, it is reasonable to trust that interesting themes and ideas touch many lives, and people who use libraries and museums are active thinkers, unafraid of ideas. In this chapter, I suggest ideas about the creation of open conversations, but I offer it with the advice I once gave to a student who later said it was the hardest ever: keep your options open. Open conversations have to fit place, people, and intentions or they will not invite participation, and unless they invite they will not work. Planning requires a flexible hand, and a disinterested ego. Open conversations are primarily about other people. Like great collections, plans for a series of conversations should follow the community. Without politics or polemics, they should help a community to address its aspirations, and introduce both challenging and informing content. In my view, this is how we learn to make open conversations happen.

AN APPROACH

In general, it is wise to begin to plan with others, including colleagues, who want to be part of the conversations, so they can feel ownership in them as only participants can. A leader in the museum or library should play some part in this, to demonstrate its importance to the institution. Talk to community leaders about their observations and advice in dealing with community members about matters of consequence and common interest. Examine any lessons taken from experienced colleagues, reading groups, and public meetings. Successful discussion-based educators can advise about techniques and topics. Eventually, you might use the conversations themselves to help in planning. Build a few minutes of spoken assessment into the end of each conversation: how did we each do as speakers and listeners? What could we change next time? What do we need to talk about in our next conversation? Who will make the plan, gather some information? What kind of cake should we bring?

There are many approaches to conversations and much work to be done before we arrive at the cake. My suggestions are mine alone, derived from work with groups in conversation over time, teaching classes (admittedly not always a convivial enterprise), and participating in reading groups as a leader and guide. What I suggest has been useful to me, and I anticipate it will be useful to others. But: look for other guides and advisors. Several are listed later in this book.

HOW WE PREPARE

Schedule a series of three or four conversations separated by one week or possibly two, allowing participants to read and reflect between meetings. Select a time, early evening is best, and set the limits: 90 minutes. Select a place within the library or the museum, somewhere chairs can be moved into a face-to-face configuration. Tables help participants to write notes, keep a comfortable space, and create a focused atmosphere. The place should be private but accessible. In museums, a gallery closed for the evening may work as well. Whenever possible, put food and drink in the room, not elaborate but well chosen and well arrayed.

Plan a topic or a theme, or a small set of foci, likely to sustain a series of conversations for the planned period. Make the focus significant but not narrow, a contemporary matter with a history. If possible, the theme should invite the telling of stories and experiences. Each week might have a question or an idea at its center, but the group may wish to continue prior themes without new additions. Art, history, and science museums often have rich topics of discussion directly in front of observers. Conversations in museums might well create an agenda that explores themes and connections among galleries or objects. However, the conversations we want are not didactic but exploratory, not tutorials but encounters. Of course, great conversations may begin with a book, a film, or an investigative report; or an informed guest might talk about the trends and issues in a particular area of expertise, or a state-of-the-art overview of a situation or enterprise. Whatever its form, the beginning stimulus ought to provide both a productive start and some further questions to pursue over the course of the plan. These subsequent questions might be gathered during the interim between meetings. Thinking and rethinking between gatherings are among the most valuable aspects of a conversation. A small bibliography of three or four books, a small set of websites, or continuing news coverage might well help ideas to emerge between meetings.

I would consider ideas like the five that follow; they reflect both my professional interests and the interests of a library or a museum, and they also accept variations easily. They are (1) learning in adulthood (what I learned and how I learned it), (2) human values (leadership, courage, and the common good), (3) historical events or documents (such as the Great Depression and the U.S. Constitution), (4) current topics (being born elsewhere, and becoming American), and (5) comparative practices (faith differences and similarities). Each of these topics can be served by reading, by experienced guests, and by the front pages of larger newspapers. Each topic also can be used to demonstrate the power of a cultural institution to bring attention and resources into the presence of learners. The best topics will have an accessible literature to inform the discussion, but they should also be inviting for people who bring relevant experiences or who are simply curious and interested. Though it goes without saying, it will be said: the knowledge and advice of librarians are essential throughout this planning.

Institutions have users, members, regulars, and a core of supporters. For a first conversation group, these are the people who might create up to half the participants; the other half might be invited from organizations, schools, or neighborhoods served by the institution. With caution, the size of a group might exceed 15 or 20, but the larger the group, the more difficult for everyone to speak, listen, and respond. As a group exceeds 15, the risk of this frustration increases. While conducting two groups at different times appears to require twice the preparation, it also provides twice the experience, especially if its leaders are different persons, able to learn from each other.

Groups communicate best within acknowledged structures—time limits, taking turns, showing respect—because they can feel confidence that a convivial process preserves their rights to speak and be heard. Prepare a few guidelines to acknowledge this requirement, and refer to them at the beginning of each conversation; at the end, ask how well the group did, and how the regulations served communication. Keep the guide simple and direct; emphasize the common agreements: civil conversations, relevance to the theme, and respect for the situation and each other. These commonalities will include fair amounts of time to speak, generosity and openness in listening, and courtesy in responding. As needed, guidelines can be amended, but with care and with the same civility emphasized in conversations.

Prepare and copy for each participant a single page to stimulate the conversation: it might include a set of quotations on the topic, or a series of different definitions, a news article or an interview, a brief passage from a document, or perhaps a poem. A combination of different information, gathered from alternative viewpoints, may incite ideas. Tables and data can also help to ground the conversation. In a similar way, an entry from an unabridged dictionary or a thesaurus presents meanings and nuances; other specialized reference works will provide more contextual or expansive information. A library's reference shelves might provide encyclopedic sources to confirm information or open relevant themes. The single page allows participants to respond to a common set of statements at the start; it also allows them to make notes as they listen to each other and reflect. Provide pads and pencils. Provide name tags or tented cards and markers to fill them out.

Time in conversation might usefully be structured into the following parts, again as part of a transparent plan: welcome to everyone, logistics of the conversation, refreshments, and restroom locations; the origins of the theme; defining the theme and the guidelines; a look at the page of stimuli; and participants identify themselves and talk about their interests in the topic. Now we can begin. Plan to take a break after 50 minutes, and then resume for 20 or 30 more.

THE WAYS OF A CONVERSATION

No conversation is the same as another.

We gather from various places and perspectives. Open conversations require fluidity and continuity to shape their processes. As topics and themes vary, so will those who attend. A convocation of equal speakers needs differences in experience and position. Invitations and announcements of meetings and procedures can be directed to civic organizations, community institutions, schools, and teachers likely to show interest. Students deserve special invitations to these gatherings in order to hear and contribute to the discourse.

We present ourselves. When, as citizens, we participate in public thinking and conversing in a library or a museum, we present our forms of knowledge, information, and opinions to each other. It is useful to begin a first meeting with three or four minutes per participant, each describing *what brought me to this topic*, *what I bring to this topic*, or both. Presenting ourselves, we refer to contexts and experiences that inform our perspectives. We express ideas and invite responses and alternative views. We ask questions of others and ourselves, and then we reflect together. When we are participants in open conversations we expect to speak, listen, and inquire in a situation of mutual respect and interest.

We withhold actions and judgments. Such gatherings are not specifically conducted in aid of civic decisions, nor are they overtly political, but they will include issues, foci, policies, and themes derived from public questions. They are reflective but not therapeutic in the clinical sense or decisive in the political sense. Open conversations, as I see them, are contemplative: they take a circumspect stance, gathering and considering reflections and thoughts that do not prescribe action or personal judgments. In these situations, talking and thinking together are forms of exposition, and sources of potential guidance for both mind and conscience in the larger, common world beyond the conversation.

We face each other. Sitting around a table is useful for notes and papers, for keeping attention focused, and for an atmosphere of equality. For a group of up to a dozen conversation participants, if a conference table is not available, one small circle of chairs might do. For more participants, a couple of concentric circles—not one larger circle—are best. Keep the diameter of the center circle between 10 and 12 feet.

We observe leadership and order. Leadership is best shared by two people, taking turns to provide structure, preparation, and management of separate gatherings. Depending on the nature of the group, volunteer leaders might vary even more, changing with each meeting as a way to build capacity and experience for participants. Rules of order must be simple and agreeable. Fairness requires that contributors share the available time equitably. A designated listener should be asked to do nothing more than listen with care and, when asked, express observations about the progress and balance of the conversation twice, at its halfway point and at its conclusion.

We value attention and focus. Open conversations require transparent plans and practices, with a defined topic, sometimes a text, and always a question at the center. A nonfiction or fiction book, essay, novel, poem, policy paper, journal or magazine article, or research report may serve as a useful focus. Some different forms—an interview, a brief news report or documentary—may combine well. But the focus is on talking and listening together, not on watching a screen or a performance. Using a designated moderator, fairness in open conversations is enhanced by timed contributions, requests for clarification, and, as needed, careful adjudications in the interests of balance.

We begin with knowledge. Open conversations begin usefully with an exposition of general knowledge—current information, classic statements, reference works, or summaries—reflecting diversity and multiple contexts. It is not useful to begin with polarities or generalized characterizations of extremes. One role of the hosting cultural institution is to assist by providing and summarizing this startup material, its contexts and sources. Contextual information is useful at all times, not only when the topic or theme of a conversation is current and fresh, but also when it is shrouded in history. All topics require some depth and extension; all topics require balance; and no topic is isolated from others, but varying degrees of relevance and pertinence might deserve comment.

We talk. After beginning with an exposition of the issue, idea, or text at hand, a conversation will contain qualities of debate: participants may express or argue positions and confirm their commitments to ideas. To assure hearing the voices of all, as suggested above, it is useful to begin with round-the-group introductions: "Tell us who you are, and what brings you to the conversation." People who wish to be silent can simply say, "I pass." Before hearing extensive points of view, this process allows people to identify themselves and to express their investment in the conversation. "I've been interested for a few months." "I read about this in school." "I have heard conflicting information." Others will respond, sometimes affirming the motives of others and linking them to their own. By the end of these self-presentations, individual voices will have been heard, and some themes or anticipations are likely to be spoken. From the beginning of talk, passion, empathy, curiosity, and ambiguity will be present. People may change their opinions or express a tentative new view, but this is not the indicator or goal of a successful conversation. Civil talk is.

We use a heuristic. The heuristic is a set of guiding questions applicable in multiple situations to check procedures, logics, connections, and perspectives. They are modeled here on a mathematical protocol offered by Polya (1960). *What is our issue or problem? Have we seen other similar issues or problems like it? What can be applied to the current issue or problem from those of the past? What is our knowledge of the issue or problem and its conditions? Is our knowledge complete? What is missing? What is unknown? What outcomes are possible?* Using a few of these questions to assess its progress and content helps the conversation to be grounded and focused. Like a checklist, the heuristic keeps the process steady and even allows a step backward to assess progress and recover a lost thread.

We pause. At times a conversation may pause to describe a query or an unknown that requires more information than is readily at hand. The ability to describe what we do not know, or what we need to know in order to think more deeply, is essential to an open conversation. At these times looking for new information or introducing the voice of an expert is an obligation for participants or the institution where the conversation happens. Context, history, and evidence are just three variables pertinent to all questions we might undertake. Pausing for more information allows a sense of inquiry and responsibility to develop. Carefully deepen the conversation in useful ways whenever possible.

We talk about things we don't often talk about. An open conversation among others we may not know well may have challenges unrelated to the topic, but entirely related to the infrequency of our conversations. Almost all the places still available for person-to-person, direct spoken sharing—the dinner table, the late-night talk over coffee or drinks, and the long shared drive—are intimate, if they exist at all. We may need to think specially about what we may feel and offer to others, and how we can say it. Our epiphanies and insights. Our observations of day-to-day life from new perspectives. Revisions in our previous ideas, our changes of mind or heart. Our early years and our expectations. Connections between abstract ideas and concrete experiences. With care, we will have the satisfaction of expressing ourselves well.

We end as planned. Open conversations conclude at a designated time, perhaps with summary statements or observations by participants or nonparticipants who serve as observers. There are no truths to be discovered or confirmed, no exhortations to be obeyed. Like the conversations themselves, conclusions are to be kept open and tentative, if not resisted entirely. An ideal conversation will retain an unfinished quality, leading to more thinking and the possibility of subsequent conversations. Time at the end should also be devoted to describing possible future topics, ideas, or themes and to candid evaluations (probably a checklist with room for comments) of how the group worked.

CONVERSATIONS LEARN FROM CONVERSATIONS

Conversations take multiple forms and may have many styles, so it is useful to look for adaptable models. Here are three examples with significant websites.

The webpage of the National Issues Forums describes its gatherings in this way: "These forums, organized by a variety of organizations, groups, and individuals, offer citizens the opportunity to join together to deliberate, to make choices with others about ways to approach difficult issues and to work toward creating reasoned public judgment. Forums range from small or large group gatherings similar to town hall meetings, to study circles held in public places or in people's homes on an ongoing basis. Forums focus on an issue such as health care, immigration, Social Security, or ethnic and racial tensions." As an example to other kinds of open conversations, the gatherings of these forums emphasize diverse, experienced people who seek together what they call "a shared understanding." Unlike the conversations described here, the National Issues Forum includes finding a "common ground" for potential action as one of their reasons to gather. The group emphasizes training for neutral moderators and provides an array of discussion guides to frame specific issues and offer a handful of differing approaches to the matter. These alternatives provide participants with a structure; they can consider the larger perspective first, then each approach, "examining what appeals to them or concerns them, and also what the costs, consequences, and trade offs may be that would be incurred in following that approach" (see www.nifi.org/forums/about.aspx).

The webpage of the National Coalition for Dialogue and Deliberation addresses the whole process of creating a conversation. Here are two of its advisories, on ground rules and the beginnings of a conversation. The emphasis is on avoiding adversarial exchanges, and moderating the tensions of strong feelings.

Establish/present ground rules. Also called "agreements," ground rules are an important part of most [dialogue and deliberation] processes. Ground rules such as "listen carefully and with respect," "one person speaks at a time," "speak for yourself, not for a group," and "seek to understand rather than persuade" create a safe space for people with very different views and experiences.

These ground rules may be developed in advance of the conversation, or they may become the primary focus of an early meeting, where forum participants can work toward agreement as the initial step toward collaboration. The National Coalition addresses the value of "sharing personal histories and perspectives," and the caution that participants are likely to feel when speaking in new settings.

> Hearing from everyone at the table is a key principle in both dialogue and deliberation. In dialogue, we begin by hearing each participant's personal stories and perspectives on the issue at hand. We ask "how has this issue played out in your life?" rather than "what do you think should be done about this issue?" or "What's your take on this issue?" This builds trust in the group, establishes a sense of equality, and enables people to begin seeing the issue from perspectives other than their own. This is especially important when participants have different levels of technical knowledge or professional experience with the issue, or when some participants are not comfortable talking openly about contentious issues. (http://ncdd.org/rc/what-are-dd)

It is useful to distinguish between "contentious issues" and contention itself or the inevitable presence of dissent. A good issue may be attractive because it is surrounded by disagreements. But the conversations we have need not be disagreeable. Formal words like "I dissent" may be useful ways to express conflict in the context of civil discourse without wrangling or falling out. People need words for disagreement without offense or contention; suggestions for beginning a discussion with self-presentation permit participants to grasp the different contexts that bring people to a topic—and to their perspectives on it.

The mission statement of The American Square, found on its website, addresses the intentional values of difference and diversity as a "community site devoted to enabling respectful, multi-partisan conversation about policy and politics." The site describes its participants as "passionate moderates, progressives, conservatives, liberals, libertarians, and nonpartisans. We are proud Independents, Republicans, and Democrats. But first and foremost, we are Americans. We reject hyper-partisanship and polarization. The enormous challenges we face can only be addressed through vigorous, honest, civil political debate." The purpose of the American Square is to construct a community online where "ordinary citizens" and "leading thinkers" are able "to engage in civil, evidence-based policy discussion. Here, Americans of all political, economic, ethnic, and geographic backgrounds can express their ideas and opinions about government and politics, learn about issues, and find areas of common ground through respectful dialogue. We will find real solutions to real problems rather than on sound bites, ego, and demonization of those who disagree with us. We will treat compromise not a sign of weakness, but as a prerequisite for progress in a democracy." (see: theamericansquare.org/page/welcome-to-the-american-square) Such statements are useful to a beginning because they remind participants that essential words and values are both useful in planning and helpful to keeping on course when conversations have begun.

Conversations created by cultural institutions may proceed along these ways with a neutral moderator, succinct summaries and materials, convivial agreements (or agreements to disagree), and patience to think through an idea and its consequences. Establishing the procedures and sequences suggested by models of this kind allows participants to understand the structured entirety of a conversation, its patterns and destinations, and the shared expectations of the group. Such patterns are especially useful for new speakers, who need a sense of structure that welcomes them and is not too arcane or private to master easily. The adjective "open" applies to themes and topics, to the flow of knowledge and information, to the open end of the conversation, and to the invitation to participate. It is important to monitor these qualities—and keep the adjective accurate.

VARIATIONS IN OPEN CONVERSATIONS

There are many forms of becoming together within the frameworks of open conversations. Generally these variations are simple: the focus of a discussion will differ in scope, from local to global, it may be stimulated by a book or an event, its form will be more flexible than a moderated discussion (for example, using films or speakers), various ways of thinking and talking will be combined, multiple ideas will appear at once, the group may use a heuristic to remind itself of its own values and logics, and the group may find its inspiration from an array of resources or stimuli. In the sections that follow, a handful of variations on the open conversation are described; many more are likely to exist, or might be imagined into practice. Resources for further guidance are suggested as well.

The Library Reading Group

This is the most familiar and successful way to gather and speak together, with a book at the center, privately in the homes of neighbors and friends, or more publicly in cultural institutions, workplaces, religious congregations, or other places of membership. Entire communities, cities, counties, and states have undertaken the large enterprise of reading across large spaces, but we have not yet seen a national reading group.

Reading groups are most importantly supported and facilitated by librarians and readers' advisors, whose knowledge of communities and public aspirations is applied every day. Combined with deep working knowledge of the library's collected resources, the expertise of library professionals makes a critical difference in the depth and focus of reading group selections and conversations.

The form and structure of a typical reading group involve a monthly book selection, chosen in consultation with readers, a discussion of 90 minutes or so, some refreshments, and informal talk beyond the discussion. Groups may focus on any kinds of reading, but the likely themes and choices include literary or genre fiction, general nonfiction, books of local interest, or bestsellers of various kinds. A number of guides to great reading choices exist.

When librarians select books for library-based reading groups, or for communities or cities, choices may address a civic value, a community issue, or the changing horizons of citizens. Their question is, *what do our citizens need to understand together?* National issues readily appear on local book group reading lists, and topical crises may lead the criteria for selection.

Reading groups in libraries can easily go beyond these conventions by showing related films, inviting guest speakers, or creating panels of local citizens, professionals, historians, or other specialists to extend the themes of the reading selection through public programs. A carefully chosen series of readings will provide an array of perspectives, developing capacity to think critically, and a desire to go beyond the selected list. A series of meetings allows the group to understand and experience an evolving perspective. Over a long period of thoughtful community reading selections, it is possible to refer to their stories or lessons in the conduct of public affairs. (Imagine a city council meeting where a councilor says, "When we discussed *The Middle of Everywhere* by Mary Pipher, we made some observations about immigrants in our city.")

A promising variation on the standard reading group, where everyone reads the same book for the same gathering, is the thematic reading group, where a single topic (such as immigration, war experiences, or ethical dilemmas) can be represented by many book titles and genres (e.g., fiction, history, poetry, and memoir). Librarians will create the list of perhaps 12 to 20 titles. Three meetings might be scheduled, and everyone reads different books for different gatherings, in some cases selecting books described provocatively by participants at previous conversations. In this variation, it is not the author, narrative, or critical success of an individual title that matters most, but the discovery and comparison of different perspectives on one theme. After a series of three conversations, a fourth meeting with a couple of experts or a mixed panel of readers might serve to bring ideas together.

The Museum Reading Group

Given the extraordinary intellectual stimuli of museums—visible masterpieces or iconic artifacts, minimal public interpretation, diverse creativity and knowledge, seemingly boundary-free collections, evidences of past problems solved, and evidences of genius at work or passion engaged—it is surprising that museum reading groups do not spring up like daylilies. (There are reasons for this, I think: our equilibrium is unaccustomed to public conversations in museums, where we tend to receive and not to express; museum collections are often presented as though their meanings are self-evident, so we are led to think that there is no need to talk much; and museums close earlier than libraries do, without evening hours for talks.)

Look critically at any museum and consider the adaptable themes present, involving literature, science, social history, natural history, industry, evolution, and powerful themes related to war, regeneration, loss, exploration, and geography. It is clear that every museum generates enough topics to fill a bookstore. Every museum is about at least one great idea, and there are likely to be books to illuminate it. In fact, the shelves of good museum bookstores are often heavy with relevant titles (offered in hope of profits, if not conversations).

It is also clear that museums and their professionals, typically unaccustomed to creating reading groups and informal conversations about museum contents, would benefit from collaborations with strong libraries in this enterprise. Small museums and historic house museums might be ideal for these collaborations; their special themes related to eras, industries, neighborhoods, and local achievements serve readers well. An inventor's house? Read about creativity, innovation, and the difference made by thoughts and perseverance. A patriot's birthplace? Consider civic commitment, the concept of the heroic, the difference made by actions and sacrifices, and the current situation for heroism.

Such collaborations can create the seeds for a learning city, and for turning an historic legacy into a contemporary identity.

The Museum *Seeing* Group

The likely experience of a museum user comprises rapid exposures and brief pauses, on the way to something, on the way from something, with a list of other somethings to see. The idea of reducing the power of the list and the agenda, and of enhancing the concept of deep, intentional focus, can be an effective way to carry out several useful intentions in museums. It is possible for groups to select paintings following focused ideas—"Things to think about domestic life," "The open road in a mobile society," or "Multiple ideas in one painting,"—that are not entirely dependent on scholarship and didacticism.

When people are gathered for an evening of looking, they should encounter a plan for observing in particular ways (with notes, with audio recorders, or in pairs for dialogues) and with specific foci for the observations. In my experience, museum opportunities to talk with others about the experiences of seeing are rare or nonexistent, and as a consequence countless observations have remained unspoken.

History museums, historic houses, technology collections, art and craft museums, and collections of diversity and cultural difference—each of these can sponsor focused conversations on ideas and concepts embedded in objects. The purpose of such experiences would not be to look *at* something, but to look *for* something, *with* someone—and make a conversation happen. The idea is based on the assumption that an artifact evokes not just a fresh response, an independent vision, but also an unfinished feeling—*I have not experienced (or seen, or contemplated) this before*—that requires a conversation and, often, another look.

A Poem on the Table

This interpretation is based on an approach to public conversations described to me by Steve Sumerford of the Greensboro, North Carolina, Public Library, the institution I most often refer to as a model for public engagement. In a setting with several round tables, each seated with six or eight persons, every person has a copy of the same poem. The poem should be fresh to all readers in attendance. Powerful, engaging, and complex poems are available everywhere.

Consider selecting a poem by Wallace Stevens, Denise Levertov, William Stafford, Emily Dickinson, Mark Strand, or Adrienne Rich; or an example from collections published by the Library of America in the American Poets Project (http://americanpoetsproject.loa.org); or a poem from *The Best American Poetry* of the year series, published by Simon and Schuster; or a poem in the Library of Congress series, *Poetry 180: A Poem a Day for American High Schools* (www.loc.gov/poetry/180/).

The choice should have ambiguity, relatively clear and accessible diction, and likely relevance to the lives of the readers around the table. Poems in languages other than English should be present in the original, and in other languages, depending on those present. After a public reading for everyone to hear, readers at the tables reread and discuss the poem for 30 minutes or more. At the end of the reading and discussion time, the entire group hears the poem spoken aloud again. Table by table, a designated reader describes the reactions of companions to the poem, noting comments around the table, and common and uncommon responses. There are, of course, many ways to read poetry, and there is no requirement to interpret a poem; but the pleasures of words and ideas ought to emerge in the discussion.

The Scholar in the Room

When a topic of value is introduced to a group, it may lead to an invitation to a guest with greater experience than the group members. A college faculty member, a local attorney, and an amateur naturalist would be conventional experts. Local authors or journalists might bring more pointed perspectives to an evening's conversation. So might a craftsperson, such as a weaver or carver who simply thinks out loud as they work. Of course, the guest speaker is a staple of library and museum programming, but participatory conversations may not be commonly created to surround such occasions.

It may be wise to remove the lectern and the laser pointer, and take the model of an expert guest speaker to the level of open public discussion. Before the occasion, ask the speaker to provide a set of ideas on a page, to stimulate the thinking the guest will bring to the conversation. Or provide a small set of questions for the guest, developed by the participants. If a community is rich in experts, this approach might form the basis for a series of discussion groups in collaboration with the guests, who can also supply the best choices for background readings, preliminary experiences, and open guiding questions.

Scholars, however, tend to affect the nature of a conversation in ways that are not always communal or collaborative; they should be invited with caution.

MUSEUMS AND LIBRARIES COLLABORATING

In *A Place Not a Place* (Carr, 2006), I offered observations about the character of collaborations between museums and libraries, an essential alliance for the future. For example, every collaboration will require tenacity among its advocates and champions in each partner institution. The champions ought to be motivated by altruism if the project is to be convivial for everyone. The interests and energies of the community should be represented in the earliest moments of planning. Institutional cultures can differ; dialogue is necessary between the partners, because communication is the most likely obstacle to conviviality. Expectations and responsibilities need to be clearly assigned, according to the skills and resources of partnering institutions. Some common ideas need to be articulated and fully shared: respect for the learner; diversity among participants; and involvement of staff as participants, volunteers, and advocates, to state just three. Such collaborations need to be visible and transparent to the community, funders, institutional board members, and likely participants. True collaborations are not light engagements: they often redefine the identity of an institution and create new expectations among users. And all of these observations apply not only to collaborations among museums and libraries, but also to collaborations between museums and libraries and opera companies, public broadcasting, nonprofit theater companies, local cinema venues, and galleries of arts and crafts.

MULTIPLE PROCESSES

In its useful and succinct *Resource Guide on Public Engagement*, the National Coalition for Dialogue and Deliberation lists more than 20 forms of civic engagement, and some of these seem richly suitable for adaptation in cultural institutions. Here are seven of these alternatives as described in the resource guide (available at www.ncdd.org/files/NCDD2010_Resource _Guide.pdf).

Public Agenda's Citizen Choicework helps citizens confront tough choices in productive ways. Participants work through values conflicts and practical tradeoffs, and develop a sense of priorities and direction. Key principles include nonpartisan local leadership, inclusive participation, and unbiased discussion materials that "start where the public starts." (www.publicagenda.org)

Conversation Cafés are hosted conversations which are usually held in a public setting like a coffee house or bookstore, where anyone is welcome to join. A simple format helps people feel at ease and gives everyone who wants to a chance to speak. (www.conversationcafe.org)

Intergroup Dialogues are face-to-face meetings of people from at least two different social identity groups. They are designed to offer an open and inclusive space where participants can foster a deeper understanding of diversity and justice issues through participation in experiential activities, individual and small-group reflections, and dialogues. (www.umich.edu/ ~igrc/ and www.depts.washington.edu/sswweb/idea/)

National Issues Forums offer citizens the opportunity to join together to deliberate, to make choices with others about ways to approach difficult issues, and to work toward creating reasoned public judgment. NIF is known for its careful issue framing and quality issue guides which outline three or four different viewpoints. (www.nifi.org)

Study Circles enable communities to strengthen their own ability to solve problems by bringing large numbers of people together in dialogue across divides of race, income, age, and political viewpoints. Study circles combine dialogue, deliberation, and community-organizing techniques, enabling public talk to build understanding, explore a range of solutions, and serve as a catalyst for social, political, and policy change. (www.everyday-democracy.org)

Sustained Dialogue is a process for transforming and building the relationships that are essential to democratic political and economic practice. SD is not a problem-solving workshop; it is a sustained interaction to transform and build relationships among members of deeply conflicted groups so that they may effectively deal with practical problems. (www .sustaineddialogue.org)

World Cafés enable groups of people to participate together in evolving rounds of dialogue with three or four others while at the same time remaining part of a single, larger, connected conversation. Small, intimate conversations link and build on each other as people move between groups, cross-pollinate ideas, and discover new insights into questions or issues that really matter in their life, work, or community. (www.theworldcafe.com)

To supplement these models, three additional resources are cited below in recognition of their specificity and pertinence to this chapter. The first and third are encouraging guides for planning in a concrete situation; the second offers strong, accessible history and theory for the civic sphere. These works might provide core readings and significant encouragement for a leader's preparation. As in many aspects of professional practice, there is no perfect guide to organizing and conducting sponsored conversations—and this is a good thing. Hard rules are not useful here. A fearless and rich conversation is likely to be artless, improvisational, unpredictable, relaxed, and convivial; when a conversation has those qualities, it is also likely to be inviting, complex, significant, satisfying, and deep.

Brown, J. et al. (2005). *The World Café: Shaping Our Futures through Conversations That Matter*. San Francisco, CA: Berrett-Koehler.

The world café is described briefly above; this guide is a detailed workbook containing designs, case examples, diagrams, guiding questions, and practical advice for immersion in this sophisticated process. The café as a method of gathering is useful in part because it can be adapted for evaluation, conflict resolution, strategic planning, leader development, and expanding the shared knowledge and natural collaboration among an organization's members. It has great value as part of an institution's repertoire of communication methods, and in some situations it is a productive form of public conversation, especially with larger gatherings.

Gastil, J., & Levine, P. (Eds.). (2005). *The Deliberative Democracy Handbook: Strategies for Effective Civic Engagement in the Twenty-First Century*. San Francisco, CA: Jossey-Bass.

The Deliberative Democracy Handbook is clearly the best available book on the concepts and foundations of public, democratic, open conversations. In 19 heavily documented chapters written by dozens of leaders, scholars and consultants, Gastil and Levine present social and cultural dimensions of an active movement for public deliberation. The chapters contain multiple examples of theories, programs, and models for conducting systematic community gatherings, with specific applications described in detail. Chapter 2 ("What Can We Learn from the Practice of Deliberative Democracy"), Chapter 14 ("Study Circles: Local Deliberation as the Cornerstone of Deliberative Democracy"), Chapter 16 ("Learning Democracy Centers: Where the Public Works"), and Chapter 17 ("Disagreement and Consensus: The Importance of Dynamic Updating in Public Deliberation") are particularly relevant to open conversations in cultural institutions.

Sandra, J. N., Spayde, J., et al. (2001). *Salons: The Joy of Conversation*. Gabriola Island, BC, Canada: New Society Press.

A successful salon is a convivial gathering of colleagues and associates, primarily for the purposes of being present with each other and talking to each other, allowing those simple things—presence and talk—to be primary satisfactions. Secondary reasons—the arts, personal development, and informal support—are possible as well. The basic model for a contemporary salon is not different from a literary circle, a reading or writing group, a round table of people with common interests, or a regular social gathering to dine and converse. It is a form of open conversation with an unlimited range of structures and foci. *Salons: The Joy of Conversation* is a practical guide to creating and animating these informal groups. While they may be organized less purposefully than the sponsored civic conversations addressed by this book, their dynamics, variations, and progress are very similar.

THINKING ABOUT BEGINNING

Remember the first words of this chapter. "The best professional advice, I have found, is tentative and conditional. Experience, the authentic teacher, happens only in a situation, a complexity in a place, among people with intentions you might fully understand only if you are there." The most important advice, then, might simply be this: be there. Be present as a communicator, be aware of how participants express discomfort, and be able to invite advice and collaboration. This chapter has been written with these cautions in mind, to be balanced by the rewards inherent in finding the courage to give a community important gifts of public conversation, social engagement, and community integrity. These gifts also communicate trust and respect for people and enhance their capacities to address each other. Whatever the cognitive worth or active outcome of a public conversation, it is trust and respect that matter and encourage people most, at the deepest levels of human exchange.

CHAPTER 7

Provocative Texts

The possibilities of stimulating conversations are endless, and their most important themes or questions are unpredictable: people may find an unexpected interest in history, or in a watershed event, or an idea that transcends times and places. One form of breaking through expectations and conventions is to find a multifaceted idea, to be beguiled by its richness and unfinished character, and then to follow it and the concepts it reveals. There are inviting reference tools for such discoveries. Among the reference works I introduced to emerging librarians over decades as their teacher, the *New Dictionary of the History of Ideas* (2004)—a six-volume successor to a 1973 first edition—proved to be a consistently engaging experience for the imagination. Each opportunity to open this work provided a reminder of the inherent value of an exquisitely planned interdisciplinary tool.

For some years, I have theorized that people are attracted to librarianship because their intellects resist the limits of traditional disciplines; my students' responses to this dictionary appeared to confirm that idea of thinking beyond academic boundaries. Its entries imply deeper alternatives to the relatively direct terms and basic approaches of standard encyclopedias. Here is one brief alphabetic sequence of essay entries, each written by a fitting scholar, and each supplemented with a rich bibliography: Genetics; Genius; Genocide; Genre; Geography; Geometry; Gesture; Ghetto; Gift, The; Globalization. Another sequence includes Masks; Matriarchy; Media, History of; Medicine (China, Europe and the United States, India, Islamic Medicine); Meditation, Eastern; Meme; Memory; Men and Masculinity. Its topics are not comprehensive but generative and provocative. (The table of contents for the entire work can be seen at the publisher's site, www.gale.cengage.com.) Each of these articles is an exposition of the ideas and the thoughts surrounding the topic, not its history or value alone.

It is not my purpose to recommend this scholarly reference tool as a starting point for community conversations—though it might serve some groups well—but to use it as an example of how rich, interdisciplinary ideas can be discovered and defined, and how certain concepts can be useful across time and circumstances. The idea of "genius," for example—a word we use casually and ironically—is extremely important for the understanding of history, change, leadership, and innovation. What is genius? How does genius cause change? Similarly, the ideas of "geography," so seemingly commonplace, are extraordinary in their complexity and import to human culture. How does geography affect economy, population and community? We may naturally expect our geographic questions to appear and expand to their largest forms; we may find them to be vehicles toward changing our big ideas. We also have to allow their complexity to guide us toward the narrower contexts that seem most promising and most fascinating to us. Our best conversations will have dynamic themes and unpredictable paths. Good tools will support their changes.

The ideas offered in each of the following sections—comprising books, periodicals, and internet sites—are forms of tentative advice, intended to encourage independent searches and discoveries. They have several characteristics that matter to conversations: diversity and provocation, unpredictable relevance, support for the idea of civil society, and ways to think about what is possible among citizens in settings of goodwill. These are resources, but they are also tools that assist us in museums and libraries to engage more fully with the implications of our collections in social contexts. They hold ideas and possibilities that will open the structures of information, the complexities of community cultures, and the expansion of our individual capacities to encounter unknowns. The more we see of useful resources and the connections they provide, the more we will feel confident as inquirers.

SELECTED BOOKS

It should be clear to any reader that the author of these chapters is a librarian who believes that there is no end to rich books that provoke, exhort, and sound off on any number of topics, guaranteed to create spirited conversations. However tempting it is to prescribe a fixed set of fitting titles, that prescriptive list does not appear here. My purpose is to suggest the kinds of books (and journals, websites, and other forms of information) that I believe will stimulate, focus, or illuminate open conversations in cultural institutions. In general, the works that follow are chosen to broaden perspectives and provide contrasts. Among engaged citizen-readers, they are likely to generate insights and alternative views and perhaps an exclamation or strong rebuttal. Their differences are welcome and their frictions are warming, at least to me. The intention of this list is not to create certain agreement or disagreement but to exemplify diverse readings of experience and opinion, and to demonstrate the importance of talking, listening, and storytelling. Each volume contains an array of evidences and, in some cases, multiple voices; and each will provide the starting points for multiple promising conversations. What will people talk about? What thoughts will these readings stimulate? It pleases me to say that I have no idea. The sole criterion for inclusion in the list is the promise of arousing responses, resonances, and remonstrations.

James Atlas, Ed. (2009). *How They See Us: Meditations on America*. New York, NY: Atlas & Co.

An international array of scholars describes their views of the United States. In the words of its editor, it is "a book about the deep bond that 'foreign' writers—that is to say, writers who are not 'American'—form with the most powerful nation on earth."

Bill Bradley. (2007). *The New American Story*. New York, NY: Random House.

Former Senator Bill Bradley uses the important idea of story to describe our systems and society, our ideas of citizenship and leadership. As we reconsider, and perhaps revise, our understanding of the American story, we are more likely to appreciate the imperfect, bittersweet qualities in our collective culture.

John Brockman. (2011). *Is the Internet Changing the Way You Think? The Net's Impact on Our Minds and Future* New York, NY: Harper Perennial.

John Brockman. (2010). *This Will Change Everything: Ideas That Will Shape the Future*. New York, NY: Harper Perennial.

John Brockman. (2009). *What Have You Changed Your Mind About?* New York, NY: Harper Perennial.

John Brockman. (2007). *What Is Your Dangerous Idea?* New York, NY: Harper Perennial.

John Brockman. (2007). *What Are You Optimistic About?* New York, NY: Harper Perennial.

These selections represent the results of Brockman's surveys of leading thinkers on the question-centered website, The Edge (www.edge.org). Because they are centered on change and the expansion of intellect, most of the observations have bases in empirical science, but they often lead beyond practical matters to the speculative, the spiritual, and possible.

Sarah Burd-Sharps; Kristen Lewis; Eduardo Borges Martins. (2008). *The Measure of America: American Human Development Report, 2008–2009*. New York, NY: Columbia University Press.

Like the census-based annual document, *Statistical Abstract of the United States* (www.census.gov/compendia/statab/), *The Measure of America* is a compendium of descriptive rankings of human development data across the United States. The values of a long and healthy life, access to knowledge, and a decent standard of living are measured using indicators like life expectancy, educational attainment, school enrollment, and median earnings. These indicators, viewed through the lenses of geography, gender, and race or ethnicity lead to a sense of differences. "Human development is defined as the process of enlarging people's freedoms and opportunities and improving their well-being," the authors state. "The human development model emphasizes the everyday experience of ordinary people, including the economic, social, legal, psychological, cultural, environmental, and political processes that shape the range of options available to us." The data, international comparisons, and lucid interpretations in this book are powerful, grounded information to sustain public conversations.

Howard Fineman. (2008). *The Thirteen American Arguments: Enduring Debates That Define and Inspire Our Country*. New York, NY: Random House.

Howard Fineman recognizes that the nation was created out of arguments, and that arguments are at the center of its governance. The questions that endure are not merely interesting or formal; they are essential to American history and pertinent to the history of other evolving democracies. "We are," Fineman writes, "an endless argument." Each chapter bears a question. Who is a person? Who is an American? What can we know and say? Who judges the law? Originally intending his book to be a report on "the DNA of American public life," Fineman found that the mood of the nation required something else: "to offer reassurance and hope to readers who may need both."

Howard Gardner. (2006). *Five Minds for the Future.* Cambridge, MA: Harvard Business School Press.

Among Howard Gardner's many valuable and provocative books—such as *Multiple Intelligences, Frames of Mind,* and *Leading Minds*—I find this to be the most valuable for explicating the diverse applications and necessary adaptations of mind. The Harvard psychologist hypothesizes five kinds of cognitive power to cultivate learning, work, family, and community: the disciplinary mind, the synthesizing mind, the creating mind, the respectful mind, and the ethical mind. This work is essential reading for anyone—educators, librarians, leaders—who works for open minds and thoughtful communities.

John W. Gardner. (2003). *Living, Leading, and the American Dream.* San Francisco, CA: Jossey-Bass, Inc.

Always engaged in advocacy for leadership informed by knowledge, John W. Gardner was an ardent, articulate writer and a consistent thinker. The work he did over many decades was deeply reflective and highly accessible; it is excerpted and summarized in this volume, edited by his daughter Francesca, and introduced by Bill Moyers. Readers will find themselves reflected in Gardner's attention: this is a book for every citizen-reader. Sections titled "The Courage to Live and Learn" and "The Release of Human Possibilities" hold passages that were formative for my own writing. The final section, "Freedom and Obligation, Liberty and Duty," includes an idea Gardner first offered more than a generation ago: "The best-kept secret in America today is that people would rather work hard for something they believe in than live a life of aimless diversion" (pp. 220–221). This book is about everyday courage and responsibility, and there is no comparable voice.

David Isay. (2007). *Listening Is an Act of Love: A Celebration of American Life from the StoryCorps Project.* New York, NY: Penguin.

The title, motto of the StoryCorps project, implies an excess of sentiment, but the conversations within justify the idea. People interview each other for the record, person-to-person and generation-to-generation, saying the things they want to be remembered for all time. As a collection, this sampling from thousands of conversations has the compelling richness of natural human storytelling and the power of authentic experience. Each one is different and each one is the same.

Anthony Lewis. (2007). *Freedom for the Thought That We Hate: A Biography of the First Amendment*. New York, NY: Basic Books.

In American cultural institutions, the First Amendment is more than a basis for diverse, challenging collections: the amendment protects words, artworks, access to provocative knowledge, and language to speak about it. It is, in itself a fine topic for conversations in cultural institutions. Anthony Lewis—distinguished journalist, observer of the Supreme Court, and author of *Gideon's Trumpet* and *Make No Law*—writes about the nearly unlimited expression of information, ideas, and words that is essential to democratic society. James Madison, Oliver Wendell Holmes, and Louis Brandeis are cited brilliantly throughout.

Michael J. Sandel. (2009). *Justice: What's the Right Thing to Do?* New York, NY: Farrar, Straus and Giroux.

Ethical choices, fair behaviors, critical decisions, and protective laws are essential in democratic societies, especially among situations causing people to live on the edges of hope and survival. Or, are they? As they appear in national and local policies, health care, and education, they are often about resources, power, and control, and not always about what is "just." It is difficult to imagine any citizen who will not respond to this masterful exposition of the morality that defines a society, a culture, and ultimately a community. Sandel puts stark decisions in the palms of his readers' hands, making them haunting, immediate, and resistant to easy compromise.

Rebecca Solnit. (2009). *A Paradise Built in Hell: The Extraordinary Communities That Arise in Disaster*. New York, NY: Penguin Books.

Among these books, it is difficult not to suggest that readers should begin with this one, Rebecca Solnit's stunning retelling of human connections and civic strengths forged by disasters. "The prevalent human nature in disaster is resilient, resourceful, generous, empathic, and brave" (p. 8). A progression of heartening but sobering observations and confirming intuitions, the book has value for discovering the possibilities of community when circumstances appear to be most impossible. In this work, the San Francisco and Mexico City earthquakes, the attacks of September 11, and the flooding of New Orleans, among other devastations, unexpectedly become records of affirmation and fear-lessness. The book is unique in its perspective and themes, and Solnit's prose is exquisite in telling them.

Studs Terkel. (2003). *Hope Dies Last: Keeping the Faith in Difficult Times. New York, NY: The New Press.*

Studs Terkel's 1974 book *Working: People Talk about What They Do All Day and How They Feel about What They Do* was a required text in all of my basic reference courses, a way to help students to think about adults whose learning experiences lay outside academic life, in the challenges and tensions of everyday choices and experiences. (A similar volume serves as a version of *Working* for the current century, *Gig: Americans Talk about Their Jobs*, published in 2001 by Three Rivers Press.) A generation ago, Terkel's theme was work and how it shapes us. In *Hope Dies Last*, published near the end of his life, the themes are aspiration and desire for a fair and just society, and the tensions that follow them. The perspectives of those who speak in the book tend to come from the political left, but they can be read as expressions of American progress and vitality that most readers will find familiar and generous.

Sherry Turkle. *Alone Together: Why We Expect More from Technology and Less from Each Other*. (2010). Cambridge, MA: MIT Press.

Sherry Turkle, Ed. *The Inner History of Devices*. (2008). Cambridge, MA: MIT Press.

Sherry Turkle, Ed. *Falling for Science: Objects in Mind*. (2008). Cambridge, MA: MIT Press.

Sherry Turkle, Ed. *Evocative Objects: Things We Think With*. (2007). Cambridge, MA: MIT Press.

It has taken decades for the emergence of excellent writers with a view of technology that assists us to see it plain, part of a continuum, part of our lives, and not a competitive, life-narrowing, dehumanizing, compromising ancillary to human nature as we know it. Such writers have a mature under-standing of tools and objects in our cognitive experiences and there are not very many of them. I offer only one here, Sherry Turkle, with the hope that others will emerge, or be discovered, though any writer of equal stature will be rare. The three volumes that Turkle has edited are different explorations of the "hidden lives of objects," collections of essays by and about brilliant people for whom quotidian objects have served as talismans and inspirations: mud, keys, toys, microscopes, chocolate meringue, the dialysis machine, cell phones, keyboards, death-defying superheroes, a stone axe head, and Murray: The Stuffed Bunny. The effect of reading it is a new relationship with our own objects as telling features of our lives. *Alone Together* does something more: Turkle offers a complex, nuanced profile of the experiential, intellectual, cognitive, emotional, personal, confidential, intimate effects of the wired, robotic, technological life. Using one of her chapter titles, it is a narrative of willing human-machine "complicities," invisibly bending us toward our tools, where we are simultaneously empowered and consoled, despite our isolation.

Alan Weisman. (2007). *The World without Us*. New York, NY: Picador.

This extraordinarily readable and deeply fascinating book asks one question at its start: "What if we (that is, all human beings) vanished tomorrow?" And then, how long would it take, and how would it happen, for all human traces on the earth to disappear, or at least to break into pieces? The answers to this question, and Weisman seems to have them all, are diverse and dependent on the atmospheric conditions, the materials in question, and the rage of nature to recover its place and powers from cities, suburban developments, farms, and forests. In the course of tracing our disappearance, Weisman reveals the invisible infrastructures of our lives, the toxic qualities of our improvements, and the unnatural nature of civilizations. Some books make us extremely self-conscious, and this is one of them—and it is also a useful and provocative reminder.

BOOKS IN SERIES

There are several series of annuals and other books that gather essays from a wide array of sources; summarize ideas and theories in relatively brief, concentrated volumes; or offer small biographies or monographs by authoritative writers.

Best American Series (Houghton Mifflin Harcourt)

The diversity and artistry of the essay are on full display in these annual titles, particularly *Best American Essays, Best American Nonrequired Reading*, and *Best American Science and Nature Writing*. Annual collections of travel writing, poetry, short stories, and mystery fiction are also part of this series. Another annual series, the *Best American Magazine Writing*, edited by the American Society of Magazine Editors, offers comparably superb, stimulating writing. Excellence in these shorter forms would otherwise be evanescent or lost without collections of this kind. Where an entire book or collection may provide too much to address in ninety minutes, an essay can be a perfect form for inspiring an evening's discussion.

Discoveries (Abrams)

A small series of beautifully illustrated handbooks, titles in the Discoveries series fulfill my frequent wish for small companion books useful to the museum learner, though these are equally excellent without a collection to explore. Like most introductory volumes, the series propels its reader on to more thinking and reading. The titles—more than 100—tend to emphasize artists (such as Leonardo, Rembrandt, Manet, Monet, Bonnard, and Picasso), but they also include the sciences, history, art forms, and leading historic biographies (see, for example, *Discoveries: Darwin and the Science of Evolution*, *Discoveries: Gandhi*, and *Discoveries: The Great Pyramids*).

Key Ideas (Routledge)

Emphasizing key ideas in social and cultural life, the dozens of volumes in this series are concise scholarly discussions made accessible to the able reader. The titles are direct, and the scope of each volume is clear: for example, *The Virtual*, *Social Capital*, *Human Rights*, *Racism*, *Moral Panics*, *Globalization*, *Citizenship*, *Risk*, and *Lifestyles*. These small volumes provide a strong basis for critical thinking about contemporary social and cultural experiences.

Keywords (Other Press)

The volumes in this series—*Experience*, *Gender*, *Nature*, *Identity*, and *Truth*—were published in 2004 as the American contribution to an international publishing project (translations appeared simultaneously on other continents) intended to advocate "a different kind of globalization." The publisher describes the premise of the works: "[Each volume] refers specifically to a word that is key to the understanding of the human condition. . . . *Keywords* explores the cultural specificity of these terms, and links them to issues that are most relevant for the region under consideration." The regions are Africa, America, the Arab World, China, Europe, and India, and the essays by chosen authors within the region address the topic from the basis of "knowledge as it has been dictated by their respective societies." The essays, for example, demonstrate that truth in the United States is different from truth in, say, South Africa.

Modern Library Chronicles (Modern Library/ Random House)

Each monograph in this series is a small treasure of synthesis and knowledge, a narrative that concentrates exquisite attention in a small space (typically under 200 pages) by a writer of extraordinary rightness for the topic. Among the prime examples are *Islam* by Karen Armstrong, *Law in America* by Lawrence M. Friedman, *Hitler and the Holocaust* by Robert Solomon Wistrich, *Baseball* by George Vecsey, *The Korean War* by Bruce Cumings, *The Age of Shakespeare* by Frank Kermode, *Uncivil Society: 1989 and the Implosion of the Communist Establishment* by Stephen Kotkin, *Dangerous Games: The Uses and Abuses of History* by Margaret MacMillan, and *Peoples and Empires: A Short History of European Migration, Exploration, and Conquest, from Greece to the Present* by Anthony Pagden.

Penguin Lives (Penguin)

These small biographies, each one around 200 pages long, pair a grand subject with a writer whose understanding is particularly fitting. For example, Larry McMurtry writes about the great Oglala chief Crazy Horse, Jane Smiley writes on Charles Dickens, Ada Louise Huxtable writes on Frank Lloyd Wright, Sherwin Nuland writes on Leonardo da Vinci, and Elizabeth Hardwick writes on Herman Melville. They are—in size, form, tone, and insight—uniformly inviting.

Seven Deadly Sins (Oxford University Press)

Each small and somewhat cheeky volume is dedicated to its own sin, and a distinguished author explicates each sin. No sin requires more than 150 pages; most require less. Michael Eric Dyson writes on pride, Joseph Epstein on envy, Robert A. F. Thurman on anger, Wendy Wasserstein on sloth, Phyllis Tickle on greed, Francine Prose on gluttony, and Simon Blackburn on lust. It is a risky and irresistible set of discussions on universal human flaws.

Thinking in Action (Routledge)

The few dozen titles in this series are uniform in size (slim) and perspective (philosophical), with pointed relevance to contemporary life and thought. Recent (2010–2011) items on the list are *On Manners* by Karen Stohr, *On Happiness* by Caroline West, *On Privacy* by Annabelle Lever, *On Delusion* by Jennifer Radden, and *On Courage* by Geoffrey Scarre. Previous volumes include *On the Internet* by Hubert L. Dreyfus, *On Waiting* by Harold Schweizer, *On the Public* by Alastair Hannay, *On Anxiety* by Renata Saleci, and *On Being Authentic* by Charles Guignon. Because the authors address pervasive but invisible cultural themes and concepts, the books in this series involve public awareness, intellectual understanding, and critical thinking applicable to diverse familiar contexts. As the titles noted here might convey, there are potential comparisons and perhaps tensions (delusion vs. courage, anxiety vs. happiness) to be explored in the series.

Very Short Introductions (Oxford University Press)

There are hundreds of these little handbooks, each providing a "trenchant and provocative—yet always balanced and complete" discussion of a significant issue or idea, such as folk music, American immigration, leadership, forensic investigation, global catastrophes, the Reagan revolution, and an array of topics in art, science, faith, politics, history, ethnography, and virtually every discipline. As the series title implies, the length of each book is just over a hundred pages.

SELECTED PERIODICALS

For the purpose of our conversations, periodicals have the qualities of currency and brevity, a point of view and observations that typically do not appear in other forms of news. And yet they also indicate possible depths that invite further reading and thinking. When surrounded by supplemental readings, a rich article from *The Atlantic* or *The New York Times Magazine* may have a provocative and resonant effect. Readers will look for more, the short form allows rereading, and online responses can enlarge the range of opinions that address the article. Only a small number of periodicals are cited in the list that follows; the interests of a group of readers will suggest others, and there are still places where a large array of periodicals can be reviewed.

The New York Times (www.nytimes.com) and *The Washington Post* (www.washingtonpost.com)

These daily newspapers are national and international in scope; they are standard daily reference points for many readers. They are supplemented by blogs, multimedia features online, and magazines and book reviews. The *Times*, especially, considers itself to be "the newspaper of record," and has sought to maintain a high level of authoritative news coverage and excellence in journalism. While each newspaper provides essential worldly content, each is also a way into the topics and ideas that shape our cultures, communities, and neighborhoods. With the array of national and international news resources cited on the website *Arts and Letters Daily*, described below, and whatever local newspapers to be found, it is relatively easy to develop comparisons among emergent issues and news coverage. A comparative study of front pages can suggest different editorial decisions and perspectives, as can contrasting editorials and opinion pieces. But more important to the topics of open conversations, each contemporary event that appears on the front page of a major newspaper is likely to have a history in politics, faith, war, ethnicity, national aspirations, or culture. For example, a recent article on page one of the New York Times describes a presidential visit to India, evoking histories of Mohandas K. Gandhi, British colonialism, civil disobedience, Pakistani-Indian relations, geopolitical partnerships, Southeast Asia, and international trade. These themes in turn evoke other matters of ethics, national character, cultural history, nuclear capabilities, and political power. (*Columbia Journalism Review* [www.cjr.org] is an example of a source that offers critical perspectives on everyday journalism, under the motto "Strong Press, Strong Democracy.")

The Atlantic (www.theatlantic.com), *Harper's* (www.harpers.org), and *The New Yorker* (www.newyorker.com/magazine)

These magazines publish articles on a wide array of topics, researched and written with depth and authority. All have distinguished histories and impressive archives; all are known for their practices of serious journalism. In long, leading essays, they address contemporary policies, events, leaders, the arts, cultural changes, and the complexities of politics, technology, and the environment. Briefer articles about culture, books, and media are equally stimulating. These readily accessible journals (and many other titles listed at the *Arts and Letters Daily* site) easily provide the grounding for open conversations. Explicitly partisan journals, *National Review* (www.nationalreview.com) and *The Nation* (www.thenation.com) for example, can also be paired to introduce polarities of opinion on identical issues.

Daedalus (www.mitpressjournals.org/loi/daed)

Daedalus is a quarterly journal published by the American Academy of Arts and Sciences comprising original scholarly contributions by members of the Academy, accessible to the general reader. Issues are entirely devoted to covering a theme with authoritative essays on topics of large public importance and human concern. The journal builds useful connections between scholarly discourse and public policy, especially in addressing the future. Of special interest is the Fall 2007 issue of *Daedalus*, "On the Public Interest" (Vol. 136, Issue 4).

Lapham's Quarterly (www.laphamsquarterly.org/about/)

A title first published in 2008, each issue of *Lapham's Quarterly* (like *Daedalus* and *Parabola*) provides diverse perspectives on a single topic, many drawn from classic literature. It is eclectic and thorough, approaching themes like "Sports and Games" (Summer 2010), "Crimes and Punishments" (Spring 2009), and "Ways of Learning" (Fall 2008). The selected passages come from philosophers, artists, essayists, leaders, psychologists, poets, and bureaucrats, and are selected for one criterion: relevance to the theme. However, the works are most often "abbreviated" and selected, though said to be "faithful to the original texts." Despite this caution, the content and imagery of *Lapham's Quarterly* are provocative stimulants to both conversation and further reading.

Orion (www.orionmagazine.org)

The words "Nature/Culture/Place" appear mantra-like on the cover of this bimonthly magazine, just under its title. Beautifully produced and lavishly illustrated with stunning photographs, *Orion* is a satisfaction to open, in part because it has no advertising. This inviting title provides articles and commentaries that might be said to contain themes of the earth, but it goes beyond the simple descriptors "environmental journal" or "nature magazine." *Orion* makes clear that environment is culture, and our respect for it follows from the other forms of respect we express in our lives. An anthology, *The Future of Nature: Writing on a Human Ecology from Orion Magazine*, selected and introduced by Barry Lopez, was published by Milkweed Editions in 2007.

Parabola (www.parabola.org)

Parabola is a quarterly, thematic magazine that describes itself as "the meeting ground for all of the world's great spiritual traditions, as they illuminate the central questions of human existence." Emphasizing the study of personal psychology, faith, myth, and tradition, its contents typically include stories, interviews, essays, poems, and art, often focusing on major thinkers and practitioners. Issues have been devoted to exemplary topics such as food, sleep, theft, the elderly, memory, and forgetting. When thematically appropriate, issues of *Parabola* can contribute the somewhat oblique and often surprisingly relevant perspectives of mythology to conversations grounded in practices and issues of everyday experience.

SELECTED WEBSITES

It is challenging, and perhaps unwise, to provide a directory of useful, provocative sites on the internet, for obvious reasons: there are so many, and they are in constant change. Consequently (and at the risk of imprudence), the following list is selective, a brief collection of promising places. It is also eclectic and personal, intended primarily to cite successful web resources, but also to suggest (1) possible examples for guidance in further searching, and (2) the robust nature of the internet as a stimulus for civic conversations. Sites on the list have a mix of origins, including apolitical humanitarian foundations, dedicated associations, resource providers, and bibliographic lists. All of them show attention to public issues, public voices, and the ways we have of discovering trusted, useful information. Organizations listed here sponsor and create electronic newsletters, conferences, publications, websites, and research. Some also make grants. The citations are current at the time of this book's completion; any errors of interpretation are mine.

America Speaks (americaspeaks.org)

An advocacy organization founded in 1995 with a record of focus on several themes (such as rebuilding New Orleans, strengthening democracy, public voices in policy making), the current anticipation of the organization is "to partner in the implementation of large-scale citizen engagement events around the nation on a range of critical policy issues, convene thought-leaders on issues of democratic renewal, and pursue research and innovation to advance the deliberative democracy field." The group also proposes "the development of a national infrastructure that would allow citizens to be quickly convened to discuss and influence issues of pressing importance to all Americans." The website is an exemplary and well-developed hub of resources, tools, case studies, and advice. Many publications are available for downloading at the site.

Animating Democracy (www.americansforthearts.org/ animatingdemocracy/)

This website is sponsored by the Americans for the Arts Institute for Community Development and the Arts, and it is intended to support activities of art and culture that sustain public engagement and civic dialogue. Unique programs based in arts and humanities attract diverse audiences and "animate" democracy when inspired by the issues of everyday experience. By advancing experimentation in the arts, strengthening arts organizations and cultural institutions, conducting research, and holding dialogues with civic leaders, Americans for the Arts strives to advocate the presence of arts and artists in the engagements of civil life. A "National Exchange on Art & Civic Dialogue" was held by the Animating Democracy project in October 2003, in Flint, Michigan.

Arts and Letters Daily (www.aldaily.com)

The motto of this essential site is "Veritas odit moras," from Seneca's version of the Oedipus story, meaning "Truth hates delay." Founded by the late Denis Dutton, it is a searchable resource for current articles, scholarship, reviews, and commentary. As its motto suggests, it is timely, a reasonable way to keep up in the humanities and related disciplines. Under the aegis of the *Chronicle of Higher Education*, the site provides a list and direct web access to essays in "philosophy, aesthetics, literature, language, ideas, criticism, culture, history, music, art, trends, breakthroughs, disputes, [and] gossip." In a sidebar, there is an extensive directory, providing immediate access to a very long list of newspapers, magazines, book reviews, columnists, weblogs, and live media. This site has been my homepage for many years, and allows me to find a handful of articles each week that draw my deep attention. The list of additional sites and resources is overwhelming and invaluable.

Books for Understanding (www.aaupnet.org/booksforunderstanding.html)

A project of the American Association of University Presses, this site offers timely bibliographies of scholarly research on emerging topics in news and public debate. Recent lists address "Freedom of Expression and the First Amendment," "The Supreme Court," and "Oil"—all topics that require empirical and reliable analysis, grounded in scholarship that often informs diplomacy, policy making, and national debates. It is useful to remember that scholarship is often compellingly and passionately written, driven by the commitments of scholars and academic presses to the public interest. The organization strives to answer the need for accurate and reliable information in response to crises and critical issues, calling it "scholarship behind the headlines."

The Case Foundation (www.casefoundation.org)

The Case Foundation exemplifies a new kind of activist philanthropy, striving to inspire public engagement and change the way public giving occurs. The foundation is deeply engaged in social citizenship and in the derivation of programs and ideas directly from the public. Its September 2010 report, "Citizen-Centered Solutions: Lessons in Leveraging Public Participation from the Make It Your Own Awards," follows from a project that "challenged people from all walks of life to discuss what matters most to them, decide what kind of community they want, and take action together." An earlier paper, "Citizens at the Center: A New Approach to Civic Engagement" (2006), made recommendations based on contributions from people invited to discuss their concerns and to employ useful tools and technologies in pursuit of solutions. The report "also warns against top-down solutions that require people to 'plug into' existing programs or campaigns." A blog called Social Citizens (www.socialcitizens.org/blog) is an initiative of the Case Foundation, carrying the rubric "Immerse. Converse. Disperse."

The Center for Information and Research on Civic Learning and Engagement (www.civicyouth.org/about-circle/)

The mission of this center is simply stated: "CIRCLE (The Center for Information and Research on Civic Learning and Engagement) conducts research on the civic and political engagement of young Americans," and it is well supported by an array of initiatives addressing such themes as "Concepts of Citizenship," "Civic Knowledge," and "Group Membership and Social Networks," among several others. A guide to research experts, youth demographic data, and data on initiatives for community service and civic education appear on the Center's website.

Deliberative Democracy Consortium (www.deliberative-democracy.net)

The Deliberative Democracy Consortium is "a global network of researchers and practitioners working to advance deliberative democracy." It offers a wide array of documents in support of this cause: "Recentering Democracy around Citizens," "Civic Engagement and Recent Immigrant Communities," "Creating Spaces for Change," and "Promise and Challenge of Neighborhood Democracy" are listed and available for downloading on the site at the time of this writing. It is also the source of the *Deliberative Democracy Handbook*, *The Change Handbook*, and the *Journal of Public Deliberation*. The view of deliberation is specifically political and instrumental to public policy, intending to strengthen the voices of diverse citizens in public discussions about ideas that matter to civic life. The consortium also strives to communicate to citizens that public deliberations affect policies.

The Democracy Imperative (www.unh.edu/democracy/)

The Democracy Imperative is a network of scholars and campus and civic leaders who advocate dialogue, deliberation, and building democracy as a way to strengthen public life through higher education. The organization's founding followed conversations on an array of public problems, such as citizen disengagement, the effects of partisanship, polarization of the electorate, disparities and limitations of social class, civil liberties and academic freedom, and the threatened environment. Themes of democratic foundations, strategies for conflict resolution and dialogue, and civic learning are among the values of the organization.

Difficult Dialogues (www.difficultdialogues.org)

Difficult Dialogues is an initiative of the Ford Foundation, intended to promote dialogue and pluralism. Concepts of interest to the initiative are "fundamentalism and secularism, racial and ethnic relations, the Middle East conflict, religion and the university, sexual orientation, and academic freedom." Campus projects are listed under titles such as "Promoting Pluralism and Academic Freedom on Campus," "Religious Diversity in the Public Research University," and "Integrating Difficult Dialogues into the Core Curriculum: Race, Ethics, and Religious Values."

The Edge (www.edge.org)

The Edge, as its name implies, is a place where provocative and, yes, edgy knowledge is featured. Almost more a collection of minds than a gathering of people, the Edge Foundation promotes inquiry and discussion on an extraordinarily diverse array of topics. Its most accessible and interesting element is a portion of the website called The Question Center, where multiple responses to wide open questions are gathered: "What questions have disappeared?" "What is today's most important unreported story?" "What is the most important invention in the past 2,000 years?... And 'why?'" The Brockman books cited above are derived from the exchanges documented on The Edge.

Everyday Democracy (www.everyday-democracy.org)

To banish divisive and contentious public hearings, Everyday Democracy advocates inclusive, participatory approaches toward social problem solving across individual differences in background and perspective. Believing that racism is an embedded obstacle to robust democracy, the organization helps communities "to pay particular attention to how structural racism and other structural inequalities affect the problems they address." The foci of Everyday Democracy include poverty, economic growth, education, equity, child development, police-community relations, and youth and neighborhood issues. Its vision includes the sustained presence of dialogue and problem solving over time, and interaction with leaders and officials to influence public policy through shared information and committed work.

International Association for Public Participation (http://iap2.affiniscape.com/index.cfm)

IAP2 is an organization striving to promote engagement in an array of circumstances, from local to worldwide. Taking a distinctively professional approach to public participation in decision making, the organization articulates a set of core values for the practice of public participation and a code of ethics to support them.

The John Templeton Foundation (www.templeton.org)

The Templeton Foundation is an intriguing benefactor supporting discoveries related to what it refers to as "Big Questions of human purpose and ultimate reality." Seeing its philanthropy as catalytic, the Templeton Foundation supports diverse areas of research, "on subjects ranging from complexity, evolution, and infinity to creativity, forgiveness, love, and free will." While the philosophical dialogues and contributions it inspires tend to be among the highest level of expertise, the foundation strives to share its insights freely. Through the Big Questions Essay Series, the Templeton Report, and the Templeton Book Forum, the foundation promotes "open-minded inquiry and [its] hope for advancing human progress through breakthrough discoveries."

The Kettering Foundation (www.kettering.org)

Not unlike the motives of the Templeton Foundation, the Kettering Foundation asks big questions. At the top of its website on November 10, 2010, for example, the foundation posed the question, "What does it take to make democracy work as it should?" Asking what it might take for people to shape a collective future for themselves, the foundation conducts research "from the perspective of citizens and focuses on what people collectively can do to address problems affecting their lives, their community, and their nation." It offers reports and research studies that emphasize the role of higher education in the process.

National Coalition for Dialogue and Deliberation (www.thataway.org)

The NCDD is among the most important resources available on the web, providing the rationale, encouragement, resources, and guides for practicing group conversations. The NCDD is an active group, sponsoring events, active lists and networks, a presence on social media, and conversations in several cities each year. As an example, the *Resource Guide on Public Engagement*— published in October 2010 and available for download on the website—is a thorough tool, including "Resources to Get You Started," "Collaborations That Work," and "Core Principles for Public Engagement." (The listing "Best of the Best Resources" is exactly that.) This document's value as an instructional manual is enhanced by its engagement streams, a "matrix of proven practices," and a brief but evidently comprehensive guide to variable styles and processes of conversations; 22 are listed. This may be the essential place to start when public conversations are first considered in any cultural institution.

National Conference on Citizenship (http://ncoc.net)

A bipartisan organization with a long history and a charter from the U.S. Congress, the NCoC's purpose is to "track, measure and promote" the civic life of the nation. This focus is used to enhance social and civic, to encourage public service, and to advocate for greater citizen involvement in the political process. Among its signal accomplishments is the annual publication of the nation's *Civic Health Index*, available for downloading on its site and a useful document for stimulating conversations in itself. The National Conference on Citizenship also holds an annual conference for leaders in the field of civic engagement.

National Issues Forum (www.nifi.org)

National Issues Forums compose a nonpartisan network of local public forums where public policy issues can be considered and debated. "[R]ooted in the simple notion that people need to come together to reason and talk," the forums offer public opportunities for citizens to come together in discussions of choices and ways toward "reasoned public judgment." A National Issues Forum can range in size from small study circles to town hall gatherings, focusing on a single issue such as public health, immigration, social welfare, or cultural tensions. Moderators are trained and neutral; NIF-prepared discussion guides are used to address multiple approaches to issues, and participants work through the costs and balances of each approach.

On the Commons (http://onthecommons.org)

Although the word "commonweal" is archaic, the commons movement might be said to embody that old-style value. "The commons," its website says, "is what we share together. From parks and clean water to scientific knowledge and the internet, some things are no one's private property. They exist for everyone's benefit, and must be protected for future generations." The purpose of the organization is to broaden awareness of these communal entities, and to encourage wider stewardship for them. In contrast to market cultures, a "commons" exists when a population chooses to manage a resource, a utility, or an environment collectively and democratically, with respect for such values as equitable access and use, and the expectations of future generations.

Pew Project for Excellence in Journalism (www.journalism.org)

The Pew Research Center sponsors the website Journalism.org, where an array of material on the state of the news media is collected. Of special

interest is their annual report, *The State of the News Media* (www
.stateofthemedia.org/2010/), about the status of American journalism and
its current health. The intention of the site is to observe and document
changes in communication and to provide a resource for citizens and other
to make their own judgments about the data. The site is a guide to these data
and their interpretation, to important markers in the evolution of the media,
and to key findings in the current communication environment. A feature on
press ownership (www.stateofthemedia.org/2010/media-ownership/
dashboard.php) is of particular interest.

Philanthropy for Active Civic Engagement (www.pacefunders.org)

PACE is an organization of foundations and donors with interests in fostering civic engagement through philanthropy. Its site leads to publications
and reports—such as "Funding and Fostering Local Democracy: What
Philanthropy Should Know about the Emerging Field of Deliberation
and Democratic Governance"—intended to inform and influence the
philanthropy community.

Project on Civic Reflection (www.civicreflection.org)

"Civic reflection" means the use of literature as a way to consider and discuss the large, common questions of public life, a practice that assists
citizens to talk with greater assurance about values and choices, and to think
with a larger array of ideas when addressing community needs. The organization emphasizes the use of the readings and conversations within organizations and among "people with common civic work," allowing them to
communicate better with each other, reflect on their reasons for civic
engagement, and reconsider mutual goals. Advocating reading as a stimulus
for conversation, this is the only site with a link to the venerable Great
Books Foundation (www.greatbooks.org) and its tools for book-centered
conversations.

Public Agenda (www.publicagenda.org)

Public Agenda addresses citizens, policy makers, and educators in fields
affected by public policy, striving to fill the gap between the often contrasting views and definitions of experts and leaders and the perspectives and definitions of the public. This distance often leads to disaffected and resistant
citizens confronting frustrated leaders and policy makers. Public Agenda
does opinion research intended to clarify public values, allowing conversations to proceed on grounded information about an array of issues:

education, climate change, the budget deficit and national debt, and the public view of foreign policy. Reports of these inquiries can be used to begin public conversations, as can the organization's "Issues Summaries" on such topics as crime, education (K–12 and higher education), gay rights, medical research, the right to die, and other critical themes in American life. Public Agenda also sponsors the Center for Advances in Public Engagement, an academic arm, where research reports on such topics as "Public Engagement and America's Growing Latino Population" and "Promising Practices in Online Engagement," both from Summer 2009, can be found.

Public Conversations Project (www.publicconversations.org)

The mission of the Public Conversations Project includes guidance training and inspiration for constructive engagement to address issues of public importance. Using practices adapted from family therapy, its processes address the situations of "people whose differences have led to polarization and stereotyping" with the belief that they "can develop better relationships with each other when they participate in effective dialogue." The themes of its engagements comprise matters of serious but often distorted public debate: "abortion, forest management, homosexuality and faith, biodiversity, the use of animals in research, the Israeli-Palestinian conflict," and others. Their intention is to make change possible by reducing stereotypes and demonization, increasing mutual understanding through dialogue, and creating possible groundwork for collaboration.

TED.com (www.ted.com)

"Our mission," the website says, "is spreading ideas." TED began as a gathering of inventive specialists in technology, entertainment, and design, but its expanding scope now has no apparent limits. The organization holds annual conferences and supports "the award-winning TEDTalks video site, the Open Translation Project and Open TV Project, the inspiring TED Fellows and TEDx programs, and the annual TED Prize." The attitudes of the organization fit the model of community conversations well. "We believe passionately in the power of ideas to change attitudes, lives and ultimately, the world. So we're building here a clearinghouse that offers free knowledge and inspiration from the world's most inspired thinkers, and also a community of curious souls to engage with ideas and each other." TED sees itself as "a global community . . . welcoming people from every discipline and culture who have just two things in common: they seek a deeper understanding of the world, and they hope to turn that understanding into a better future for us all."

SELECTED DOCUMENTS

Foundations and organizations are frequent sponsors of research reports, handbooks, and other noncommercial documents intended to stimulate citizens and organizations to engage in civic conversations. An incomplete sample of recent reports appears below. Note that titles tend to vary and publication is irregular. Downloadable versions can often be found on the internet by entering the report title in a web browser.

America's Civic Health Index: Broken Engagement.
National Conference on Citizenship, 2006.

America's Civic Health Index: Renewed Engagement.
National Conference on Citizenship, 2007.

America's Civic Health Index: Where We Stand.
National Conference on Citizenship, 2008.

America's Civic Health Index: Civic Health in Hard Times.
National Conference on Citizenship, 2009.

America's Civic Health Index: A Civic Nation.
National Conference on Citizenship, 2010.

The Arts and Civic Engagement: Involved in Arts, Involved in Life.
National Endowment for the Arts, 2006.

Citizens at the Center: A New Approach to Civic Engagement.
The Case Foundation, 2006.

Creating Spaces for Change: Working Toward a "Story of Now" in Civic Engagement.
W. K. Kellogg Foundation, 2010.

Democratic Dialogue: A Handbook for Practitioners.
Betty Pruitt and Philip Thomas. United Nations Development Programme, 2007.

Engaging Citizens: Meeting the Challenge of Community Life.
The Kettering Foundation, 2006.

Recentering Democracy around Citizens.
Deliberative Democracy Consortium, 2010.

Resource Guide on Public Engagement.
National Coalition for Dialogue and Deliberation, 2010.

We Have to Choose: Democracy and Deliberative Politics.
The Kettering Foundation, 2008.

CENSUS DATA

Often viewing and interpreting data and data trends can stimulate observations and conversations, especially when they are employed in the contexts of news articles and other nonfiction reading. The following general sites suggest the wide array of data available to view electronically.

National and international documents, data collections, and narratives can be explored at U.S. Government Federal Document Depository Libraries, typically found in universities, state libraries, and other research settings. Depository libraries are listed at http://catalog.gpo.gov/fdlpdir/FDLPdir.jsp. An experienced government documents librarian is the best guide to these collections.

The home page of the U.S. Government Printing Office (www.gpo.gov) is the place to begin a preliminary exploration of U.S. documents. Other national governments, the United Nations and similar international organizations, state governments, philanthropic foundations, and many governmental organizations also publish reports and documents in support of public information.

The U.S. Census Bureau provides online census data, publications, and various data tools at its website, www.census.gov. World census data is also available at www.census.gov/ipc.www/idb/worldpopinfo.php.

Data gathered by the United Nations are available through its website, http://data.un.org, including data from the Food and Agriculture Organization, Indicators on Women and Men, World Meteorological Association, Organization for Economic Co-operation and Development, World Health Organization, International Labor Organization, and UN High Commissioner for Refugees. Using these organizations as search terms in a browser will also lead the user to data. Worldwide data on environment, energy, workforce, economy, gender, crime, HIV/AIDS, and the international status of children are available from these sources. See http://data.un.org/Partners.aspx for the sources of data provided by the United Nations.

For general web searching, entering geographic terms such as "international" or "United States," population terms such as "children" or "elder," and a topic such as "rights" or "health" in a browser will lead to documents of this kind.

Reminding Ourselves

The value of these provocative texts and sources is more than their content. They hold a critical sensibility in common, and their perspectives are supported by data. There are difficult issues, urgent scholarship, and uneasy observations in these compilations and investigations, presented in ways that claim our attention and evoke our ethics. When we are thoughtful citizen-readers and participants, we can often make strong use of these reminders, finding that a part of ourselves is to be discovered among them.

When we open these tools on the desk or the desktop, we discover evidence of the value of process, the importance of public talk, and the ways we have of using discourse to live up to our lives. Our talk asserts alternatives and it also weighs them. Our talk makes plans and carries us along to fulfill them. When we are provoked by what we have read on the page, and when it is shared among others, we place our responses on the table for everyone to see. We place our authentic selves at risk as well, not only by our words but also by our silences. If we do not listen among the spoken lives of others, we invalidate not only their trust but our own integrity as well. If we do not speak, who are we? How will we change? The public processes of open conversations may be informal, but they have the quality of ritual and ceremony. They confer a sense of membership, even if transient, in a community of speaking and listening.

When we speak, we replace anonymity, abstraction, and neutrality with a human characteristic—curiosity or caring or compassion—that by its expression alone changes and advances us. We may think that we have no words for what we have made out of our experiences, until we do. Sometimes we will be observing change all around us, with no sense of what it means, until we realize that something inside ourselves has also changed. Until we express ourselves in public, we may not truly exist in public; without words or their equivalent, we are weightless, we are shadows. Our strengths lie in whatever capacity we have to alter our cognitive and social lives, and in our capacity to resist speed, isolation, and shallow thoughts. Even our adult lives require us to enter periods of incubation, unfolding, and the natural processes of exploration and (if we are fortunate) immersion, intensity, and ambiguity.

Among the great number of cognitive losses in our lives, one is worst: the loss of intellectual experience as a social activity, done with others, cooperatively, collaboratively, and collectively. How can we work and change without a surrounding community, without the full contexts of knowledge at hand, or without a sense that our first career is to learn and think? Without that surrounding place, that sense of vocation, and the evidences of context, how can we break through insularity? Read this. Think with me. Break through.

CHAPTER 8

Look at the Unknown

Some years ago, Charles M. Vest, then the president of the Massachusetts Institute of Technology (MIT), issued an unusual annual report on the state of the university. Instead of announcing the many grand patents, accomplishments, and prizes won by distinguished faculty, he offered the unfinished questions, the puzzles, and the conundrums—the unknowns—they were chasing and would continue to pursue (Vest, 1995). Some problems were dire and elusive; they still are. "We do not know which classes of earthquakes are predictable," President Vest wrote. Some problems remain urgent and contemporary; they have grown more important in the interim. "We do not know how to extract all the energy from existing fuel sources." Other questions—about the internet, language and thought, cancer genetics, antimatter, and the age of the universe—are probably different now, but never likely to go away. They are emblematic of the human enterprise that surrounds knowledge (or, more accurately, unfinished and still-open knowledge). It was inspiring to read about this report from MIT, because it reminded me that there is no one who does not harbor and nurture persistent unknowns. Everyone, I thought then and now, is capable of reflection and inquiry about the unknowns they carry.

Cultural institutions are the places where we might best come together for convocations on the countless unknowns and unfinished issues that remain—in the humanities, the natural and physical sciences, the social sciences, and the life of faith. Like those evolving questions at MIT, we cannot resolve them; that is their perfection for us. We need the reminding of long-lasting questions, the patience of reflection, and the crafting of possible knowledge. We need the best questions for trying out, for connecting to other knowledge, and for sustaining as long as possible. We make truth out of what we can see, grasp, hear, feel, connect, and understand. Yet before that crafting comes the asking, the creating of a way to express something that, if we could know it, would make a difference in our experience, perhaps the essential difference. Asking a question is creating a way. There is nothing of greater importance than our making of this way toward finding or crafting a truth to embrace.

Open conversations require simple stimuli, most often in the form of comprehensible, nearly naïve questions, created (as an artwork is created) for the depth of response and invitation they evoke. Many years ago, two years into my poor career as a public school teacher, I read the most provocative chapters, like "The Inquiry Method" and "What's Worth Knowing?" in a provocative book, *Teaching as a Subversive Activity*, by Neil Postman and Charles Weingartner (1969). My yellow underlinings remind me in 2011 of what I found persuasive in 1970. Now most of my notes and marginal exclamations embarrass me, having at last come to a critical distance from my early teaching life, but the following passage marked in my book is still valuable to me 40 years later.

> Our intention is to help make visible a strategy of inquiry. What this means in the context of the new education is this: in the world . . . there are fewer and fewer closed systems that have any relevance either to knowledge or to life. Our students will need the most frequent opportunities to think about problems in an open way; that is, to make choices and to find solutions. Closed problems simply leave out too much to produce a viable answer to any question except one that is so abstract that the answer doesn't make any difference to human beings as they go about the business of trying to cope with an ever-changing environment. (Postman and Weingartner, 1969, p. 119)

An answer-centered education is a closed system; in contrast, the library and the museum offer knowledge as an open system, configured by knowns and unknowns, containing a changeable array, often directly responsive to a good question asked. Near this quoted passage, the authors also say that their intention is to turn students themselves into open systems, unlocked and capable of self-rescue and self-reinvention. Forty years on, there is even greater need for open human systems as we live and work and make our way.

The book led me to ask my middle school students in 1970 to ask their own questions. I found myself as enchanted by what they asked as I was baffled by their complexity as learners. Suddenly questions became the essential mechanisms for what I wanted to cause in classrooms. I gathered unlimited questions from my students, typed them single-spaced onto 17 purple ditto masters, and ran them off, then made tiny, pennant-like posters for selected questions and stapled them on bulletin boards around the room.

"Look up," I said, "it is an environment of your own questions." The questions comprised an entire living curriculum across all the disciplines and foci of our class, and beyond. It shames me now to acknowledge that I was not skilled enough to use the energy, the great gift, of my students' questions ("How do poets think?") to live up to their promise. Now I am merely hopeful that some of those students survived that year of my teaching with their best questions intact. While my confidence in school teaching disappeared after two more years, my belief in the formative nature of questions remained.

Had I known what I was doing as a teacher, my students and I might have pursued several things together. We might have organized our questions according to subjects, unknowns, or common terms. We might have paired related questions. We might have considered why some questions were "better" questions than others. We might have considered what answers or responses to the questions might evolve over time with our attention. We might have asked how the objectives of questions differ. We might have modified the questions to improve them, or to alter their scope. We might have thought about the kinds of data a question requires. We might have come up with the questions we needed to address before we addressed the question we wanted to answer. We might have considered the differences between an "answer" and a "response" to a question. We might have considered the difference an answer would make to our lives, to our town, to civilization. I don't think we did any of these things, and then I left the school system, and school teaching soon after.

Some years later, now a professor, after several years of library reference practice, I formed a set of questions that I shared with my graduate students as we discussed the nature and process of reading groups. My intention was to offer a broad set of stimuli that might be used when conversations needed new directions, a little clarity, less density or partisanship, or simply more air. I wanted each question to create a pause for assessing a conversation and to allow participants to reset its content or direction with minimal discord. The questions are also designed to accomplish specific parts of a conversation in progress, to enable a previously silent person to speak, to allow a dominant speaker to step back and sit down, to invite expressions of alternative points of view, and to help participants to see how a conversation has a theme, makes progress, and leads to hidden areas of knowledge and experience. My generic questions are open for revisions and adaptations in any kind of discussion. Only a few are needed in even the most contentious conversations.

Let's see if we can summarize what we have heard so far. We started out with [this idea] and now where are we? We began with [this question]. How has it changed? What other questions do we need to ask now?

What idea that we heard earlier might we return to? What idea has stayed with you most? What idea do you want to revisit?

Does anyone have another idea to add to that? Something else for comparison? Did anyone hear anything else in the conversation so far? Is everyone in complete, unqualified, absolute, perfect agreement with what we have heard? No? Well then, how would you like to add your opinion?

Some of my questions now seem better unspoken, or if spoken, unaddressed.

*How do you describe the differences, if any, between what do you **think** about these ideas, and what you **feel** about them?*

How do you see new ways to understand this topic?

But some are still useful.

How do you think this issue might look from another person's point of view? From another political or ethical position? From a different gender? From a different economic, racial, or religious perspective? From the perspective of another generation? From elsewhere in the world?

What difference does an alternative point of view make to the way you think? How might it change your approach to our topic in order to reflect a broadened perspective?

If we were to continue this conversation for another 15 or 20 minutes, what questions should we ask and try to answer next?

Librarians, mechanics, doctors, theologians, attorneys, police, flight attendants, bartenders, panhandlers, reporters, cruciverbalists, philosophers, tailors, investors, scientists, teachers, students, cabdrivers, and beggars all depend on questions for progress in their work. They ask, variously, to determine symptoms, facts, situations, behaviors, spelling, wisdom, location, evidence, comfort, directions, background, observations, perspectives, needs, wants, comparisons, sequences, purchases, tastes, and spare change. The answers they receive to their questions allow progress toward various ends: diagnoses, justice, fairness, protection, safety, satisfaction, services, complaints, assessments, profits, fit, sales, storytelling, information, a sandwich—and more questions. For these people—for most people who ask questions—there are neither perfunctory questions nor mechanical answers, nor is one question ever likely to suffice. The exercise of intelligence, especially in a group of thoughtful people, and most especially in a thoughtful institution, requires respect for good questions.

We respect a question when we recognize it as a bridge, understand the distance across, envision the engineering of that span, and disregard the height of the chasm.

We know that a question is the result of an imaginative, creative, ambiguous, stimulating, unfinished experience. It exists before us in a brief suspension, then it moves forward.

We observe that a question is often a sentence that expresses knowledge and its opposite simultaneously.

We know that a good, courageous question is not easy; that it can define and even ennoble the person who asks it; and that it is rarely an expression of ignorance.

A generative question leads us further, engages us more with the process of responding, addresses something we understand from our lives, and speaks beyond our conversation to the culture we are part of. The generative question makes us pause.

A single question often implies a constellation of other, necessary, related questions. Most questions cannot stand alone for long, and will need expansive, ancillary questions.

Questions change toward complexity. As they evolve, so do we.

The more clearly we ask a question, the greater our awareness of what a useful response would mean. And we feel more challenged to live up to the question.

Don't ask first, "What's the answer?" Ask, "Is an answer possible?" And then ask, "What difference would an answer make? Why do we ask this question?"

A good question surprises us and wakes us to something unspoken.

These notes are meant to emphasize a simple idea: questions are common, but not always easy. Great questions are uncommon, and certainly not easy, but they can stimulate, refresh, expand, and create possible thoughts. However, they rarely work perfectly for us, the chasms they suggest being so vast. A large and complex question may require more than one attempt at articulation. Even if it is highly relevant, its complexity can stop the flow of a good conversation. Similarly, a question that is too pointed or too personal can divert the conversation toward private experiences. Questions that flaunt erudition can discourage contributions from reluctant speakers, rather than inspire a risk worth taking. And there are several categories of themes and ideas that we may find difficult to talk about, though they often construct the best parts of a conversation. It is difficult to clarify how we make connections between an abstract idea and life experiences that exemplify the idea. We may be reluctant to express revisions of our previous ideas, changes in our minds or hearts. We may not be able to say how we have felt or what we have observed when we have had surprising feelings or powerful insights. The day-to-day, even though it may contain great changes over time, may be invisible to us. We may hold our own crafted truths to ourselves, though others would welcome them. We tend to be unconfident that our experiences matter. We dodge ourselves. We keep secrets, even from ourselves. It is difficult to shift from plane to plane (from personal, to public, to academic, to abstract, to scholarly, and to quotidian) as we think and speak with others.

Open conversations of the kind that I advocate may require a strategy of questions, or at least a sensitivity to how important a strong question can be when we are thinking together. I. A. Richards called words "speculative instruments" (1955), and they are especially exploratory and provisional in questions. As a question or theme emerges, for example, it is useful to think of it as a fresh machine, a new vehicle of words, comprising critical terms, subtle but intensifying adjectives, and verbs that move, unsettled in our minds. We imagine and explore a question before we can address it. It is sometimes useful to take a question apart like a bicycle, dissassembling some nouns or other components or replacing them with something slightly different. Oil it, propel it, and check the tires and brakes. Questions comprise variables, assumptions, conditions, and unknowns. When we loosen and tighten these elements, we demonstrate the effects of language on our asking, and we determine how far we can travel with it before more adjusting is needed.

Consequently, it is important to understand that, as a good question evolves and improves with tinkering, it also refracts a slightly altered unknown, because each variable in the question implies a difference in its function as a mechanism or an instrument of focus. It is useful to stop and ask what question among a handful is most important, and what is it *really* after? What are *we* really after? When conversation is vigorous but inflexible, no single question will last very long, and its end can come as a disappointment. A purpose of a better, more flexible conversation may be to improve the quality of our questions, and then to generate related questions, the out-of-left-field questions, recognizing that our best questions will recur and inevitably reshape our thinking. Then we are like astronomers gazing at a constellation of questions, even though each will differ from others in distance and magnitude. There are some questions, I can imagine, that both mechanics and astronomers might find useful.

And here is one other note on words in questions: if we have no words, we have no questions. Though we may wonder without limits, we are able to ask only questions that we have the words to say. What we cannot say, we cannot ask. When it is put on the table between us, a question is only the words and structures we can master to express it. So we pay great attention to words and their values: in open conversations, they are our essential tools.

Here is a heuristic question from a mathematics text: "Look at the unknown. What is the unknown?" (Polya, 1960).

Breaking a question down may not be very useful; a good question cannot lose its parts without losing its character. It may help us to find or describe the unknown that each question seeks. Unknowns differ and the difference matters, even though what we can say about the unknown (obviously) will be limited. Some unknowns are contexts and applications. *Under what circumstances? For what purpose?* Other unknowns are definitions. *What do we mean by "answer"?* But some unknowns are reasons and causations, qualities, and complexities. These are complex. Some unknowns are definitive, as in *who, what, when, where, how, how many, how much, how big, how often, what shape and color,* and *yes* or *no.* Some are reasons or causations, as in *why*. Some unknowns are qualities or conditions, as in *value* or *worth*, in *what currency*, for what *purpose*, with what *expectation*, in support of *what cause, positive, negative*, or *neutral*. Some unknowns will always be complexities, difficult to describe. *Predictions. Relationships. Comparisons. Conditions. Consequences. Processes. Speculations. Perceptions. Feelings.* Some questions seek guidance and advice. *What should I do? What would you do? How should I feel?* If we are aware, we prepare for the question turning toward complexity, as good questions tend to do.

What do I anticipate? If, in goodwill and trust and hope, I ask a question of you, I have hypothesized two things. First, I think there is an answer or a response to my question. Second, I believe you are capable of providing it, or something like it, or something useful to me as I move forward into the unknown as I understand it. Perhaps we will be companions, useful to each other's progress. We are all—the question, the person who asks it, and the person who receives it—part of a sequence, part of a system. *There is this thing I hope to know. You may help me toward it. I believe you can assist me by telling me what you know or what you think. I hope you will join me in this thinking.* Now we have arrived at a form of reciprocity, a form of personal contract, enacted by our questions with one another.

Look at the unknown. What does the unknown look like? What will be present if we find it? Will it have a particular form? Will the unknown be words? Will the unknown be numbers? Will it be an insight? An opinion? An explanation? A description? How will we recognize it when we find it? How many different kinds of responses will satisfy the unknown? Will only one unknown serve this problem? Are there multiple unknowns? Might we address them all? How does the question itself suggest the qualities of the unknown, its context, or form? What kind of evidence will be useful in reducing the unknown? Empirical? Personal? Narrative? Historical? Projective? A guess? Where will it come from? How will we trust it? Where will we find it?

Nothing happens in an open conversation without an articulated question at its center. It concentrates attention and allows early processes of definition and variation, and an investment in its value, rather than a rush toward an answer or a response. A multifaceted theme or idea may harbor many questions, each an invitation to think and speak. Certain questions are constant heuristic tools that allow us to treat questions attentively, permitting us to trust the process, trust the question, and trust the conversation. At times we may need unchanging questions and an observed protocol in order to assure that the question can be held in our thoughts, even if briefly. We begin a sequence of steps, of which definition is the first.

What qualities make a good question good? If we want to be interested in a question for a long time, it deserves our best attention. If it is to be respected and trusted for its intention and validity, it needs a relevant context. If we want our question to have a useful purpose, it deserves our craft.

A good question should have an unknown that attracts us, a relationship to other questions and other questioners, and a place among other inquiries and inquirers.

Write and rewrite your question. Revise your question. How is your question like a magnifying glass, changing the details we see in the unknown? Define its key words and concepts in ways that others understand. Does your question require an introduction or a context in order to seek a response? Write it in different ways. Revise it again. Write it in ten words. Write it in five words.

Does your question capture an authentic, consequential unknown? How does it matter? An authentic question should have a purpose, a function that you can describe. The unknown ought to be compelling and motivating to you. It should draw and hold your attention, even after you have a response to your question. Why is this unknown something you must reveal? Why is this question worth asking more than once? What is its necessity?

Is your question generative, with implications for other questions? Do further questions follow from your question? Does it generate deeper questions? How is your question a part of a logical sequence or progression of questions? How is this question one of a constellation of related and relatively equal questions? What questions precede or follow your question? How is your question like a key among them? What might a previous or subsequent question address?

Some questions have an open end. Some are diagnostic. Some seek information. Some questions challenge. Some imply or posit action, something that could be done. Some questions address the best order or priority of things. Some ask for predictions of what could happen. Some questions hypothesize things that did not happen, things that might happen, or things that could happen under certain situations. Some seek the implications of assumptions. Some ask for generalizations based on evidence (Christensen, 1991).

The sequence of questions has consequences for thinking. We move toward complexity, pausing to understand details, examples, and potential errors or deviations. We strive to resist the rush to close the question. An answer may not be possible. Our purpose may be to illuminate the question, to observe its presence in multiple contexts and situations, to find patterns in these situations, and to observe how the question might shape them. In what ways and places can we observe the question and its effects?

Is your question evocative? A good question has your voice behind it, but it also has a voice of its own and the voices of others. Has anyone else asked this question? Has it appeared elsewhere, in another way, at another time, or belonging to someone else? And yet when you ask it, how does the question become yours? Ask a second question. How does working on one question help to solve another?

Is your question resonant? What is the history of your question? Where did it begin in your experience? Reading? An event? A teacher? A conversation? Resonant questions will have histories in beliefs or assumptions, in myths, or in factual evidence. They may arise from ambiguity or conflict. What are the history and context of your question? What are its tensions, consequences, and implications for you as its author? Does this question imply a process, a way of gathering evidence, a source of information, a standard of relevance?

Look at the unknown. A good question expresses knowledge, not ignorance. The naïve question (without assumption, without cynicism) allows us to begin, create a new foundation for our thinking, and clear the conversation of prejudgments. These are assurances for the life and promise of our question. Assume that you will continue to ask this question as long as you need to ask it. When you no longer need to ask it, assume that there is another equally good question waiting for your voice. Then define the new unknown.

CHAPTER 9

This Afternoon

As this book began, I asked my reader to think with me about the intentional experience of the user in the art or history museum, or in a branch of the public library. Think with me, I asked, of the person whose purpose is to seek experiences to increase knowledge and awareness, or to create personal change. That user, focused in the work and experience of the moment, is never far away from any of us, and we know that it is not a perfunctory moment for us to notice. We think with the user. Around three or four o'clock this afternoon or any afternoon, we will be able to imagine exactly what is happening in libraries, archives, and museums nearby, perhaps even in our own institutions—wherever users gather—and we can further imagine these things happening in libraries, archives, and museums everywhere in the United States, and perhaps around the world as this hour comes around.

In public libraries, kids have left school behind and have come to work on projects or homework, to explore the web, and to be with each other, and (surely) to be distracted by each other. If they are younger children, perhaps their parents are with them. There are already others in the library, we imagine, using its computers, looking for work, pursuing something they cannot yet see. We cannot see it either. And in an hour or so, adults may be stopping in on their ways home, to pick up children and to check for a book they heard about during the day. If they can linger, they might read an out-of-town newspaper or the news in Spanish; look over the automobile evaluations—especially for used cars; maybe consider a career course at a community college; peruse and select from the CD or DVD collections; or ease their worries with authoritative information about the health care of someone they love. We cannot verify these things, but experience suggests the afternoon is like this in most ways. People are using American public libraries.

In academic libraries, the day moves easily toward night, because the library does not close until midnight, and its users are likely to be less driven by the imminent tasks and requirements of the day. They are managing what is expected of them, and what they expect from themselves, over an entire term. Expectation and anticipation drive them, but it is mostly vague and hidden. They may be in libraries starting to do some research, keeping up with their friends, reading textbooks or reserved readings, following up on a suggested idea or even an article, a book title, a name, a place, a website, or an event that may illustrate an idea. Perhaps an optimistic professor has cited an article or book in class, and a student is looking for it. Most of these users are likely to be unaware of the electronic reference tools at hand, at least until a reference librarian shows them. They are surely unaware of the paper reference tools at hand. There are faculty, graduate students, and other scholars in these places as well, looking hard into complexity, looking hard for words they have not yet seen, with the hope that just one of those words might illuminate whatever sliver of the unknown they have chosen to pursue.

In archives, a different group of users has gathered this afternoon; probably older and less certain of their task than others; more exploratory, they have different problems to understand and solve. Hunters and scholarly gatherers, they want to see rare collections of documents or unique images, read a war diary, hear a digitized recording, and see matching sepia photographs of some gathering long over, some person long dead. They want to find the evidence of past life, someplace or someone who lingers in a particular time, and they want to assemble the traces of something that remains beyond place or time. They want to confirm the birth order of a lineage, the record of couplings, births, deaths, and life spans. These may be modest adventures, but they are certainly adventures, and as in all adventures, there are unknowns and surprises waiting everywhere.

This afternoon in the art museum, attentive and intrigued people may want to see a collection of ceramics or portraits, perhaps to inspire their own work in clay or oil, or they want the solace of quiet privacy they find without asking or searching, in the presence of Cypriot icons, African masks, Italian portraits, or American landscapes. They may want to return, as I often want to do, just to see one thing: a box by Joseph Cornell, a painting by Franz Kline or Cy Twombly, or a video by Bill Viola. Such masterworks are challenging to me, as are works by Holbein or Breughel, or the handwork of countless, nameless carvers. In the history or natural history museum, or in the science center, people are gazing at evidence that has implications for the civic environment, the ecology or economy, or the future world that is being shaped as they live. It is possible, day after day, for a museum user to turn anywhere, to look for a long time, and to think anything at all.

Lives are happening in all of these places even as we think about them, and they are all mysteries to us. They are all hidden from us; and yet they are all partly visible to us, in the living community that holds and nourishes its users. And as this place nourishes them, it also flourishes. Those lives move outward, toward something outside themselves; wherever we work and think, lives become different here. Out of needs we might barely articulate or be unable at all to say, our *thoughtful, mindful* lives in these places become different—don't ask how, there is no single way—and even these places become different, because they contain our energies. As we think of the afternoon, we might begin to understand the possibility that libraries, museums, archives, and their steady purposes are immensely present in the configuration of countless progressive, evolving lives.

WHAT IF

What if, at this hour of the day, everyone in these places, child and adult, in our place and in all of the nation's places like it, as if guided by a thwarted instinct for communication and connection, were to look up suddenly unbound from their purposes, turn to another person, and say, "If you don't mind, please tell me what brings you here today." And in the same fresh way of being present for each other, what if the person asked were to respond easily, "I have been working on this" or "I am reading about this" or "I am fascinated by this." And then, what if, for 10 minutes or 15, a conversation—at least a million or two simultaneous conversations across the nation—were to happen this afternoon, about the unknowns and evidences at hand, the experiences and the practices in progress, the unknowns resisting light or suddenly illuminated, the processes and accomplishments so carefully sought? And then, with a wish of good luck, each would turn back to the process and experience at hand—the reading and gazing youth, the reading and gazing adult, the searcher or scholar in preparation—everyone thinking a little differently, in order to work more on whatever has brought them there. And then perhaps it is time to get to supper, where they might tell someone else about this momentary conversation earlier in the afternoon.

This could be a dream—in normal experience we don't speak to strangers, we don't like to be interrupted, and our privacy is precious to us—but, if we are dedicated to imagining the possible, when are we not dreaming? And if we could create such possible situations for communication that make work and thought less insular, and cultural institutions less isolating, would we not consider them? In *Home Town*, the Pulitzer Prize–winning nonfiction work by Tracy Kidder (1999), the author imagines taking the roof off every place in Northampton, Massachusetts, the place he is excavating as an observer. The passage, coming somewhat early in the book, appears to be a revelation of what he will later confirm and understand more deeply about the place.

> A great deal lay hidden and half-hidden in this small, peaceful town. Well before you understood all of it, you would feel you understood too much. Northampton wasn't New York or Calcutta. It wasn't even as large as the little cities to its south. As places go, it seemed so orderly. But what an appalling abundance it contained. If all of the town were transparent, if the roofs came off all the buildings and the houses and the cars, and you were forced to look down and see in one broad sweep everything that had happened here and was happening, inside the offices, the businesses, the college dormitories, the apartments, the hospitals, the police station, and also on the playing fields and the sidewalks, in the meadows and the parks and the parking lots and graveyards and the boats out on the river, you'd be overcome before you turned away. And not just by malignancy and suffering, but by all the tenderness and joy, all the little acts of courage and kindness and simple competence and diligence operating all the time. To apprehend it all at once—who could stand it? No wonder so much remains invisible in towns. (Kidder, 1999, p. 79)

What is it we would see, if all the libraries and museums across the United States, for just those 15 minutes, had their roofs taken off, and we could consider somewhat breathlessly the people we might take in, the people in conversation, as we gaze at each one? And if—like the angels in the great Wim Wenders film *Wings of Desire*, loitering in the public library—we could overhear their thoughts, what would they say, what would we know about their hopes and aspirations? Would we be able to understand even half of the many ways of self-understanding, self-expression, desire, crisis, and self-rescue being demonstrated as we look on and listen in? Or would we too turn away before we are overcome by the complexity of it all?

HUMAN CONTEXTS

We know that the overwhelming, overabundant world is powered by irreducible facts: by budgets, salaries, percentages, square feet, troops, tests, shortages, horsepower, miles per gallon, surpluses, deficits, births, deaths, bailouts, and deficits. And yet everything we know and learn that moves us from birth to death as individuals, everything we think of as worth knowing or essential to pursue, and everything that makes us feel and confirm our own vitality, is surrounded and inspired by irreducible human contexts, not facts alone. Human contexts: the tendrils that connect our perceptions to our memories, summon or lead us to the thoughts of others, and take us way beyond ourselves and our lives, first to our families and communities and even to our nation and world and other spheres of our progress and renewal.

The contexts we think through are part of the cognitive habits shared among those who imagine and work in museums and libraries. We rarely see things without the hands or histories associated with them. Nothing stands alone, without description, place, or purpose. Each of us lives in multiple contexts, but contextual lives become deeper in cultural institutions. We see, think, know, and feel through them; no fact has isolated meaning or value, no shard of evidence has a separate place, because we know nothing without context. From context comes our complexity, mystery, and possibility. Context, history, and complexity walk with us.

They certainly walked on January 20, 2009, at the inauguration of President Barack Obama. In observance of the lives lived, lost, and found over the injustices and challenges of race in American history, John Mavroudis's cover of *The Nation* on February 2, 2009, depicted an invisible host of martyrs and advocates surrounding Mr. Obama's arrival at the presidency. Context suffuses the imagined scene. Justice Thurgood Marshall administers the oath as Dr. King, Malcolm X, Rosa Parks, Medgar Evers, Dred Scott, Homer Plessy, Susan B. Anthony, and Mohandas K. Gandhi stand by. Sojourner Truth and Nelson Mandela are there. So are Jackie Robinson, Chief Joseph, the Little Rock Nine, the Greensboro Four, Henry David Thoreau, John Brown, Marcus Garvey, Viola Liuzzo, Thomas Paine, Eugene V. Debs, and Lyndon Baines Johnson. And, down front, are the youth as well, never having grown old: Andrew Goodman, James Chaney, Michael Schwerner; Carol Robertson, Cynthia Wesley, Addie Mae Collins, Denise McNair; and Emmett Till. Only the imagination of context brings them all, along complex and differing paths, to this one moment where they all had earned the right to be present and remembered.

Context is invisible, and yet it is definitive. It explains complexity and value, even as it obscures simplicity and ease. Context *is* complexity, no matter what other words we use for it: memory, implication, association, connotation, resonance, difference, insight. These are the surrounding invisibilities that can turn all our hard certainties into spidery filaments, and yet they create all possible progress. What is visible is the hard evidence, perhaps; but it is in the invisible evidence that we can find the truth: in the connection, implication, imagination, and reconstruction of what is beyond witnessing. Contexts are elusive and yet decisive. The traces of experience are constantly transmitted back to us, and we do what we possess our minds to do: we observe, we nurture, we move beyond the evidence given. We fold and refold the letters we find, and we assemble the passages of the past. We think and search for continuity.

What is this gift of complexity? And what are we to do with it? In the evidence we assemble—of our hopes or our observations—and in the rediscovered desires we might recollect, each of us finds the meaningful record of our life. We see no piece of evidence alone, and so the possibilities of complexity invite us to look into the entire mirror. We recombine the captive evidence at hand with the free intellect in motion, we use language to tell what has brought us to this point, and then we act to move ourselves forward.

It is difficult to tell just how we transform evidence and information into knowledge, and experience into story, yet it is how we communicate as learners. The evidence always comes with a narrative, and we try to understand it. We are learners when our language expands, when we have words to say complex things we have not said before. Not to speak is to be a captive of the unspoken. Not to discover the truths of our own time, or not to strive for understanding, is to allow the hidden parts of experience to make us vulnerable. When we learn to think of one life as a thread—not fragile but a tough, essential strand whose traces we can follow—we can see a life's course in context, and imagine other lives in their own contexts. It is a useful practice to imagine the patterns and variations of a life woven even this afternoon, and to see how it enters the living culture and its historical record. Understanding this thread of our own presence in the patterns of society and community helps us to begin our own rescue from silence and absence.

VISIBLE COMPLEXITY

At the Seattle Public Library's Central Library recently, I saw an electronic artwork suspended above the help desk in the Charles Simonyi Mixing Chamber, a room devoted to the public's use of electronic search tools. The work, *Making Visible the Invisible: What the Community Is Reading* by George Legrady, comprises a series of cascading texts dropping from the tops of six large LCD screens. A page provided in the room describes the artwork; it is also described on Mr. Legrady's website, www .georgelegrady.com.

Making Visible the Invisible captures the circulation data of users at the Seattle Public Library and transforms it into four animated "visualizations," displayed on the six video screens above the help desk. Each visualization lasts a few minutes, moving more quickly than the eye and brain can synthesize, like a stock exchange ticker running at the bottom of a TV news screen. What becomes visual in Legrady's work is the flow of evidence that indicates how Seattle's library users search and borrow what they need. The first visualization displays and continuously updates the quantities of books and media checked out during the past 60 minutes of the day, with background colors on the screens changing to signify time passing. The second visualization is more substantive, comprising titles of the library materials—moving horizontally across the screens from right to left—checked out of the library during the past hour. The titles themselves are color-coded to differentiate among books and media, and items checked out at the same time appear near each other. The vertical placement of the title is an indication of its Dewey number.

The third component of the set is titled *Dewey Dot Matrix Rain*, and it is best described by Legrady himself on his webpage:

> The screens are subdivided according to the Dewey Classification System consisting of 10 columns across and 100 bars vertically placed to represent the divisions of each category from 0 to 99. Checked out items' titles come on the screen chronologically . . . "falling from the sky" if they do not have a Dewey number [that is, if fiction], otherwise popping on screen at their Dewey location, which has the effect of brightening the bar's color that represents their Dewey classification. Books are in yellow, DVD in green and other media in blue. By the end of the animation, the bars are color coded to provide an overview as to which Dewey categories received the most circulation. (www .georgelegrady.com)

Legrady's fourth visualization is called *Keyword Map Attack*, displaying the keywords of checked-out titles, positioned and colored according to Dewey subcategories. "White lines move across the screen, connecting the keywords to the classification of the books they came from." The artwork reflects the people of a community using its library, selecting and borrowing materials for use in lives outside the library. Unfortunately, we do not know the processes of searching, the winnowing and trying-out, but the display gives us a rare visible example of the human cognitive flow in Seattle on an ordinary day. What becomes almost tangible on the screens is a community in quotidian change, becoming something together, investing time and attention on subject matters and knowledge in order to change their experiences, capacities, and skills. If we could observe this—the invisible becoming visible—in similar artworks in one hundred cities, or one thousand, we might see the nation engaged by its own intellect and its own need for knowledge, story, and aspiration. Until then, Seattle might stand as an example for us all.

INVISIBLE AND VISIBLE

Democracy requires intellect in its citizens, an awareness of the values that drive and motivate humans, and the several qualities we have come to describe in combination as an open mind. We are able, I think, to live up to these challenges, even from our own small living thread. We can ask questions, listen, and we can ask again. We can avoid judging; we can encourage the narrative to continue. *Tell me more*, we can say. We can see how one life might vary from another in family, in economics, and in education, and how it differs in health, in civic participation, and in employment and avocation. We all differ in these and other parts of our lives, but they do not make a difference that prevents us from understanding each other.

Democracy requires that we spin and weave our own strands; yet we are also in part woven into the strands of others. Our hopes, anticipations and hardships may be private, but we can cull the stories of lives from brief experiences with others. Whole families and communities are in these stories; so are places, professions, journeys, sorrows, and satisfactions. And yet, it seems to me that, even with so much to say, we are largely without places to speak and present ourselves. We are also without ways to express what we see and know, in ways that reach toward the experiences and knowledge of other people in the same culture. Consequently, I believe that, unless we rescue voices and experiences, we will not live up to the possibility of sharing a common world, or filling it with something beyond our selves.

In my eyes, museums and libraries are the cultural instruments most able to approach the complexities and ambiguities of our experiences, the most likely places to allow our stories to emerge and take form. They are places of artifacts, records, and documents, but they are also not-places, meaning that when we occupy them we are in process and motion; they cause us to think beyond ourselves and to remember beyond our own lives. Cultural institutions deepen, inform, and encourage, even elevate, their users toward reflection. As we experience them, we are likely to become more complete, more open; our awareness and language are likely to expand. Museums and libraries are resonant places: they imply affinity, continuity, and safety; they promise a place of sustenance and advocacy. They suggest the possibility that there is more to understand if we might speak together.

Writing on the site of *Slate* magazine after the 2008 presidential election, Emily Yoffe (2008) described the emotional phenomenon of *elevation* that accompanies sudden, hopeful change, as in a large achievement that brings with itself a sense of hope and possibility. Yoffe wrote, "Researchers say elevation is part of a family of self-transcending emotions. Some others are awe, that sense of the vastness of the universe and smallness of self that is often invoked by nature; another is admiration, that goose-bump-making thrill that comes from seeing exceptional skill in action." Yoffe cited scholar Dacher Keltner, who said, "We had to evolve these emotions to devote ourselves into social collectives." And Jonathan Haidt, a moral psychologist, said, "Powerful moments of elevation sometimes seem to push a mental 'reset button,' wiping out feelings of cynicism and replacing them with feelings of hope ... and a sense of moral inspiration." Perhaps there are also "resetting" moments of this kind that appear to us in the form of a challenge or a crisis, and evoke small but evolutionary steps toward our own particular forms of resonance.

From the beginning, our national experience has always been defined by the tension of voices and ideas. Simplistic history has made some of us believe that amity and accord reside in the Constitution, a document created of unchanging wisdom. Others know it was flawed from its start and remains subject to revision. A visit to the National Constitution Center in Philadelphia is a reminder that it is a living and sometimes aching document, always meant to be new and refreshing to its people, always open, never finally interpreted or unambiguously complete. Above all, it is a monument of language. We turn to this document with the questions that we find the words to say. What is a citizen? Who judges the law? What are the limits of individualism? In our history we can see that the founding of the United States started in an argument, and it has never stopped. Perhaps we are meant to be a little cranky about what we want our living ideas to mean, and to argue with passion about their ambiguities. For this, we need voices and ideas.

Our never-ending public, democratic, founding questions are similar to the more personal questions that we can see as the unfinished issues of American life. Individually, nationally, we are always in progress. We may understand that we have been shaped by our faiths, our families, our race, our reading, and our educations—but none of those has done us any good if we are not left with constant and pertinent questions. We ask ethical questions of conduct, questions of what we are meant to become, how we are meant to teach and help, what we want to happen, how we can bring it about, and how much of destiny is an evolution of our own gifts.

I think we cannot choose otherwise; there is no choice except to evolve. We ought to believe that we are always at the edge of becoming stronger; and because we grow strong in hidden ways, we rarely understand fully that we have more competence and more capacity than we are typically called upon to show. For our competence to emerge, in my view, we need to be engaged in the kinds of conversations that confer new language that matters. It seems to me that our task in cultural institutions is to change the public lexicon, moving it toward a common way of speaking of knowledge and change, and of becoming something together. Unless anesthetized by entertainment or beaten by despair, human beings are capable of self-questioning, self-observation, and self-renewal.

Of course, museums and libraries are not alone in strengthening the civic mind and spine. Places of faith may also be seen as cultural instruments of this kind, where a resonance that offers solace, hope and responsibility resides. Hospitals are also social instruments whose resonance can imply well-being, health, strength, and longevity; they make healing possible. The resonance of such places lies in their practices and the intangible promise they offer, a promise that can evoke our response. But museums and libraries alone are cultural instruments whose resonance lies in their limitless complexity of ideas and experiences; to map them (or display their statistics, as George Legrady has done for Seattle) would be partial at best. They are secular and public, and their work is not to heal or worship, but to help and provide. They require no avowal or condition, and they exist for the common life and aspirations of a community. Although their deepest contributions to American life remain invisible to most of the nation, they are essential parts of American democratic practice; they hold our stories and national memories, they communicate both evidence and value, and they elevate our capacity to observe and remember together.

At their most powerful, human beings are capable of immense acts of self-rescue, finding the idea that revitalizes a life and lends it strength. We survive in part because we think; we overcome obstacles because we think well, usefully, and with awareness. Each of us may know a person who exemplifies self-rescue; each of us may have survived against the odds on our own. It seems true to me that self-rescue prepares us to rescue and strengthen others; we transfer our strengths in these encounters. It is the human being changing, in my view, who stands at the center of our cultural instruments, at the center of every cultural institution: the human being becoming, whose resonance is courage. For the observations and processes that will help us to flourish, we require human voices in inviting places. In the presence of these questions and the ways they affect us, I see cultural institutions as places for public critical thinking, and for the reflection that brings people together in progressive reciprocity.

PROGRESSIVE RECIPROCITY

In one of my final terms as a professor, I walked to my classroom and my waiting class around dusk. I was usually late to class, because on my path, right in the center of the Chapel Hill campus, a group of students—sometimes eight, sometimes twice that—would gather to juggle. Of course, even late as I was already, I had to watch. The jugglers would juggle the usual things: balls, pins, hoops, starting with three, then more; then additional jugglers would join in the same exercise: now four jugglers standing opposite each other two by two, throwing things and catching them and throwing them back, each time keeping the speed and spin steady enough for the other to catch, but also (it seemed to me) slightly increasing something in the toss. Things would be dropped; things would be picked up. Things would be fumbled, then the move would be invisibly corrected. But the effect on the jugglers was progressive, and reciprocal. They grew stronger and more adept at juggling through what I called "progressive reciprocity." The tension of skill and learning shared among them was mutual, self-created, and completely fabricated, but essential to the important task at hand: juggling.

I propose to reinvent American cultural institutions as places for the expression of American voices, and to explore—from no prior assumptions or points of view—the ways we have of discovering possibilities, and changing our perceptions of complexity. My idea is to use American cultural instruments, already dedicated to the invisible actions and meanings of lives, to recover the lost voices of Americans, in mutual, self-created relationships of progressive reciprocity.

Think with me for a moment about a single challenge we will have for the rest of our lives. A year ago I visited my friend, who was then director of education at a museum still in planning as I write, the National September 11 Memorial and Museum at the World Trade Center. We talked about the great challenges and ambiguities of the work of that museum. What will it hold? What will it teach? What *might* it teach? What kinds of truth—and how many truths—will it assist users to craft as they contemplate? How will the severity of memory affect the open mind of learning? What will sustain the balance between knowledge and question? What unknowns will it summon? What information will it provide, and in what situation? What will it evoke that is invisible? What different resonances will survivors, firefighters and police, children, New Yorkers, and Muslim Americans find in the experience? How shall we construct meanings together there, make ourselves learners there, and ask of ourselves, "What has happened here?" as though we knew nothing and had to learn our feelings and construct our knowledge out of nothing?

The day before that visit, I had considered similar questions with educators at the Museum of Jewish Heritage, a Living Memorial to the Holocaust, in Battery Park at the tip of Manhattan. How are Holocaust memories changing? What are the meanings of the event in a world of multiple, simultaneous, commodified modern genocides? As survivors die, how will the losses of living voices affect our thinking about Holocaust memory? During this visit to New York I also spoke to educators at the Queens Museum of Art, where they are planning a public library collaboration within the art galleries. This will happen in a vast, densely populated community where the children in public schools speak about 140 different languages at home, where 55% of the population over five speaks a language other than English at home, and where the public library collects materials in nearly 50 languages. What is the purpose of a library or a museum in such a community? What might the community become together, with the assistance of its cultural institutions? How do a community's cultural institutions become its cultural instruments?

I believe we need to ask these questions everywhere, especially when we remember where we began, thinking of all the human ideas and values that will appear in the library this afternoon. It seems to me that in these places, and in every place that resembles them across the nation, those who care about history, knowledge, art, culture, and the continuities of democracy have an opportunity to learn what the complex human voice brings to the object, to the search, to the image, and to the past. The voices add dimension and detail, add resonance, and express an individual integrity of observation and interest. In these places, even the newest Americans are aspirants, for themselves and their children, to what America promises.

This is what we require in our places of public learning: complexity, passion, empathy, curiosity, ambiguity, and the large unknowns that each of us carries at any given moment. We should be asked to live up to these possibilities, to give attention to the promises of the unknown. We might create opportunities to speak to each other about the knowledge we seek. Clearly, my ideas are not new. In American public libraries during the early decades of the twentieth century, people became something together, against the odds, against the challenges of immigration, prejudgment, and an economy on its way to a crash. And I know there has never been anything simple or simplistic about the United States; its complexity is overwhelming and extraordinary because it has always been grounded in process, expansion, and the persistence of democracy, as in its own becoming as a nation. It has lurched toward fairness in my lifetime and will continue to challenge itself with good ideas and bad.

If our nation is continuously unfinished, our cultural institutions are about the process of coming into the knowledge that will fill out our imaginations, so we might live in accord with our time. In contexts large and small, the nation cannot hide its errors or losses, it cannot hide its fears, nor can it obscure its resources and energies. We will always want to see the nation evolve openly, through informed acts carried out with purpose, fearlessly, by thoughtful people. What it cannot bear, it seems to me, is fear of others whom we do not yet understand, or a failure to be curious about the possible dimensions of lives we cannot yet see. To be called incurious— implying pre-knowledge of the answers before the statement of a problem, or of simply not caring to consider the crafting of truth from evidence—is the most damning epithet I can imagine.

And so it seems to me that our institutions and those who work in them this afternoon should consider themselves to be provocateurs, "knowledge provocateurs" (in the words of Michael Baldwin) who are meant to "stimulate public interest in sociopolitical issues and responsible citizenship" (Baldwin, 2006). If we want to cause trouble for the incurious, the kind of trouble we need in order to transform and rescue citizens and readers, it is important to expand and deepen our response to the public challenges of poor or shallow information, disinformation, and mindless media. The nation ought now and forever to be engaged in unprecedented public problem solving. Though it is often evoked, the Great Depression is not really comparable to the current era because the nature of information is so much more complex, and the challenges to our economy seem so far from our own hands. It seems to me that libraries and museums have an essential proprietorship and fiduciary responsibility (not unlike banks, except knowledge cannot be depleted or devalued by blunt avarice) over resources that steadily expand and regenerate as users require more, and ask more of us.

Our institutions can help to bring communities to their questions, to the knowledge that helps to inform their responses, and to the ideas and values that will shape our policies and plans. We especially require new thinking for discovering the experiences that will last within us, for rebuilding our institutions, and for creating new possibilities—think of them as fields of ideas—out of which we might find and nourish what our great communities, institutions, and people want to become. Children should be present to see adults do this, so they will never think that critical thinking and its public applications begin elsewhere, with other people. Children might also come to know that libraries and museums exist for exactly this kind of transformation by deepening what and how we think about and work to resolve human differences.

For all we hear about Main Street, there is only one kind of place where we might go to discover our own voices. Cultural institutions must have a role in reconstructing American trust through face to-face forums and community conversations. If the nation is capable of becoming engaged in this immense work of rediscovering itself and what we have become, we must be there, thinking with each other. We still have our resources and our tools; we will continue to have an economy of banks and auto makers; and we have an economy of information, moving too fast to see, at least until we do our jobs and slow it down. It is likely that we will use the adjective "troubled" to describe them. We still have greed and capitalism, but we still have generosity and compassion. We still have people moving into our nation to become us, and perhaps, unknowingly, to rescue us by transforming us. But what do we have of each other?

We need to replace ruthless or selfish individualism with becoming something together. As we can see in pockets of our past, it will not be the first time we have done this. Perhaps it will begin one afternoon with stories told in places where we live, to others who sit near us. *What is your story? What happened to you? What are you working on? What have you learned from it?* We will be unafraid to speak in the safe places we have made for discoveries, reflections, and voices. If we teach ourselves to speak, listen, and think together, these are the places that will open us to ourselves—the places that will open something unspoken within ourselves—and move us toward the possibilities of self-rescue that every civilization needs.

CHAPTER 10

That Difference

Each of us needs the capacity and circumstance to imagine and construct a whole life. We need this capacity for our discoveries; it is also about our capacity for respect and affinity. When we understand that we are always at work on ourselves, we can regard others who are similarly engaged. In conversation and discovery, we address our unfinished selves among other unfinished selves. We admire and we learn from other lives in flow.

A cultural institution creates a situation of difference. We mind and remember differences. Almost all change we understand as learning is a change in our understanding of patterns and variations, our understanding of difference. We do not hunger only for different information; we hunger for different structures, different perspectives, and the different ideas that nurture other people.

Our memory, attention, and senses recognize differences. Thinking of ourselves as people who learn, we attune ourselves to differences. *This is new. There is new, unprecedented information here. There are unusual observations to be made. This idea makes a difference.* We see differences when we make comparisons; we see differences in human beings; we see them in ourselves. Learning is seeing a variation in pattern, perceiving the surprising difference. *I have never seen this before.*

Our lives and strengths are proven in the presence of things we do not understand. Open to thinking, we are in motion toward possibilities never seen before, and toward things that have not yet happened. If we are closed and disengaged, we move toward nothing new; we risk stagnation. We remain safe among routines. Improvisations are important acts of variation in a learning life. Our experiences are experiments.

The world we experience is living and fluid; the collection is captive. Our institutions and language keep knowledge and the living record still; what we come to know in museums and libraries is grounded in the captivity of that evidence. Because it is captive, it can become knowledge for us only if we restore its contexts and its energies. The learning that matters most to an evolving life, the experiences that most change us, are proven in tension between the fluidity of our experience and the captivity of the evidence. The captive experience allows and prepares us to perceive, or to imagine, the wild.

We learn by interpreting living contexts. We take our observations beyond the institution, into a living context, departing from the captive evidence, and going beyond it by imagination, inquiry, and conversation. We also learn by departing from the institution in order to participate in a living culture. Here the tasks of the learner and the tasks of the institution are similar: to evoke and grasp the world that flows beyond the captivity of the place, and to find meanings or purposes in the continuously unfolding situations of experience.

The living world is known in an unfinished, open state. We may perceive the moving energy in the captured thing, the aggregate energies of a whole collection of things, and (possibly) the origins and motives of those energies. In objects, artifacts, examples, specimens, and collections, we see the human dimensions of a hand or mind, and within them we may find the infinite implications of these dimensions across time. Thinking and organizing, we mind the evidence and its implications. We ask, *What continues here, having left these traces behind? Where is the infinite at work here?*

In cultural institutions we dwell, like Emily Dickinson, in possibility. When we can see a gathering of objects, an ensemble of evidence, we connect and reflect. These invisible actions, connections, and reflections are inspired. They are interpretations and inventions required by provocative objects and information. We are surrounded and seized by the insistence of evidence. We have no choice. Like witnesses, we must look and remember.

Learners, like witnesses, perceive differently. We see things differently, in different kinds of contexts and light; and we live and express different experiences of the evidence. We craft different understandings of what we have seen. When they are fresh and consequential, our observations transcend the common and lead us where we did not expect to be. A good collection is evocative; it evokes us in new forms. We might say, as Louise Rosenblatt says of reading and the reader, "An intense response to a work will have its roots in capacities and experiences already present in the personality and mind of the reader" (Rosenblatt, 1995, p. 41). A cultural institution enables the intensity evoked by a sudden, unsuspected possibility to emerge; our astonishments help to complete us as persons. Even when astonished, we ask questions.

Knowledge has motion and course, a narrative, and an origin. We want to know about its past as well as its future. The meaning of evidence is charged; it appears as an expression of energy, possibility, and change. It is charged with a story, and therefore holds possibility for us. We can encounter and grasp knowledge as part of something passionate and compelling, happening now, in our presence. Holding evidence in place, a museum or a library makes variations and improvisations of thought possible. Observing, we come to infer what cannot be present. A collection is always more than itself, and the object or text is also more than itself.

The energy of an object, a book, or a work of art is apparent in the difference of perception and feeling created in us. A great work makes a difference in our thinking when we go beyond its edges. An ensemble of works will resonate within us. A deep collection will stimulate resonance among its pieces and stir all contexts with its intensity. Even a small collection creates opportunities for comparison, reflection, observation, and speculation. These tensions and complexities are also sources of energy. Without our capacity to contain these differences and sense this energy, we would understand less, we would see less far, and we would carry less with us as we live.

In museums and libraries, thinking is the work at hand. An institution driven by thinking articulates both the known and the unknown. It envisions itself engaged in the circulation of the human record, striving to become what Jean Lave and Etienne Wenger (1993) call a "community of practice." In cultural institutions we enter a community of thoughtful interpretation, a setting where "learning needs to be understood in relation to the development of human identity. . . . What people learn about . . . is always refracted through who they are and what they are learning to be" (Brown and Duguid, 2000, p. 138).

Thinking, we adapt and transform our experiences. We combine evidences to make something stronger than its pieces. We discover what is already present in each of us, and we use it to extend and deepen our integrity. No matter how much we know, new understandings can rock us, can rock our assumptions and expectations. We would be shallow to wish it otherwise. We want our world to be rocked. It is difficult work, knowing and feeling and being rocked: it means projecting, hypothesizing, imagining, and questioning, then finding balance.

Intellectual experiences are sustained by collaboration. We need to see the evidence of another intelligence at work next to ours; we need to see our own thinking among other intelligences at work, in order to understand what we might independently become. We need to see enough to say, "This is a form of intelligence of which I too am capable."

We want more and more. The challenge of finding structure and order requires us to reach into our memories and nearby memories. Assume the mind is a collaborative, improvisational entity. It remakes itself as needed, in the presence of other minds, using all available materials at hand, seeking information, expressing questions, and looking for differences. We come to understand that multiple perspectives on single objects or ideas are equally possible. We come to understand that all complex knowledge harbors a still more complex unknown within it. We are insatiable—we understand that the reduction or removal of any element of our gaze will diminish our possible knowledge of it; therefore, we will always want more evidence before us.

Our lifelong human task is to become more capable, and this requires us to work constantly at our edges, and to strive to see what we have not yet seen. When we dare to behave and think as ourselves alone, we become original, we break from mindless pattern, imitation, and expectation; and only then can we have integrity. We go to our library or to our museum in order to see what unfolds within us when we are there—we are folded up, and we unfold before the object or the book, becoming capable of saying something new about ourselves. Living at such edges can awaken us. This unfolding, and the new topography revealed in us as we unfold, is one promise of cultural institutions. Another word for this unfolding is "experience."

Cultural institutions are not about what they contain; they are about what they make possible. Institutions construct narratives that help us to locate and recover our memories, passions, and commitments. A library makes the user's future conversations more informed, the user's thoughts and actions more engaged, more particular. A museum allows us to experience variable forms of genius, the assumptions and actions of the past, and their implications for our lives. Not only is *what* we have seen important; it is important *that* we have seen it. Our experiences illuminate and revise us. Our institutions contain and extend our evolution; they hold and imply our capacity for change.

We need to see beyond the usual. Years ago, I found these words of the painter Robert Henri on a wall in the Phoenix Art Museum: "There are moments in our lives, there are moments in a day, when we seem to see beyond the usual. Such are the moments of our greatest happiness. Such are the moments of our greatest wisdom. If one could but recall his vision by some sort of sign. It was in this hope that the arts were invented. Sign-posts on the way to what may be. Sign-posts toward greater knowledge." Libraries and museums hold evidence in trust that a thoughtful person will think again, and will remember the past; and in trust that another person might pause to "see beyond the usual" and understand that difference in that moment.

As our lives become more complex, we imagine ourselves living and acting fearlessly within them. Our lives can themselves become inspired works of art and improvisation, dynamically and unpredictably open, capable of change, renewal, and transformation until they end.

CHAPTER 11

Where a Space Opens

Neither silence nor isolation can nurture or keep the great genius of democracy; it appears and reappears in the engagement and rescue of voices, in conversations where we create, express, and define our selves. A community is impoverished without informed conversations in safe places. The open conversation is an artifact we create ourselves because it fulfills our promise and allows us to grasp a shared integrity, rather than integrity in isolation. Given no chance to evolve through dedicated talk, neither the democracy nor the person will live fully. In silence, new ideas remain latent and unchallenged, old ideas vanish without transfer, and the courage to speak is gone. What is the difference we will have made? What is the possibility that will inspire us, if our work is to attain a more constructive and more trusted institution? Without a difference in what we do, thoughtless noises will increase until we cannot hear, reason, or reflect.

Think with me about this difference. It becomes possible for us to move forward, to make progress in our lives, and to arrive at integrity when we imagine that trust is not beyond us, and that it will be sustained only if we think openly and with daring about the future. While it is surely simplistic and risky to say that progressive lives are constructed by mere hopes, or by plans and desires, we also cannot imagine a life without them. In fear of disappointment, however, we often keep these things in privacy and denial to protect them and ourselves. We may feel that we are made vulnerable by our aspirations and dreams—and yet we cannot make our way dreamless. A space for our strengths must open to us.

Hopes, we might say, are prospects of the possible; they are imagined considerations, motives grounded in anticipation, need, and want; they are enabled or disabled by the presence or absence of trust. To lose hope is to accept the futility of wanting and questioning; to lose trust as well is to disable our engagement in the construction of change. I believe that such despair also degrades the intellect and creates a deep need for rescue. If cultural institutions are themselves grounded on promise and service, if they create responsive situations for the exploration of the possible, they must also come to see themselves as agents for the personal progress, and at times the rescue and recovery, of citizens. For both the person and the institution, without wanting something specific to happen, it is unlikely to happen. Without expressing the possible, even if we say the words to ourselves alone, we are unlikely to become aware of the possibility. What we want together, we need to express together in an open situation worthy of our trust.

Experience tells us it is better to be hopeful than to be fearful, and that, moreover, we need a certain kind of fearlessness to thrive. The genius of our institutions lies in their provision of fair places where people are given opportunities to think and explore, leaving fear at the door. Though we may never be fearless enough to cease questioning ourselves, the risks of change and transformation require us to go beyond the things that limit us to dullness.

Dreams, hopes, experiences, progress, and integrity are all words that I tend to associate with changes in our minds. If anyone can use just one of these words to describe a search, or an unfinished part of the intellect, or the thinking or motivation that brings them to a museum or a library, it is clear to me that something important is going on. The great challenge of our lives as learners is cognitive management. Keeping our learning and growth near the core of our experiences, we frame and reframe our world as an evolving drama (with acts, scenes, and dialogue) or a building (with foundation, structure, and windows) that we design and make for ourselves. In cultural institutions, cognitive management occurs in a relatively fluid environment, open to exploration, inference, and intuition. Our fresh knowledge depends on what we already know; our ability to engage with the drama relies on our empathy; our skill in building depends on what we may have built before. Cognitive management in this fluid environment must be fluid itself: we are not moved by control or curriculum, but by suggestion and connection; we are not lured by certainty or completeness, but by possibility. For me, this is the definition—and the integrity—of learning through the course of one finite life.

Consequently it is never enough simply to place a deep institution and its energies at the center of a community. If it ever was enough to believe that our work there was *to serve*, it is no longer enough. The great Children's Museum in Indianapolis taught me this: our best service is always with our users, not simply for them. Even a great institution that embraces change and advancement may not evoke trust or provoke engagement. The deep institution that challenges its users may be arrogant, the teaching institution that instructs may condescend, and the clever institution that manipulates its users may also exploit them. Cultural institutions earn trust through part-nerships, in alliances with users. One part of an alliance is explicit and func-tional: assuring that processes and evidences that make a difference in the user's knowledge are enabled to happen. The user may need assistance in defining terms, comparing complex evidence, or recombining knowledge gathered from different disciplines. Another element in the alliance between user and institution is an implicit guiding ethos, including the user. It might comprise aspirations and patient guidance; it certainly will include unequivocal respect. What do you wish to happen here, and how can we help? Each part of the alliance—process and evidence, guidance and respect—advances the other; they are equal as well in the institution's goal, a combination of illumination and elevation of knowledge.

TRUST, COHERENCE, CONTEXT

No one is likely to trust an institution that does not reveal itself to its users. Knowing how a curator or a bibliographer interprets a mission and builds a collection ought to be known to the public, one of several transparent pro-cesses. Professionalism, so often unclear to a public, should be clarified as a way to develop a public understanding of what libraries and museums pro-vide and assure in order to serve a community, and how the idea of service takes form in the lives of individual professionals. That is a form of breaking through that challenges every cultural institution we know. No one is likely to trust an institution that speaks as though only to itself, excluding its users. Any cultural institution that opens its doors must rethink its voice and its vocabulary, presenting itself as a partner in a mutual dialogue. Speaking and listening in a community are acts of public access, equivalent to provid-ing access to a collection. Whatever informs the institution and its mission cannot be hidden without a loss of confidence.

No one is likely to trust an institution that does not acknowledge experi-ences outside itself. Hour by hour, the world evolves; but its differences are rarely apparent to people inside a library or a museum. Users have to emerge from the place and turn on their car radio or personal player, or check the Internet in order to encounter fresh information in a fresh world. Libraries especially should hang a television on the wall, and tune it to CNN, BBC, or another world news service. Among the wall decorations needed in American libraries are charts depicting worldwide literacy statistics, publishing and web data, weekly media bestseller lists, bookstore flyers, maps to other libraries, and current news articles about the knowledge and information environment—because that is the sea we swim in.

No one is likely to trust an institution that has no room for learning and reflection. For the user, an open and reflective space is always welcome in the course of a complex experience. In museums, small galleries of one or two objects, or books and ideas, can provide that respite. In libraries and museums alike, we welcome a place for coffee or tea. Such experiences provide a moment of time and space for reflection and self-renewal. When we are in cultural institutions, our experiences are our work; they are serious and at times exhausting, because they are often so exhilarating.

But an institution also requires what Donald A. Schön described as a reflective conversation with the situation (1983, pp. 150–151). When a new situation has been designed and created based on assumptions, expectations, and decisions—or "moves," in Schön's idea (p. 131)—the institution needs to listen when the new situation "talks back" to its designers. Our relationships with situations are transactional, and an institution seeking to evoke trust keeps its attention steadily engaged with the ways users respond: a place, a situation, its users, and its community constantly make moves and talk back to what they experience in the setting. When we think like architects or designers, we come to understand a situation by trying to alter it. We are *in* the situation we strive to understand, and our moves help us to shape the situation we want to create, but they also help us to understand it as well. Trust does not necessarily follow from steady and unchanging practices but rather from an evolving attention to the continuous flow of engagements inside and outside an institution. The potential for transforming an institution is more likely to be revealed outside its walls than within.

The word *trust* is perhaps too casually used here; it implies a fiduciary relationship between an institution and its responsibility to live up to the culture and society it serves. From our own experiences, we know that trust seems to evolve as conversations become increasingly coherent and compelling: we develop trust when we encounter knowledge and experience that seem to hold together and emerge to suggest a perspective we can recognize. We want to be participants in that coherent conversation, if only by our presence as witnesses. We want to contribute to the shared situation. Coherence does not imply our agreement or persuasion, but it suggests a basis for the conversation to continue, a ground for our own stance. The elements of coherence that impress us most, in my view, are those we can organize as recognizable contexts or even clusters of ideas. I believe that such aggregations are the most powerful of all qualities of information, more useful to us than the linear ideas of relevance and pertinence. Contexts are deep and fluid situations, never entirely defined.

We all live and act in contexts, amid the contexts of others. We think and act in multiple contexts simultaneously. When we know something, we know it embedded in contexts. Some contexts are personal, familial, and vocational. Some are intellectual, literate, and informational. Some are events and the historic environments that surround them: the Great Depression, the Eisenhower years, the War to End All Wars. Some are scientific and technical, contexts created and revolutionized by knowledge: nomenclature and taxonomies; advances and breakthroughs; genetic patterns; scientific methods; and substances and their properties. Some are cultural: we recognize styles, forms, and movements; we identify masterpieces; we understand the qualities of genius; we sing along with the "Ode to Joy" and Aretha Franklin. They live in the human interior, roaming at will. Contexts allow us to build coherence and trust, and to ground ourselves in a world where continuities and connections extend and refresh (and occasionally ambush) our thinking. We cannot explain or trust a world or a perspective that does not hang together in ways we can grasp, a world that is incoherent or discontinuous. But we can enter such a world in part because we carry a rough map, tools, and ways to think.

The work of intellect is to make connections, to make our perceptions deeper and more complex, to understand the possible lives of others, to recognize our unfinished work, our continuing questions, our ways of discovering self-knowledge by engaging with others outside ourselves. Further, it is the work of intellect to express our incompleteness and cognitive hunger, and to recognize it in others. These expressions will never be heard, nor will any risk be taken, under situations of fear, the opposite of trust. Trust is an artifact essential to authentic becoming, breaking through, and speaking out; it is necessary to overcome the fears of change and feeling that so often restrict our promises to ourselves. The cultural institution that does not strive to generate trust has misunderstood its own purpose and integrity, and its promise.

FEAR

I have come to see almost all of our presence in libraries and museums as expressions of one or another form of wanting, or hoping, or anticipating. I believe that we go there to aspire, perhaps in ways we have not fully understood. Wanting is another form of imagining, and cultural institutions serve and nurture that particular kind of wanting. But we are also linked to cultural institutions by many kinds of fear; it is difficult to imagine a person who has no experience of them. I think first of the fear of not knowing, of having missed an opportunity to know something or to see something. There is also the fear of knowing too little, possessing the surface, but not the depth, of an idea. We may be fearful of stagnation, having nothing new to experience in our lives, or having nothing uniquely our own to embrace or contemplate. And yet we may also fear that we have no way to restore freshness to our thinking. We fear the loss of design our lives, and the feelings of passivity that follow. We fear classification into social categories prescribed by age, or identity, or faith: we do not wish to be written off, disrespected, or disavowed.

These are not the fears of age; they are the fears of everyone. Each of us fears alienation and the distances that may isolate and distort our sense of participation in our own society. Because the world moves with increasing speed, we fear being left behind, unable to know the questions we need to ask, or where to ask them, or how to interpret a response. We fear that, under threat or confusion, we may forget our own voice and have no way to clarify ourselves. Although we do not wish to be erased, we may too easily look past our vitality, our places, and our capacities because something happened to obscure them and nothing has revealed them again. We may compromise our aspirations because we believe we have lost any just claim on living up to them.

To counter all of these fears, and to keep ourselves safe, we must create and sustain integrity, commitment, complexity, and depth, and dwell within them. These are also reasons to augment and extend cultural institutions toward even greater provision of information, confidence, and inspiration, as places where citizens are free to think deeply and independently about anything at all. Consequently, in the daily work of living, supported in our need for self-renewal, we can tolerate the risks and challenges that allow us to transform ourselves, to build bridges, with help among empathic others. We build our institutions to provide this safety and these bridges, but their strengths as instruments of dialogue and change are often underimagined and not always apparent, even to those who work within them. In a society typified by economic instability, aging generations, evolving demographics, undereducated youth, and pervasive insularity, our cultural institutions must openly strive to keep a community free to think, enabling its people to imagine the possibilities for public awakening and growth. When we change our institutions, we reconstruct our possibilities and even our conceptions of community.

The promise of cultural institutions is not proven or broken easily; it evolves in a long history of actions and expressions, of conversations with communities, with users, and also with the best thinkers and theorists of contemporary culture. Any change in our places will surely take time as well, but is important to recognize that, although much in the relationships between an institution and its communities will be invisible, human beings and their interests are not entirely mysteries. The necessary engagement required by living a thoughtful life is easily understood, if not easily developed. To begin in a common place, created for a common civic good, is an essential step. We find these common places for ourselves when we think apart, move beyond the immediate, consider alternative ways to practice, and read.

A SPACE

In my case, the most important, most formative professional book I know is a slim work of educational philosophy, *The Dialectic of Freedom* by Maxine Greene (1988). It is formative in the ways of neither technique nor practice, but in the ways of thinking about the larger purposes of professions and situations in service to inquirers, seekers, and questioners. We underestimate the thirsts and motives of such persons, and misunderstand the importance of such professions and situations. Greene is an eloquent and deeply thoughtful advocate for demonstrations of the self in a flowing world, "an awareness of a world lived in common with others, a world that can be to some extent transformed" (1988, p. 4). Her view is broad, yet expressed in human words we do not struggle to understand. She writes about the need for each of us to "create an opening" (p. 11) in order to be a human being, to think—and to oppose, as we may need to—in order to discover our capacity for public engagement, and therefore complexity, interdependence, and the challenges of compromise.

Greene's book is driven by a feeling of crisis and an understanding of the distance between the promise of democratic discourse and the shouting that too often replaces it. Her compelling intention is to expand the capacity to imagine a different way to talk under conditions of freedom. She writes, for example, about members of the French Resistance during the Nazi occupation and their belief that an "apparition of freedom" (citing poet René Char) had suddenly "visited" them as never before in their lives. This appearance of freedom occurs in acts of association and attachment between people, acts that expand conscience, integrity, and responsibility among each other.

> [F]reedom shows itself or comes into being when individuals come together in a particular way, when they are authentically present to one another (without masks, pretenses, badges of office), when they have a project they can mutually pursue.... There must be a coming together of those who choose themselves as affected and involved. There must be an opening of a space between them ... deeper and more significant than merely practical or worldly interests. (pp. 16–17)

Coming together in a particular way has historic exemplars in resistance to oppression and cultural stagnation, political resistance, and civil rights, but it also has relevance to the customary situations that cultural institutions provide, situations where we, almost literally, find ourselves without cognitive maps or bearings to find our way. We carry memories of places and lives, grounding experiences that are the foundations of identity. We carry aspirations we cannot describe, and promises we may have made to ourselves. Our actions and reflections in cultural institutions often draw on these memories and allow us to confirm or revise our lives among others.

Personal conscience and integrity are especially embedded in our perspectives on memory and history, and we have the capacity to reframe the past as we come to understand it better and as our knowledge changes. One essential quality of adult learning is that it is *adult* in its vantage point: an experienced person expects complexity and welcomes it, recognizes ambiguity and attends to it.

To recognize the role of perspective and vantage point, to recognize at
the same time that there are always multiple perspectives and multiple
vantage points, is to recognize that no accounting ... can ever be
finished or complete. There is always more. There is always possibility.
And this is where the space opens for the pursuit of freedom. (Greene,
2008, p. 128)

One fresh perspective on our own possibilities is an understanding that we
can reframe our life stories as we come to see them from authentic, alternative perspectives. The possibility of breaking through the structures of our
worlds and their assumptions and claims on our attention—the artificial
orders of bureaucracies, the sickening constraints of bias and discrimination,
and the cold and ungenerous politics of anger—cannot become real to us
without our first imagining it in such detail that it is shared, incubated, and
spoken into reality among others.

I believe we are damaged when we see our capabilities through the eyes of
our parents, or our intellects through the eyes of our teachers. I also believe
it is a compromise to see and understand the work we do through the
assumptions and values of our colleagues. And if we see cultural institutions
as educators, as didactic extensions of schooling, with their curricula and
forced attendance, we need to reframe our place in every mind including
our own. Our work at times is to change the framing of things and overcome
the ways our great institutions are reduced to a minor presence in the world.
When the stories of our institutions are reframed, it is possible for them to be
seen as instruments for cognitive and intellectual freedoms.

NAÏVE QUESTIONS OF PRACTICE

At the end of my teaching, I created a course called Seminar on Information and Culture, intended to help my students to understand the variable
dimensions of knowledge and information in the contexts of human life.
I wanted them to go beyond the technologies, management techniques, and
protocols of librarianship to consider the evanescent ideas of service, communication, and cognitive development in a knowledge environment. The
course themes were certainly variable, but they always emphasized the ways
we understand reading habits, adult development, knowledge, and literacy.
I wanted my students to understand the differences that information can
make in a single life, in a family, in a neighborhood, a community, a culture.
As librarians do, I selected our readings widely from an array of fields:
anthropology and history, cognitive development, sociology, education,
and reading. We began by creating a sense of ourselves as professionals
responsible for knowledge and how it appears in lives.

A purpose of the seminar was to pose large, naïve questions—rare in professional schools—intended to provoke thinking about the relationship

between our beliefs and practices. I wanted my students to think deeply over the dimensions of individual encounters with learners, encounters they had not yet experienced. *What is going on here? What is going on beyond this encounter? What is helpful in this situation?* I have found such basic questions to be valid ways to focus discussions of our professional purpose. Too often unasked, the questions involve concepts we need to speak aloud at least once in a professional life. *What does it mean, and how does it matter, to grow intellectually? How do we understand and evaluate our experiences? How do we talk about learning, growing, and becoming? What is our task as professional agents and advocates for learners? How do we expand or explore our professional values as we serve, learning from practice? What does it mean when we help another person? What can I impart that is not a document or a tool or a skill? What is my responsibility to the user? In an era of personal information styles and strategies, handheld tools, and viral misinformation, what is the value of the library to the person? How can libraries express their advocacy for learning in communities? In what ways do libraries and museums make differences for us? How do our institutions serve as cultural instruments?*

These are, among many others, some of the unknowns I have carried for decades, hoping to transfer them to my students. They are among my unfinished issues; they will never leave or be resolved. In addition to the authors I have mentioned in previous essays—Maxine Greene and John W. Gardner especially, but also Jerome Bruner, Mihaly Csikszentmihalyi, Erik Erikson, Nel Noddings, Barbara Rogoff, Donald Schön, Frank Smith, and Lev Vygotsky—I find a rich literature to suggest as readings for those professionals who share one or all of my questions. Our professional preparations for work in cultural institutions need a strong and eclectic reading list, including commentaries on democracy and culture, critiques and theories of education, the cognitive psychology of everyday experience, and learning over the entire adult life span. In my experience, such deviations from orthodox texts have been rare.

Books and conversations will not fully answer my questions, nor will they address all of the questions grounded in communities among living learners. Only dedicated practice will; but books and conversations will prepare me for practice, help me to overturn my weak assumptions, and allow me to invoke new rules of evidence. All continuous learning happens in the living world, where we find the place to make differences. Every professional field needs to find its identity beyond the limited literature of technique and technology, because service is complex and the preparatory programs most people experience are never long enough, nor do they connect firmly enough to practice. *What am I to believe about the lives of other people? What in my work serves fairness and justice? What are the choices and consequences? How much risk can I bear?* We are not asked to write papers or read research about such questions. Clearly everyone who serves the needs of people, their interests and questions, should be interested questioners themselves, especially focused on the implications of their experiences for practice. We do not always need to read many books to understand critical perspectives; but we need to select excellent, accessible reading that lingers in our acts and plans. We need to find the most accessible and provocative writing, and the most promising ways to bring it into our thinking.

READ WITH EACH OTHER

The reading group is an ideal setting for understanding the power of narrative and the possibilities of retelling the stories that have been told to us. When we read and speak of our reading, we address the narrative of another person from a narrative of our own, a process for building our own integrity in parallel to the written life or experience of another. We do this reading biography and nonfiction; we may do this when we read fiction as well. Reading the same book together places the author in the room, with premises, evidences, and interpretations. When professionals think together, plan together, and become something together themselves, we are collaborating in the presence of something larger than ourselves. In this collaboration, it is especially important to read beyond the narrow literatures of our professions.

A reflective person who completes studies in order to enter professional service in a cultural institution is likely to have survived a relatively dry intellectual program, without significant emphasis on the lives of users. As one of my students wrote to me, just before dropping out of a highly ranked program, "It's a different experience, these classes without feelings." I found this to be accurate, sad, and ironic all at once, believing as I do that our fields of professional study are rich with feelings and strengths, full of extraordinary ideas, and deep wells for drawing up the critical concepts and questions of practice. Much that is essential to public lives is lost in our schools, associations, and publications, entities that seem to create so little that matters in the changing lives of citizens.

Consequently, my advocacy is that professionals need to read together—within and among a community's institutions—in order to extend the sense of purpose and possibility they bring to their institutions and to grasp the value of public engagement. Were I still a teacher, I would plan a seminar for my students with several themes: the human in change, learning in practice, conversation as a professional form, the idea of innovation in an open world. In one institution, in one life, it is always possible to interpret the potential for something new. What has been given to me? What are my strengths? What can I make of this? What can we begin together?

Our practice itself—working among thoughtful users and practitioners alike—will be deeply strengthened by constructive reading. My observation is that we share very few core readings, but this does not mean we share very few core ideas. But we need to read together in order to grasp and make them common. In this penultimate chapter, I suggest readings that I believe will stimulate useful conversations about the ways we control and vary the narratives we are given, how we might compose a narrative of our own, how we might understand the value of conversations in a working democracy, how communities function and serve the commonweal, the prime importance of language in becoming something together, and possible ways to explore the public sphere we occupy together. These are, of course, not the only themes to imagine.

While the works I mention here are purposefully chosen, they are also personally chosen: for me, inspired thinking follows from these books. They give me perspectives for thinking. Because I am slow to change, these works are like crowbars; they help me to open the heavy, nearly immovable doors to new concepts. For another reader, they may be productive in different ways, or not at all—but they will also lead to other works, and other ideas. They are my suggestions for generating the open conversations—the talking life, in Toni Morrison's phrase—that always must follow from stimulating reading.

They will occupy a small professional shelf. In this chapter only the most valuable are listed, knowing that there are more to be found without my advice. My intentions have been to gather works that inform our understanding of social and personal contexts, address the values of a democratic civil society and the public sphere, and inspire us to imagine the unfinished issues within and without our institutions. It is not an exclusive, comprehensive, or prescriptive list, and there is no preferred order. Each of these books will lead to others, and to writers whose skills will suggest new approaches to open conversations as yet unimagined.

A SMALL SHELF

Danielle S. Allen. (2004). *Talking to Strangers: Anxieties of Citizenship since* Brown v. Board of Education. Chicago: University of Chicago Press.

Nothing we are likely to talk about will last as long as race among those things we barely understand, nor will it be replaced as an unfinished issue for the nation. When we speak of social equity and civil society in a democratic context—and even when we don't—"interracial distrust" is likely to be the hardest, deepest issue in the room. Education, history, income inequality, violence, marriage and the family, popular culture, health, military service, immigration, music, law, and incarceration: the human experiences of racial difference and discrimination show up in most of our places and are always worth talking about. And yet, though it is an unfinished, ubiquitous issue, race is uneasy. Nothing we are likely to talk about will last as long among those things we barely understand. Danielle Allen begins *Talking to Strangers* with photographs of the Little Rock school segregation drama of 1957, graphic images of divided experiences of democracy and citizenship, shattering the myths of a better past and an indivisible people. Her work is ruminative scholarship, addressing history, language, self-interest, and sacrifice. An understanding of "friendship" emerges as a way to understand and speak to differences. "Our real social capital problem," Allen writes, "is simply that we have come to believe that self-interest comes only in one form, namely the rivalrous variety, when, in fact, it inhabits a spectrum from rivalrous to equitable. Any effort to culti-vate friendship preserves a valuable cultural understanding of that spec-trum" (p. 138). A classics scholar, Allen discusses Ralph Ellison's *Invisible Man* to frame the idea of sacrifice, a fine use of literature as a channel to deep observations. In an interview on her publisher's website, Allen answers the question, "What should democratic citizens, in the first decade of the 21st century, do?" She says they should, "Ask themselves, when they interact with strangers, whether they have treated them as they would a friend. Explore political questions by trying to make the best possible argument, on any given question, from the perspective of someone with whom they dis-agree or whose experience of life in America differs fundamentally from their own." (See www.press.uchicago.edu/Misc/Chicago/014665in.html.)

Robert N. Bellah et al. ([1985] 2008). *Habits of the Heart: Individualism and Commitment in American Life*, 3rd ed. Berkeley: University of California Press. Robert N. Bellah et al. (1991). *The Good Society*. New York, NY: Knopf.

These books—complex and detailed, thorough and rich—might be called moral profiles of American culture and character, as derived by sociologists from the lived experiences of citizens. They may not be recent, but they remain incomparably insightful, as tensions continue to configure our lives and shape our culture. They are also works that describe a kind of civic faith, the motive to live with awareness of human moral force in a public world. *The Good Society* begins ("Introduction: We Live through Institu-tions") and ends ("Conclusion: Democracy Means Paying Attention") with assertions that do not disappear.

John Seely Brown and Paul Duguid. (2000). *The Social Life of Information*. Boston, MA: Harvard Business School Press.

The relevance and value of *The Social Life of Information* has lasted a decade for me and will continue to be purposeful, reminding professionals

that compelling human forces—the needs and interests of living cultures—
"play a critical role in shaping not only society, but information itself, making information useful and giving it value and meaning" (p. 33). Information
has use and meaning only through the human dimensions placed upon it;
therefore it is reductive to regard it as an abstraction, a science. One value
of the public conversation is to imagine those dimensions, and to use them
to combine forms of information and experience—that is, to construct
knowledge—not as it is known on screens, but in the contexts of lives.

C. Roland Christensen, David A. Garvin, and Ann Sweet, eds. (1991). *Education for Judgment: The Artistry of Discussion Leadership*. Boston, MA: Harvard Business School Press.

This explicitly "educational" book frequently addresses instruction, but
in my view it is more certainly about the essential conditions of teaching
and learning. We learn in situations that are contextual, social, interactive,
and ethical. Situations for learning are also subject to the design and
process, and the agency of a patient (and ego-free) leader. The emphasis is
best placed on the book's subtitle, especially the word "artistry," and how
a discussion constructs situations where informed judgments and participa-
tive questioning can happen. In a chapter titled, "Every Student Teaches
and Every Student Learns: The Reciprocal Gift of Discussion Teaching,"
Christensen writes, "No matter how factually accurate and time tested our
data, how clear cut and disciplined our analytical methods, or how practiced
and skillful our pedagogical techniques, true learning emerges only when we
honor the human factor" (pp. 110–111).

E. J. Dionne, ed. (1998). *Community Works: The Revival of Civil Society in America*. Washington, DC: Brookings Institution Press.

This small book, like O'Connell's below, is page by page among the most
powerful of all listed here, because it is composed of 18 essays written by
scholars and politicians across disciplines and viewpoints (Bill Bradley, Jean
Bethke Elshtain, Gertrude Himmelfarb, Colin Powell, Rick Santorum,
Theda Skocpol, Michael Walzer, and Alan Wolfe among them). The mix
means that the book contains multiple perspectives, briefly stated, distributed
in a way that informs the idea of "civil society" but also holds it accountable
in realistic expectations. Nothing is resolved here, but ideas are put into play,
with all their imprecision and complexity intact, and all their ambiguous
surroundings. These support both talking points and worldviews.

Michael Edwards. (2009). *Civil Society*, 2nd ed. Cambridge, UK: Polity.

This scholarly approach to people gathering in common cause is one of many examples; the catalog of my local university library is rich with similar books. (Not the case in my public library, however.) Edwards is admirably concise and yet clearly respectful and inclusive of the array of theorists, classical perspectives, and contemporary implications of both local and global civil society. Multifaceted and multivalent, "civil society" in its applicable forms tends to represent "civic activism" and engagement in democratic dialogue and political reform. But the less political fundamentals of conversation in the public sphere are presented as well, in the value given by Edwards to place, engagement, and contention: "[P]rotecting space for diversity while negotiating common rules and standards is perhaps the most important question facing humankind in the twenty-first century" (p. 81). The idea of a good society driven by an "inclusive and well-articulated associational ecosystem" is among the most powerful ideas in *Civil Society*. The bibliography is extensive, excellent, and current.

John W. Gardner. (1963). *Self-Renewal: The Individual and the Innovative Society*, rev. ed. New York, NY: W. W. Norton.

Among his earliest books, *Self-Renewal* is emblematic of John W. Gardner's many contributions to rationality and intelligence as the foundation of common efforts. It is also part of his legacy to rational citizens, leaders, and organizations, a perspective on the renewal of thought and policy in the hands of a responsible democratic people. "The institutional arrangements of an open society are not themselves the means to renewal. Their virtue is that they nourish free individuals. And such people are inexhaustible sources of renewal" (p. 27). Gardner was an advocate of learning throughout life, of mining the tension between individuality and commitment, and of trusting the power of human beings to construct fair settings for useful work and social progress. This book and its successors epitomize both wisdom and faith inspired by the energy of civic enterprise.

Tracy Kidder. *Home Town*. (1999). New York: Random House.

Northampton, Massachusetts, is its own place, with its own history and people. Here the view is local, and the issues are cultural and social. The theme is universal: the person in the community, living among others, working for survival. In Kidder's exploration of the characters and processes of this town—while telling of no extraordinary events, no charismatic figures, and no great changes—the interactive genius of a small American community becomes clear. Such places keep us safe for living a life. The profiles Kidder gathers define the ways lives grow and change in passage and in tension, and how the surrounding safeguards of order and survival protect them from falling too far. *Home Town* is about familiar continuities and patterns, structures of commerce and law, and the aspirations and achievements of the town through its people. But it is also about the smallness of a town, the privacies and torments invisible to see, and its reciprocities and transitions in the everyday. Readers might well begin here.

Knight Commission on the Information Needs of Communities in a Democracy. (2009). *Informing Communities: Sustaining Democracy in the Digital Age.* Washington, DC: Aspen Institute.

"The United States stands at what could be the beginning of a democratic renaissance, enabled by innovative social practices and powerful technologies" (p. 62). I will add that it will also be enabled by community visionaries, librarians among them, who understand the critical nature of accurate information and accessible information tools in the creation and continuity of this renaissance. The Knight Foundation's interests are grounded in journalism, but this report makes clear that knowledge of the everyday—government actions, public health, the economy, and cultural change—is essential to democratic membership and social participation. Among the commission's recommendations is a set grouped under "Enhancing the Information Capacity of Individuals," providing provocative and challenging goals for assuring personal access to the "information richness" of the nation. "America's libraries," the seventh recommendation says, "need sufficient funding to serve as centers for information, training, and civic dialogue" (p. 47). Under "Promoting Public Engagement," the commission writes, "Engagement within a community can take infinite forms. ... What follows from disengagement is the flip side of these community assets. Instead of trust, there is alienation. Instead of cooperation, there is indifference. Instead of knowledge, there is ignorance, misunderstanding, and higher levels of social conflict" (pp. 52–53).

Jack Mezirow and Associates. (2000). *Learning as Transformation: Critical Perspectives on a Theory in Progress.* San Francisco, CA: Jossey-Bass.

Of the many necessarily imprecise ways we have of understanding the essential effects of adult learning, "transformation" comes closest to its heart. Transformative learning enlarges our capacity to question ourselves and our assumptions, to recognize different dimensions in others, and to think critically about ourselves as agents and engaged learners. We reconsider and reconstruct our premises as we come to understand the experiences and identities of others. In "Learning to Think Like an Adult," Mezirow writes, "Imagination is central to understanding the unknown; it is the way we examine alternative interpretations of our experience by 'trying on' another's point of view. The more reflective and open we are to the perspectives of others, the richer our imagination of alternative contexts for understanding will be" (p. 20). Using the life of Nelson Mandela as an example in the chapter titled "Transformative Learning for the Common Good," Laurent A. Parks Daloz describes conditions of transformation: the presence of the other, reflective discourse, a mentoring community, and opportunities for committed action (p. 117). "Deep change," Daloz writes, "takes time, strategic care, patience, the conviction that we are not working alone, and the faith that there is something in the universe, as Robert Frost said, 'that doesn't love a wall' " (p. 121).

Martha C. Nussbaum. (2011). *Creating Capabilities: The Human Development Approach*. Cambridge, MA: Harvard University Press.

This extremely important and deeply ethical book critiques the standard model for assessing human development—as Gross Domestic Product rises, so does quality of life—and replaces it with the "Capability Approach." Its questions are simple: "What is each person able to do and to be?" (p. 18) "What does a life worthy of human dignity require?" (p. 32) Responses are complex by design, and valued for their complexity. The woven strands that compose a life and a society do not exist except in relationships to each other and so defy simple reduction. For cultural institutions, the implications of these questions will be profound. If libraries and museums come to regard "each person as an end" (p. 35), what must change in our places? If the expanded capability of the individual is our intention, how must we think of and encounter our users?

Brian O'Connell. (1999). *Civil Society: The Underpinnings of American Democracy*. Hanover, NH: University Press of New England.

The importance of *Civil Society* today is that it reminds us of idealism and expectation at the end of the twentieth century, still valid and still worth our aspirations. O'Connell provides the view of an activist more than the view of a theorist; the conversations and organizations he describes are purposeful, intended to build something and to affect something in the social and political world. The lessons here are even-handed: while some see civil society as a middle ground, O'Connell points out that its foundation is the work of many structures—government, philanthropy, enterprise, and institutions. In a robust civil world, it is a partnership that keeps a common focus on the thriving of the individual, and the elimination of barriers to flourishing. Like John W. Gardner's essays, O'Connell's book is rich with quotations, including Havel's concept of the need to "rehabilitate the human dimension of citizenship." *Civil Society* also sends the reader on to other theorists. Without his reference I would not have found Robert Putnam's (1993) primary characteristic of civic engagement (drawn in part from the observations of de Tocqueville), that enlightened self-interest is "self-interest that is alive to the interests of other." (Putnam, 1993, p. 88). O'Connell's own "essential characteristics of free and effective societies" begin with "[c]ivic space where citizens with similar interests and concerns can find one another and are free to pursue what they believe is in their and the public's interest" (O'Connell, p. 4).

Andrew J. Perrin. (2006). *Citizen Speak: The Democratic Imagination in American Life*. Chicago: University of Chicago Press.

"We imagine the society we live in through discussion, communication, and observation" (p. 51). Andrew Perrin's work is admirable for is intelligent extension of social lessons out of empirical research. Public talk, or "civic speak," is an act of democratic imagination, a group phenomenon, and it is essential for a public realization of democracy. Social discussions of the kind that Perrin observed provide a forum for the expression of cautions, responses, and uncertainties, and a realization of agency, the power to affect change. The democratic imagination, he says, is capable of reinvention, recombination, and creativity that "flourishes in the context of other creative minds" (p. 144). "An imaginative citizenry is, at root, a social goal: it is the product of richly patterned and connected relationships among people and groups," Perrin says (p. 149). The conditions for fostering civic creativity require access to ideas, exposure to complexity, a focus on institutions, and patience with unpredictable progress. "A strong program for building the democratic imagination should engage citizens' interests and emotions along with their information-processing capacities" (p. 150).

Danel Yankelovich and Will Friedman, eds. (2010). Toward Wiser Public Judgment. Nashville, TN: Vanderbilt University Press.

Twenty years after Yankelovich's *Coming to Public Judgment*, this collection revisits the question of how citizens think usefully in the presence of issues and their complexities, what the editors call "deliberative democratic work." (p. 7) The collection begins by describing the sources of distortion for our understanding of public thinking: shallow media, callow leaders, and reductive research. While it is easy to assume that accurate information, debate and analysis by experts, and media coverage will lead to sound public opinion, Yankelovich writes that "The key dynamic in public opinion formation is an emotion-laden, value-driven, time-consuming process of overcoming our natural inclination to denial and wishful thinking over extended periods of time." (p. 16) The time, values, complexity, and evidence required for reflective engagements with tough issues will vary greatly, but the processes of deliberation are likely to be characterized by inclusion, multiple framings of information, and confrontation between denial and informed engagement. Especially for complex matters, the learning curve may be slow and difficult, but it leads to greater public certainty when it is complete.

THE STIR OF CONVERSATION

There is no end to this book without more reading. Even nearing its conclusion, I find something new: a translation of Andre Cossette's *Humanism and Libraries: An Essay on the Philosophy of Librarianship* ([1976] 2009). I am drawn to it because it was originally written in my own formative time as a student of cultural institutions, but it is now translated and published almost as a voice from that time, a reminder to recollect my reasons for entering the profession. "Only the well informed," Cossette wrote a generation ago, "can take steps to radically change their situation in society." It is the work of democratic institutions, he continues, "to provide this additional opening to the world that allows for informed choices in a state of clarity" (pp. 55–57, passim).

I am grateful to read these words. "To provide this additional opening to the world" is the true mission that has engaged me for decades, though it has not always been clear. In part, my life is a confusion based on striving to find the best ways to keep that promise. And now, after one decade in the new century, to contemplate the idea of arriving at "informed choices in a state of clarity" seems to be as pure a fantasy as any other from the 1970s. In contrast to my original naïve intention to conduct a life of generous service, learning, and knowledge, it is now avoiding ambiguity, struggling for balance, and sustaining constancy that draw my energy and, more often than not, lead me to defeat. I wish us all a state of clarity.

Thinking further of lost time, I have also been tempted to list among the works here yet another volume from the even more distant past, *The Autobiography of Malcolm X* (1965); I will assume it is well known to all. Among the greatest books of the twentieth century, it is an important document of human development and transformation—an inexorable path of continuous becoming—derived from experiences in our own society during a time that exists in living memory. There are such lives, there are such experiences, that will stand over a long time for us among the legacies we need to endure as citizens and dwell within as readers. My own life could not be more distant from the life of Malcolm Little, Detroit Red, Malcolm X, or El-Hajj Malik El-Shabazz, but I am humbled to recognize in him the essence of a life that is forever imperfect, unfinished, uncompromised, and vital, always seeking lessons to speak clearly among others.

I recognize and covet this generative quality—as I do the elusive state of clarity—in the lives of artists and writers, humanistic leaders, and other people of strong belief and service with others. I anticipate long lives of generosity and intellect in the best of my students. Their work—our work—is to create the stir of conversation. When I am calm and unafraid, I continue to look for these things in myself. Each day our lives are able to remain open to the words of another voice, they will also remain unfinished in service to our most important responsibilities.

CHAPTER 12

Civility

Altruism. Amity. Awareness. Comity. Compassion. Complexity. Consistency. Cooperation. Courage. All of these, and more, matter to open conversations. When just a few of these qualities are present, so is the possibility of civil exchange and provocative engagement, and in any conversation, their presence makes a difference to the integrity of the collaboration. *Courtesy. Dedication. Deliberation. Empathy. Fairness. Generosity. Goodwill. Mutual respect.* This is the vocabulary of civility and its possibilities, and we are capable of acting with all of them in mind. It is also a list of the conditions and requisites, the aspects of the situation required for open conversations to happen in places we create and allocate for them. *Mutual responsibility. Openness. Optimism. Patience. Reciprocity. Trust.* Like all abstract, ideal words of this kind, this vocabulary calls up its opposite: *anger, arrogance, carelessness, convention, mindlessness, passivity, presumption, shallowness, silence,* and more. These opposite words are also within us if we are feeling human beings. Of these, arrogance, passivity, and silence are most damaging to civility, most undermining to trust. When they appear, they will fragment any hope we have to navigate the complexities of our world. We break through them in order to become what we need to become.

Language and civility are not just casually connected. Our social structures and conduits of progress are fabrics of language. Our ways of serving the lives of users in cultural institutions are typically ways of language. Words are functional tools in our searches and descriptions, of course, but more than this, our language is an essential constructor of the ideas of the possible that lead us forward. They are essential as well for grasping the past: experiences and memories disappear over time if we do not give them words, images, and indelible connections to our identity. We know from the decade that began on September 11, 2001, that experiences and their deep effects construct our integrity. The mindless and the shallow never serve us well. If a democratic strand naturally threads us into a vast national self, an insular life is a denial that reduces our substance as a society. We are not isolated in either losses or gains, and we are diminished when we remain silent. We never stop considering our possible public selves, and it is past time for cultural institutions to live up to the possible ways of sustaining them.

In a recent State of the Union address, President Barack Obama used words that matter to the civil flourishing of the nation. His words might have been spoken by any leader of any party who recognizes the substance of progress in a democratic society. Citing the differences on display in governing, he said, "The debates have been contentious; we have fought fiercely for our beliefs. And that's a good thing. That's what robust democracy demands. That's what sets us apart as a nation." Then, reflecting on the effects of public shootings in Tucson, the president said, "Amid all the noise and passion and rancor of our public debate," we were reminded that "each of us is part of something greater. . . . We believe that in a country where every race and faith and point of view can be found, we are still bound together as one people." He went on to describe a world in unpredictable change and a society in need of renewal, but he returned to this significant theme: "We are the first nation to be founded for the sake of an idea—the idea that each of us deserves the chance to shape our own destiny."

The talk to Congress began with these themes at its center: differences and the need for conversation and comity; altruism and loyalty to each other and to principles of reasoned discourse; common aspirations and challenges; and the need for adaptation to change in an uncharted future. And then the address moved toward the implications of these foundations: to the need to advocate for learning and intellect throughout society, to the challenges of widespread literacy and connections to technology, to providing essential access to tools among the information poor, to the reformation of schools, and to the adaptations of commerce amid global markets. Finally, the president spoke of the timeless process of change, as any president would: "We should have no illusions about the work ahead of us. . . . None of this will be easy. All of it will take time. And it will be harder because we will argue about everything." Possibilities and aspirations began and ended his address, alluding to "ordinary people who dare to dream." Among his final sentences were these: "The idea of America endures. Our destiny remains our choice." The address, unsurprisingly, contained many expressions of national ideals, emphasizing common interests, education, and adaptation to new world dimensions.

What would it mean if these words, "our destiny remains our choice," were to become true in every life? There are concepts embedded in our public language that should cause us to pause for reflection, if only to ask, *If this is true, how do we make the choice of our destiny? If this is true, how do we act in order to feel a part of something greater? If we are founded on these ideas of democracy—discourse, renewal, and mutuality—where do they appear in my life?* These are not rhetorical questions, even in the context of a ritualistic presidential address. The questions that follow all of these expressions are broad, but they should be asked by every legislator, leader, teacher, and policy maker in the nation: *Where do we find a place and a purpose where citizens can experience these essential national values? And when we find that place, how shall we speak and listen there?*

CIVILITY MEANS SOMETHING

On a Saturday morning, a young man carefully selects and loads a small yet lethal firearm, conceals it on his person, takes a taxi to a mall where people are deeply experiencing ordinary life, and uses the weapon, firing more than two dozen rounds into the gathering. A member of the U.S. House of Representatives is gravely harmed; a respected judge, a small hopeful girl, and four other people are killed; many more are injured. What the nation does in consequence—and perhaps the most important part of all that it does in consequence—is to discuss civility, discourse, responsibility, and the nature and consequences of public talk. It does not seem to be a particularly useful discussion, because it rapidly falls into the predictable channels of discourse—accusation, defensiveness, and counteraccusation—familiar to anyone who has thought about the freedom to speak and the right to bear arms. The possible presence of mental illness in the alleged gunman confounds the public conversation, as do the hardened preexisting political opinions of many shallow speakers. Consequently, nothing fresh or bold is spoken to seize the attention of the nation, and no openings are created for new stances. And so, unspeakably sad losses become unspoken frustrations, and ineffectual but symptomatic conversations about civil conduct, speech, and gun control dwindle to silence, though the issue remains unchanged, the dead remain dead, and the wounded society strives to recover. Looking back after a few weeks, the events retain a sense of familiarity, and a sense of disheartenment without consolation.

And yet the event and its aftermath did create a discussion on the blog of James Fallows, a national correspondent for *The Atlantic* (see www.theatlantic.com/james-fallows/). It began with a few basic questions about defining civility, and went on to ask for the contributions of readers. Other questions about the practices of civility were unasked but tacit, such as the value of rules for civil conversation, and how they might be created. People wrote, offering evidence that an urge toward civility exists among some of us, and further evidence of dismay amid loud political commentaries, frustration with cautious editorial writers, and despair over the loss of generosity and care in civil life.

The cautious, conditional comments sent to Mr. Fallows by his readers made the problem of civility in public speech immediately clear. A few plain themes, but very few absolute rules, became visible. Much of the discourse was about threatening language, and some correspondents addressed the ominous use of symbols of death in advertising. Such symbols—targets, guns, swastikas, and nooses—are not subtle; their offense is visible. A drawing of a guillotine is not a civil image but a threat of bodily harm: the possibility of free conversation is over when it appears. One benefit of these lethal pictures is the clarity they give to our thinking, because they assist us to recognize what is clearly uncivil, what distorts the conversation beyond rescue. Any threats of death and allusions to physical harm go to the top of a small list of forbidden expressions.

In civil society, it is talking that matters most, and so it is also where we are likely to find the most tension and discomfort with regulations. Forbidden themes are few. When I note that language, the freedom to speak out, is the focus of civility in many of these responses, it is not a surprise. Politics, civility, decorum, courtesy, ethics—and all of the ancillary concepts we might name—have words, utterances, statements, and documents as their central evidence, and we live in a nation where free speech is prized and protected. (This protection sometimes surprises us and tests our tolerance. As I write today, for example, the Supreme Court of the United States has determined that church-sponsored antigay protests at the funerals of American soldiers constitute protected speech.) The theme of civility implies our ability to express vital, restrained, ethical talk, spoken as a way of making plain to others the ideas and responses we have harbored privately. We want to express ourselves unclouded by threat or innuendo, and we want someone to listen and to respond, also without fear. Talk deserves our care because it makes us as vulnerable as it makes us powerful. Once uttered, the privacy of words is gone, and so is the privacy of the speaker. The listener's privacy is also at stake if a response is required.

Those who wrote to Mr. Fallows seemed to agree that every speaker is accountable, when transforming a private opinion into a public statement, for observing the human context where it is uttered. Speech is heard in a diverse civil context of beliefs, faiths, commitments, values, and allegiances, spoken and unspoken; it also includes the feelings, intellect, and awareness that others bring to their social lives and commitments. This context is where we speak and where our speech has consequences; obviously it is a space to be entered with caution and deep respect.

Even if rules of public conversations were to be endorsed and accepted, thereby forming a code or protocol for public civility, their management and observation will not come easily. If a code is created, it needs to be endorsed by citizens as fair, inclusive, and unthreatening. Even then, its values would have no meaning unless they are proven in the practice and acceptance of participants. Beyond practice, a code of civil conversation would require that people who violate it are not rewarded for their abrogations, although they may not be easily held accountable. Coercive enforcement would be a civil problem itself—but there might be a larger value to having such a code, regardless of its powers.

Perhaps, as one writer suggested to Mr. Fallows, a common endorsement of a civil speech code by many millions of Americans would create the weight of public expectations that leaders and commentators would have to acknowledge. Apart from what it permits or condemns, a code in wide general use and acceptance has the power to shape civil communication behaviors, since any violation would become apparent to a public, or to a gathering of speakers. More important, disregard for the values of a widely public code would be immediately apparent, and civil words of disapproval would be directed to the deviant.

While civility is complex, its practice has bases in social etiquette, discretion, generosity, and kindness. We are not outside it, and we must come to understand civility from within; more likely, we *live* through careful civility in our daily lives as a form of justice and self-respect, and we work to sustain it. Based on my interpretation of what people wrote to James Fallows when asked to define civility, it means these things.

Civil speech is generative and has lasting effects. Children who hear us speak will carry lessons from what we say. Consequently, we should speak as though our own children were present to hear us, or as though our most respected friends will hear us and judge us on the responsibility and accuracy of our words. It follows that we must make a conscious attempt to speak only true things, or things that are not demonstrably untrue, and when truths or evidences are unclear, we need to say so.

We all have biases, commitments, and matters of faith or ethics that lead our actions. Perhaps a full acknowledgment of our personal interests in a topic or an idea should be disclosed when the circumstances require. In some cases—even if we believe we are speaking only for ourselves—full disclosure may suggest that we need to mention a formative experience, an ethical or even faith tenet, or our employer's interests, and maybe our profession, if these influence our remarks. However, a person's membership in a group, party, race, nationality, faith, cause, or workforce does not imply solidarity with or similarity to other members.

Conversations are about topics, not persons. We need to learn to speak of and with others as individuals whose perspectives differ from ours, not as people who are inherently opposite. People may not be attacked in a personal way; disagreement with a person's point of view does not require disparagement of the person or the belief. Demonizing, humiliating, bullying, threatening, or shaming an opponent for an idea creates inherent danger for the conversation. Even the raised voice is a form of violence.

Consequently, there are some absolutes. Incitement to hate or to harm directed at others, even in the guise of opinion or belief, is forbidden. Without evidence, incendiary or accusatory words are forbidden, such as those implying treason, criminal acts, mental impairment, or pejorative descriptions of intellect. Accusatory epithets like "traitor," "liar," "tyrant," and "crook" are deeply serious and require evidence; "socialist," "fascist," and other generalized terms related to political systems are incendiary, and forbidden. Arguments solely for the purpose of provocation are forbidden; we focus on reason, not emotion. Alarmism, the intent to create a constant state of fear and expectation of an imminent disaster, causes people to reject civility and is forbidden.

We acknowledge counterarguments, and we respond with respect. Different points of view are not to be eliminated or destroyed; better and more desirable perspectives are to be advocated. Statements that shut down debate or deliberately take an argument beyond its topic violate the promise of mindful participation, as do "straw man" arguments, attacking someone for a position they do not advocate.

We remember that it is possible for us to be wrong, and that the purpose of debate is to communicate and clarify differing perspectives, not to defeat. If proven right or wrong, we and our opponent have learned something new, thanks to the other; we accept the learning gracefully.

This is my tentative interpretation, not a credo. What is certain to me is that we need to learn to talk in ways that allow us to be precise but not rigid, strong but not closed, equally speaking and listening. Vile speech is vile—and protected. But vile speech does not assist a conversation to happen. Open speech requires civility if it is to be sustained over time, however rightfully or freely a speaker may attack our words. One purpose of civility is not to close the conversation. We need to understand that our exchange will be crafted in language, heard and considered, and judged to be true, false, or something between. When our speech is grounded on knowledge or information without distortion, and expression without insult, perhaps it is more likely to come closer to being accepted in the discourse.

Knowledge as we present it in civil conversations may come from an inquiry, from research, or from a wiser, more experienced voice; but for each of us, our truths come to be ours only through crafting and practicing them, using words to forge them, and (as needed) hammering them out with more language, more knowledge, and more wisdom into something that is functional, well grounded, and adaptive to the unanticipated contexts of life. Contexts serve both to create and to change our crafted truths. Words are parts of the engine that is a sentence, part of the dynamo that is an argument. Mastery requires time and practice. It also requires tools like dictionaries, thesauri, handbooks, encyclopedias, and a host of works in a well-stocked reference collection. This leads to a truth about libraries, the places where dictionaries are kept: they do not keep language, they do not keep knowledge, nor do they keep truths. They keep tools for constructive and expansive dialogues; they are places where language is treasured and clarified for our craftwork. They keep a conversation in flow, or on track. Humbling though it may be, no argument is beyond the need for information and knowledge. When forms of information are needed in the conversation, a librarian knows how these things are found.

Another truth about civility, in my view: kindness matters. Early in life, if we are given the right attention, we learn not to interrupt others, to look in their eyes when we speak, to refer to them with respect when we disagree, and to accord them a dignity that increases trust and conversation. We sit around a table, and though we may have different origins or intentions, we share a civilized responsibility as citizens in a forum; we use an inclusive "we" rather than an accusative "you." To speak fairly and openly is to invite a response. No amicable change in opinion or point of view can happen without a mutual place and vocabulary, and the amicable presence of each other.

A common code of civil discourse, unlikely as it is, might serve to strengthen the intellect of the nation. While it is least likely to pervade the ubiquitous internet, it can be a visible part of cultural institutions as they engage users in the living questions of contemporary life. This might extend them usefully into communities and schools. Perhaps our media, if they are under the management of responsible people who embrace the practice of an ethical profession, will find a handful of guidelines to say out loud or print above the masthead, and then live up to them. Those examples of media—in print, on the air, on the web—that seize the citizen as a form of prey ought to be called out, in public. So should predators in politics, for the harm they do to civic trust.

A passing blog reference to a work by P. M. Forni, *Choosing Civility*, led to these ideas, as clear as they can be, and easy to present as the foundation of civil talk in any public forum: "Courtesy, politeness, manners, and civility are all, in essence, forms of awareness. Being civil means being constantly aware of others and weaving restraint, respect, and consideration into the very fabric of this awareness. Civility is a form of goodness; it is a gracious goodness" (Forni, 2002, p. 9). Perhaps the tendency to believe truly and deeply in our own correctness of opinion—and our urgent and uncompromised right to express it forcefully—has darkened the grace and goodness that Forni identifies with civility. Recall with me that it is "the worst" who "are full of passionate intensity," as described in the Yeats poem, "The Second Coming." The purpose of dialogue is not to win a fight, but to speak from the intellect and heart. No?

I added only one comment to Mr. Fallows' blogged colloquy, a possible mantra to state silently to myself as a point of practice, just before responding to others: "You may be right, but it is so easy to be wrong." I wanted to remember the fragility of discourse, and to ask the question that should appear among open conversations: "Can we help each other to understand this?" We must emphasize "this," "this idea," "this question," and "our topic" as ways to remind each other that we are challenged to speak about ideas, not fears, or threats, or insubstantial secondhand opinions. Our talk is at its best when it is tentative and uncertain, as we ask ourselves to speak our part in crafting something solid to build upon. On what knowledge do we base our question? On whose evidence or experience do we base our understanding? In what ways can we make something together?

We are civil in order to sustain our own selves, neither demeaned nor compromised. We are also civil in order to assist others to sustain their own best selves. Disagreements will happen, but they may not happen outside our mutual humanity and our capacity to be generous and fair. This is why we need to talk, but it is also why we need to learn to talk.

LEARNING TO TALK ABOUT LEARNING TO TALK

Among the most difficult things we need to speak about among others is what our learning has been and what it has meant to us. It is a form of self-presentation I think we must undertake as people who change. Where did we learn something? Who helped us to learn it? We need to see ourselves as capable of particular kinds of growth toward complexity, and having a record of being a learner. Early in this book, I spoke with dismay about the common and casual ways we hear the word "learning," as though one word is enough to describe this complex process thriving inside us and engaging us each day. We often deny respectability to the learner dwelling within us, out of disregard for our own intellect, or out of relief that we have put schooling behind us. And yet, the learner within is always there.

When we look again at the array of living strands I have suggested among the continuities of one life, and when we project our own lived experiences onto the grid, we must see places and times when our learning was deep and necessary and very hard, though we may have called it by another term. We adapt, we pursue, we become. Our museums and libraries also need new words, and new ways of seeing the people whose experience means a certain way of becoming different, a way that goes beyond the adequacy of "learning" as a container of meaning. In the words we need, we may find a generative metaphor (Schön, 1993, pp. 254–283) that allows us to redefine our purpose as individuals and as institutions.

In *transformation* we may dissolve one way of being and emerge in a new way of experiencing and accounting for our world. We speak of change, of growth, of developing, of becoming someone else, and of recognizing a new identity. Our transformations may be slow, but they will have signposts and watersheds we can recognize.

Our *explorations* imply a robust form of experience that carries the air of risk and departure from the everyday, as though in adventure or exotic challenge. But there are countless ways of stepping off the edge of the known world to explore it, sometimes by uncovering a hidden pursuit, testing one-self against a difficult task, or discovering the reserved parts of our strength we had not needed before. Although we are often pushed unexpectedly into an exploration or an adventure (as by military service, emigration, revolution, or family crisis), our seriously daring lives will begin from within (Welty, 1983, p. 114).

When we recollect our experiences of learning, we may focus on a time when *finding a solution* to a problem happened. This has the quality of clarity: a problem contains an unknown, it requires a solution, and we take a step forward. But it is not only the arrival at the solution that matters, except as a brief landmark; the processing matters more. When we recollect solving a problem, we may need to expand our sense of our experience to include our breaking through conventional thinking, our expanded understanding of how to proceed in the future, and the satisfaction of unraveling a tangled complexity.

To break through, to reorganize, to untangle, to perceive a structure in chaos, is to change the problem, also a way to solve it. The generative metaphor of *construction*, to me, may describe change best. It is certainly an adaptable descriptor. Using it, we can talk about building a foundation, erecting a scaffold, connecting frameworks, and fabricating our structure. We might follow a blueprint, assemble the parts in a pile, piece it together, or make spaces out of wilderness. The importance of constructive learning is that we are active in making something, gathering experiences as lumber, making connections through tools and skill, and modifying the construction.

At times we say that knowing is to see—see a difference, see a possibility, see the point—and this sense of *vision* is a way to say we have learned. I see. It was revealed to me. I gained this insight. I found a new perspective. I looked again. I saw a different horizon. Learning in some ways is to perceive that we have learned, and—wait, let me draw you a picture—now it looks like this to me.

What civil discourse promises to those who engage in open public conversations is an opportunity to speak in ways that reveal the human possibility of growth among others, in collaboration with others, in a world that is shared equally by others. We may learn to express the ideas and lessons that become real to us because our awareness of processes such as thinking, deciding, and describing has become clear.

> The challenges of beginning this conversation were . . .
> The hardest part of this topic is . . .
> What I have observed most clearly is . . .
> Every process has its tensions, and I found these . . .

We learn that we have an intellectual style and a preferred way to encounter new ideas. We can trace our path from the first conversation to the last.

We notice how our attention is drawn to particular themes, key ideas, insights, and watershed moments. We learn to ask for help in understanding. Unexpected discoveries surprise us and teach us. Often the most provocative experiences contradict our expectations and raise new questions. In some cases, what we don't expect to discover is our own depth, our own need to speak and be heard. And, there is knowledge. We learn that there is a rich and useful record of work to read, showing a mix of the useful, the conventional, and the brilliant. We are led on. We may have made connections to previously unexplored parts of our experiences, or questions we had hidden away, and these are our next inquiries because we are learners.

CLOSED TO OPEN

The challenges I see are not small things to do in our cultural institutions: to create an alternative to closed discourse, to allow citizens to find their voices and develop their intellects, and to respect the value of a democratic idea that is never finished or complete. The differences between closed and open conversations reflect a cultural institution's founding ideas of knowledge, its willingness to transmit new capabilities to its users, and its capacity for encouragement. Authoritarian or unconvivial leaders may create closed environments for professional communication, making it difficult to inspire the public open conversations I advocate in this book. We do not need to read Kafka to know these differences between closed and open. Our formative experiences of closed, judgmental institutions often remains present in our lives and causes us to shape our practices about the places where we work. We may first be challenged to break through an organization's administrative limits.

When conversations are closed, language is often reduced and suffused by authority, and deadened by convention and efficiency. It is frequently bland and formal, sometimes condescending. Spoken exchanges—even routine guidance—may be constrained and uninviting. But words and meanings in open conversations are constructed by speakers to fit a particular context or situation. In an open conversation, language is expansive and evocative, a tool of encouragement for exploring complexity as deeply as possible. Metaphors are generative and collaborative; didacticism and authority are not.

In closed inquiries, procedures constrain and rule. Progress is most likely to be linear, moving toward resolutely empirical knowledge and logical explanation. The human factor is hidden behind the work to be done. Scientism is one model of inquiry in places like this, but in its hardest and narrowest forms, without exploration, elaboration, interpretation—or even curiosity. In open inquiry, observations and lives are irreducible. Inquiry in open forums aims to find out in a common effort, combining expertise, exploration, articulation, analysis, synthesis, and critical thinking.

Knowledge is always incomplete—perpetually open—and subject to contextual variations, on which it will always depend.

The truths we may find in closed conversations may rest on proven empirical knowledge, or they may follow from revealed, unshakable faith. Such truths may be revealed or transmitted by authority, unembellished and unconditional. They have the qualities of laws, and they exist outside individual experience. When, in the contrasting open conversation, a participant feels a sense of certainty, it is likely to have been crafted from an array of possibilities, by personal reflections and worldly interactions. Such truths are more like working hypotheses, where knowledge is always in process, needing refinement, tempered by experience. Such truths are constantly open.

Our recent world history—our world today—is full of closed cultures, anti-democratic, judgmental systems of lines and compartments without the shared passages, diverse stories, or personal routes that lead to individual identity. Only when such cultures crumble do we understand them clearly for what they are. Closed cultures do not tolerate variation easily. They are not founded on mutual trust, or on diverse engagements with others. They may exude defiance. But an open culture communicates a range of possibilities to its members, opportunities to move across lines of heritage, economy, or conformity. It recognizes the value of plural voices and beliefs, unconventional ideas and practices. It tolerates ambiguity and accepts change.

In a closed world, information is hoarded, useful only when it is unchallenged and unchallenging. Having neither context nor energy of its own, information is inert and without effect. When a culture is open, information is freely sought and valued for the alternatives it contains, for the breadth of reference and questioning it introduces. Human beings in open cultures require information to nourish aspirations and control uncertainties. Knowledge is built when strands of information are woven into fabric, guided as much by art, belief, and desire as by science, faith, and mind. In an open culture, nothing supplants learning and nothing suppresses thought. The open mind considers, questions, and weaves.

THE CIVIL WORK OF CULTURAL INSTITUTIONS

We are always challenged to describe the differences that cultural institutions make. Their essential importance will always be elusive, even invisible, to the consciousness of society. Changes in mind or conscience that happen because a person has seen a painting by Breughel, read a book by Tolstoy, or shared a gaze with a mountain gorilla will never appear in the records of museum or library use. The institution's collections, funding, and integrity are unaffected. Such transmissions and transformations remain hidden in the lives of users, traces of invisible civility and inaudible discourse. This is a truth for all museums and libraries: we know that invisible transactions are our work, and we know that they make invisible, undocumented differences in lives, but they bear neither weight nor effect on our value. Instead, museums and libraries are likely to be offered sentimental praise, generic approval, and benevolent support until money is in short supply.

To make a part of our transactions visible is one motive to create forums where open conversations take place. But the motive is more than this. Our work is to enrich the discourse that knowledge requires and reading nurtures. Our motive is the reminding of communities, societies, and cultures. What museums and libraries offer may be tactile, visual, and iconic, but there are dimensions we cannot see associated with every thing, and what matters most is untouchable, invisible, and shape shifting. This is what we live to understand.

I am unfinished, still, although this book is done. The work I want most to do will never disappear as themes in my life, invisible concepts I can barely communicate even now. I offer them, even to myself, as a tentative vocabulary of differences, the consequences of cultural institutions in our lives as I have observed them. They are terms, metaphors I have used before: the invisible actions of cognitive change; unfinished issues guiding adult lives; aspects of the infinite embedded in every object; structures, bridges or scaffolds to some imagined knowledge; possible selves leading us forward; stories and their traces that remain; heuristic questions and critical thinking; crafted truths; self-rescue; and the steady invitation of the unknown. I like to think that cultural institutions will continue to hold these things for me and for others, and that their full abundance has not yet been realized. They are things made possible by cultural institutions in a community, and only by cultural institutions. They are essential to communities and their aspirations, and essential to democracies and their practices.

Each of us needs to assume that a constructive living intellect is an essential condition of human life and the dearest treasure of a society. I believe that museums and libraries need to arouse and evoke the presence of the living intellect—active questions and active imaginations in civil conversation—if we want to elevate the promise of the possible in the lives of citizens and companions, and if we want to find out why it is that we cling to one another. Think with me in this way toward becoming something together. Think with me among the lasting engagements that occur between citizens and cultural institutions. Of these, the most important to me is the confirmation of an emergent courage to ask, to speak, and to become in the presence of the unknown. In this way, a human culture and its civility are expressed.

REFERENCES

Alexander, E. (2009). *Praise Song for the Day*. Minneapolis, MN: Graywolf Press.

Allport, G. (1955). *Becoming: Basic Considerations for a Psychology of Personality*. New Haven, CT: Yale University Press.

Baldwin, M. (2006). Librarians as knowledge provocateurs. *Public Libraries*, 45(2), 11–14.

Bellah, R. N., et al. ([1985] 2008). *Habits of the Heart: Individualism and Commitment in American Life*, 3rd ed. Berkeley: University of California Press.

Bellah, R. N., et al. (1991). *The Good Society*. New York, NY: Knopf, 1991.

Brown, J. (2005). *The World Café: Shaping Our Futures through Conversations That Matter*. San Francisco, CA: Berrett-Koehler.

Brown, J. S., & Duguid, P. (2000). *The Social Life of Information*. Boston, MA: Harvard Business School Press.

Brown, R. (2010). 45 years later, an apology and six months. *The New York Times*, November 16, p. A14. www.nytimes.com/2010/11/16/us/16fowler.html?_r=1&scp=2&sq=civil%20rights&st=cse

Bruner, J. (1986). *Actual Minds, Possible Worlds*. Cambridge, MA: Harvard University Press. 1986.

Carr, D. (2006). *A Place Not a Place: Reflection and Possibility in Museums and Libraries*. Lanham, MD: AltaMira Press.

Christensen, C. R. (1991). The discussion teacher in action: questioning, listening, and response. In Christensen, C. R., Garvin, D. A., and Sweet, A., eds., *Education for Judgment: The Artistry of Discussion Leadership*, pp. 153–172. Boston, MA: Harvard Business School Press.

Cosette, A. ([1979] 2009). *Humanism and Libraries: An Essay on the Philosophy of Librarianship*, trans. R. Litwin. Duluth, MN: Library Juice Press.

Csikszentmihalyi, M. (1993). *The Evolving Self: A Psychology for the Third Millennium*. New York: Harper Collins.

Dewey, J. ([1934] 1987). *Art as Experience*. In *The Later Works, 1925–1953*, vol. 10, ed. J. A. Boydston. Carbondale: Southern Illinois University Press.

Doctorow, E. L. (2008). The white whale. In *The Public Good: Knowledge as the Foundation for a Democratic Society*. Cambridge, MA: American Academy of Arts & Sciences and the American Philosophical Society.

Emerson, R. W. ([1860] 1983). Considerations by the way. In *The Conduct of Life*, in *Essays and Lectures*. New York: Library of America.

Erikson, E. H., & Erikson, J. M. (1998). *The Life Cycle Completed*, ext. version. New York: W. W. Norton.

Fineman, H. (2008). *The Thirteen American Arguments: Enduring Debates That Define and Inspire Our Country*. New York: Random House.

Forni, P. M. (2002). *Choosing Civility: The Twenty-Five Rules of Considerate Conduct*. New York: St. Martin's Griffin.

Gardner, J. W. (1964). *Self-Renewal: The Individual and the Innovative Society*. New York: Harper & Row.

Gardner, J. W. (1999). Foreword. In O'Connell, B., ed., *Civil Society: The Underpinnings of American Democracy*, pp. xiv–xv. Hanover, NH: University Press of New England.

Greene, M. (1988). *The Dialectic of Freedom*. New York: Teachers College Press.

Havel, V. (1993). On receiving the Onassis Prize for Man and Mankind, Athens, Greece, May 24. http://old.hrad.cx/president/Havel/speeches/1993/2405 _uk.html

Hofstadter, R. (1963). *Anti-Intellectualism in American Life*, New York: Knopf.

Jacoby, S. (2008). *The Age of American Unreason*. New York: Pantheon.

Judt, T. (2010). *Ill Fares the Land*. New York: Penguin Press.

Kidder, T. (1999). *Home Town*. New York: Random House.

Lave, J., & Wenger, E. (1991). *Situated Learning: Legitimate Peripheral Participation*. New York: Cambridge University Press.

Legrady, G. (2005–2014). *Making Visible the Invisible*. Installation, Seattle Central Library, Seattle, WA. www.georgelegrady.com

Leonardi, A. (2007). Future time perspective, possible selves, and academic achievement. In Rossiter, M., ed., *Possible Selves and Adult Learning: Perspectives and Potential*, pp. 17–26. New Directions for Adult and Continuing Education, vol. 114. San Francisco, CA: Jossey-Bass.

Miller, D. (2010). DOJ concedes most civil rights-era murders will remain unsolved. Defenders Online | A Civil Rights Blog. www.thedefendersonline.com/2010/ 08/10/doj-concedes-most-civil-rights-era-murders-will-remain-unsolved/

New Dictionary of the History of Ideas. (2005). Horowitz, M.C., ed. New York: Charles Scribner's Sons, 2005.

Noddings, N. (2003). *Happiness and Education*. New York: Cambridge University Press.

Polya, G. (1960). *How to Solve It*. Princeton, NJ: Princeton University Press.

Postman, N., & Weingartner, C. (1969). *Teaching as a Subversive Activity*. New York, NY: Delacorte Press.

Putnam, R. D. (1993). *Making Democracy Work: Civic Traditions in Modern Italy*. Princeton, NJ: Princeton University Press.

Richards, I. A. (1955). *Speculative Instruments*. Chicago, IL: University of Chicago Press.

Rosenblatt, L. M. (1995). *Literature as Exploration*, 5th ed. New York: Modern Language Association.

Rossiter, M. (2007). Possible selves: An adult education perspective. In Rossiter, M., ed., *Possible Selves and Adult Learning: Perspectives and Potential*, pp. 5–15. New Directions for Adult and Continuing Education, vol. 114. San Francisco, CA: Jossey-Bass.

Schön, D. A. (1983). *The Reflective Practitioner: How Professionals Think in Action.* New York, NY: Basic Books.

Schön, D. A. (1993). Generative metaphor: A perspective on problem-setting in social policy. In Ortony, A., ed., *Metaphor and Thought.* New York, NY: Cambridge University Press.

Smith, F. (1990). *To Think.* New York, NY: Teachers College Press.

Vest, C. M. (1995). The pursuit of the truly unknown. *The Chronicle of Higher Education*, 42(17), B5. http://web.mit.edu/newsoffice/1995/annreport.html

Welty, E. (1983). *One Writer's Beginnings.* New York, NY: Warner Books.

X, Malcolm, with Haley, A. (1965). *The Autobiography of Malcolm X.* New York, NY: Grove Press.

Yoffe, E. (2008). Obama in your heart: How the president-elect tapped into a powerful—and only recently studied—human emotion called "elevation." *Slate*, December 3. www.slate.com/id/2205150/

FURTHER READING

Augst, T., ed. (2003). *Libraries as Agencies of Culture*. Madison: University of Wisconsin Press.

Bryan, F. M. (2004). *Real Democracy: The New England Town Meeting and How It Works*. Chicago, IL: University of Chicago Press, 2004.

Buschman, J. E. (2003). *Dismantling the Public Sphere: Situating and Sustaining Librarianship in the Age of the New Public Philosophy*. Westport, CT: Libraries Unlimited.

Carr, D. (2008). Confluence. *Curator: The Museum Journal*, 51:3.

Carr, D. (2010). An aspect of the infinite: New Zealand talks. *Curator: The Museum Journal*, 53:1.

de St. Aubin, E., et al., eds. *The Generative Society: Caring for Future Generations*. Washington, DC: American Psychological Association.

Dworkin, R. (2006). *Is Democracy Possible Here? Principles for a New Political Debate*. Princeton, NJ: Princeton University Press.

Evans, S. M., and Boyte, H. C. (1986). *Free Spaces: The Sources of Democratic Change in America*. New York, NY: Harper and Row.

Fishkin, J. S. (2009). *When the People Speak: Deliberative Democracy and Public Consultation*. New York, NY: Oxford University Press.

Gutmann, A. (2007). The lure [and] dangers of extremist rhetoric. *Daedalus*, 136:4.

Hedges, C. (2009). *Empire of Illusion: The End of Literacy and the Triumph of Spectacle*. New York, NY: Nation Books.

Jacobs, L. R., et al. (2009). *Talking Together: Public Deliberation and Political Participation in America*. Chicago, IL: University of Chicago Press.

Janes, R. R. (2009). *Museums in a Troubled World: Renewal, Irrelevance, or Collapse?* New York, NY: Routledge.

Kegan, R. (1994). *In Over Our Heads: The Mental Demands of Modern Life*. Cambridge, MA: Harvard University Press.

Kelly, E. A. (1995). *Education, Democracy, and Public Knowledge*. Boulder, CO: Westview Press.

Korza, P., and Bacon, B. S., eds. (2005). *Museums and Civic Dialogue: Case Studies from Animating Democracy*. Washington, DC: Americans for the Arts.

Kranich, N. C., ed. (2001). *Libraries and Democracy: The Cornerstones of Liberty*. Chicago, IL: American Library Association.

Lankes, R. D. (2011). *The Atlas of New Librarianship*. Cambridge, MA: MIT Press.

McAdams, D. P., and de St. Aubin, E., eds. (1998). *Generativity and Adult Development: How and Why We Care for the Next Generation*. Washington, DC: American Psychological Association.

Pitman, B., and Hirzy, E. (2004). *New Forums: Art Museums and Communities*. Washington, DC: American Association of Museums.

Ross, M., and Woodward, G., comps. (2003). Appendix 2: Libraries build community. In Christensen, K., and Levinson, D., eds., *Encyclopedia of Community: From the Village to the Virtual World*, vol. 4, pp. 1533–1551. Thousand Oaks, CA: Sage.

Schiller, H. I. (1996). *Information Inequality: The Deepening Social Crisis in America*. New York, NY: Routledge.

Smith, G. (2009). *Democratic Innovations: Designing Institutions for Citizen Participation*. New York, NY: Cambridge University Press.

Spitz, J. A., and Thom, M., eds. (2003). *Urban Network: Museums Embracing Communities*. Chicago, IL: The Field Museum.

Thomas, D. and Brown, J. S. (2011). *A New Culture of Learning: Cultivating the Imagination for a World of Constant Change*. Lexington, KY: CreateSpace.

Thomas, N. L., ed. (2011). *Educating for Deliberative Democracy*. New Directions for Adult and Continuing Education, vol. 152. San Francisco, CA: Jossey-Bass.

INDEX

About the Author

After a dozen years as a teacher and librarian, DAVID CARR taught librarianship for three decades, specializing in collections, popular reading, and reference services. He was recognized as a master teacher by the Association for Library and Information Science Education in 1994. He consults, observes and evaluates in museums and libraries, advises community reading projects, and writes about cultural institutions and the passion for reading in adult life. He received a BA in English literature from Drew University; an MA in special education and teaching of English from Teachers College, Columbia University; and MLS and PhD degrees in library service from Rutgers, the State University of New Jersey. Two collections of David Carr's essays have been published: *The Promise of Cultural Institutions* in 2003, and *A Place Not a Place: Reflection and Possibility in Museums and Libraries* in 2006.